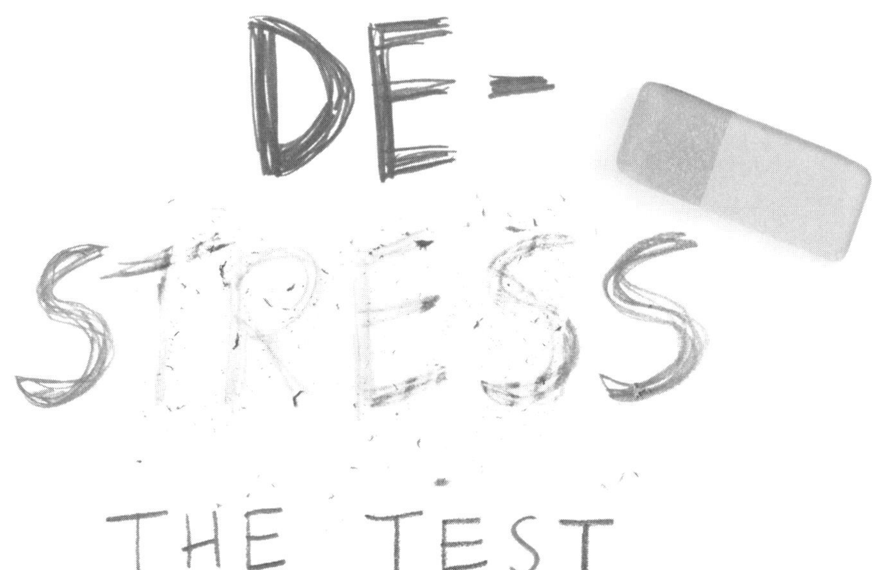

De-Stress the Test

Brain-Friendly Strategies to Prepare Students for High-Stakes Assessments

MARTHA KAUFELDT

Solution Tree | Press

555 North Morton Street
Bloomington, IN 47404
800.733.6786 (toll free) / 812.336.7700
FAX: 812.336.7790

email: info@SolutionTree.com
SolutionTree.com

Visit **go.SolutionTree.com/assessment** to download the free reproducibles in this book.

Printed in the United States of America

Library of Congress Cataloging-in-Publication Data

Names: Kaufeldt, Martha, 1954- author.
Title: De-stress the test : brain-friendly strategies to prepare students for high-stakes assessments / Martha Kaufeldt.
Description: Bloomington, IN : Solution Tree Press, 2021. | Includes bibliographical references and index.
Identifiers: LCCN 2021006645 (print) | LCCN 2021006646 (ebook) | ISBN 9781949539554 (paperback) | ISBN 9781949539561 (ebook)
Subjects: LCSH: Test taking skills. | Achievement tests. | Classroom environment--Psychological aspects.
Classification: LCC LB3060.57 .K28 2021 (print) | LCC LB3060.57 (ebook) | DDC 371.26--dc23
LC record available at https://lccn.loc.gov/2021006645
LC ebook record available at https://lccn.loc.gov/2021006646

Solution Tree
Jeffrey C. Jones, CEO
Edmund M. Ackerman, President

Solution Tree Press
President and Publisher: Douglas M. Rife
Associate Publisher: Sarah Payne-Mills
Art Director: Rian Anderson
Managing Production Editor: Kendra Slayton
Copy Chief: Jessi Finn
Production Editor: Rita Carlberg
Content Development Specialist: Amy Rubenstein
Copy Editor: Jessi Finn
Proofreader: Evie Madsen
Text and Cover Designer: Kelsey Hergül
Editorial Assistants: Sarah Ludwig and Elijah Oates

Robert (Bob) Sylwester (1927–2016), Emeritus Professor of Education, University of Oregon

I would like to dedicate this book to my dear friend and mentor Robert (Bob) Sylwester. I met Bob at a national conference in the mid-1990s. It was my first solo presentation on learning and the brain. At the luncheon, I asked if he would take a look at the research I was presenting. He happily met me in the lobby of the conference hotel that evening, and I literally sat at his feet and took copious notes while he gleaned my handouts and gave authentic, actionable feedback. A few years later, he attended one of my sessions at Learning Brain Expo. (He was pleasantly disruptive at his table group while he made dozens of origami creatures for everyone.) I still have the evaluation exit ticket from him that stated “Absolutely wonderful!!” We became good friends and loved meeting up at conferences over the years, often getting together with his dear wife of sixty-three years, Ruthie, for dinners. I could always send him articles or manuscripts I was working on, and he would happily review, edit, and make suggestions. He always encouraged me to keep writing and presenting. In July 2016, I made a special stop in Eugene, Oregon, to see him. We spent several hours laughing, sharing stories, lamenting about the state of the world, and, of course, talking about recent brain research! He passed away one month later. I am forever grateful for his unconditional support, encouragement, playful spirit, and friendship.

Thank you, Bob.

ACKNOWLEDGMENTS

The author would like to personally thank the following people.

Sarah Payne-Mills, associate publisher, for her incredible abilities to make actionable suggestions, clean up my rambling discourse, encourage me throughout the process, and keep me on track to meet deadlines. I was so lucky to have her as my editor! Thank you!

A special thank-you to Jeanne Spiller, assistant superintendent of teaching and learning, and staff members at Kildeer Countryside School District 96 in Buffalo Grove, Illinois. They provided valuable feedback at the beginning of this writing process. Thank you!

Much love and appreciation to my wonderful husband, Rick Burros.

Solution Tree Press would like to thank the following reviewers:

Scott Hagerman
Superintendent
Tanque Verde USD
Tucson, Arizona

Kathy Perez
Professor Emerita, Author, and International Consultant
Saint Mary's College of California
Alameda, California

David Pillar
Assistant Director
Hoosier Hills Career Center
Bloomington, Indiana

Anthony Stamm
Curriculum Coordinator
Ann Arbor Public Schools
Ann Arbor, Michigan

Jianna Taylor
ELA, MTSS, and School Improvement Coordinator
West Bloomfield School District
West Bloomfield, Michigan

Visit **go.SolutionTree.com/assessment** to download the free reproducibles in this book.

TABLE OF CONTENTS

Reproducibles are in italics.

ABOUT THE AUTHOR

Martha Kaufeldt is a professional development specialist and author. Since 1984, her specialty has been applying educational neuroscience to classroom practice. She travels internationally, conducting workshops and trainings on curriculum development, differentiated instruction, school restructuring, assessment, and brain-friendly strategies for teachers. She served on the Transformative Education Forum board and has been a trainer and coach for the Mid-California Science Improvement Project.

Martha was a classroom teacher for more than twenty-three years in California. As an elementary teacher, she created brain-compatible learning environments for a diverse student population. In the middle grades, Martha was a core teacher on an interdisciplinary instructional team. Her curriculum included integrated project-based and service learning, and she emphasized social and emotional well-being. Martha has also been a district staff development specialist and gifted education program director. For her work in the San Francisco Bay Area, Martha was awarded the Mason-McDuffie Outstanding Teacher of the Year Award.

She has authored and coauthored several books, including *Begin With the Brain: Orchestrating the Learner-Centered Classroom*; *Teachers, Change Your Bait! Brain-Compatible Differentiated Instruction*; *Think Big, Start Small: How to Differentiate Instruction in a Brain-Friendly Classroom*; *Best Practices at Tier 1: Daily Differentiation for Effective Instruction, Elementary*; and *Best Practices at Tier 1: Daily Differentiation for Effective Instruction, Secondary.*

She earned a bachelor's degree in liberal studies from San Francisco State University and a master's degree in human behavior from City University of Seattle.

To learn more about Martha's work, visit Begin With the Brain (www.beginwiththebrain.com). To book Martha Kaufeldt for professional development, contact pd@SolutionTree.com.

INTRODUCTION

Test-driven classrooms exacerbate boredom, fear, and lethargy, promoting all manner of mechanical behaviors on the part of teachers, students, and schools, and bleed schoolchildren of their natural love of learning.

—SACKS

The test. Students dread this phrase, whether it refers to chapter tests, finals, standardized tests, international assessments, Advanced Placement (AP) exams, the ACT and SAT, or other testing experiences. The test-taking culture embedded in most primary, secondary, and higher-level education systems inevitably creates an overwhelming high-stress response for many students—and their teachers. Educators want their students to do well and be able to demonstrate mastery during these rituals; however, they recognize that the administration of *high-stakes tests*—those considered to have great consequences for students, staff, or schools—triggers stress and anxiety that can negatively influence students' performance, not to mention affect their brains and bodies. Teachers administer important high-stakes tests to gather data about instructional success and individual student achievement. Preparing for these tests can trigger stress and anxiety not only for students but also their teachers. This book will investigate the impetus for testing culture and, therefore, the resulting test anxiety and provide a wide variety of classroom suggestions and instructional strategies to *de-stress the test.*

The Expansion of Testing Culture

Since the 1960s, the use of international and national tests has swelled, with countries deeming high-stakes tests as critical for determining students' futures and school accountability (Smith, 2016; United Nations Educational, Scientific, and Cultural Organization, Education Sector [UNESCO], 2020). By the early 2000s, over sixty countries were participating in the three largest international assessments: the Programme for International Student Assessment (PISA), the Progress in International Reading Literacy Study (PIRLS), and the Trends in International Mathematics and Science Study (TIMSS), with participation increasing 50 percent by 2012. Globally, one in three schools administers standardized exams. As William C. Smith (2016), senior lecturer in education and international development at the University of Edinburgh states, "There is growing international consensus that participation in international testing and the use of a national assessment system are essential in a legitimate education system" (p. 10).

In the United States, there were many factors that led to an increase in the development and administration of standardized tests. In the mid-1800s, school reformer Horace Mann, secretary of the Massachusetts State Board of Education, instituted the first reported use of a written examination and introduced standardized testing to Boston public schools, modeling the Prussian school system (which had students progress through different grades based on age). By 1918, more than one hundred standardized tests measured achievement in the principal elementary and secondary school subjects. The University of Iowa launched the first major statewide testing program for high school students in 1929, and tests were available to and being used by other states by the late 1930s. After World War II, the population grew immensely due largely to new immigration, and, like in many other countries, the yearly tests provided valuable information about instructional methods, school success, and student achievement. Schools used test scores to organize, diagnose, and classify students. Schools could be separated and place gifted students and poor-performing students on different "tracks," which added to the controversy of testing equity. Technology from IBM and Scantron revolutionized the testing industry. With this new equipment, testing programs were better coordinated, and test-score data were reported and used in a variety of ways (U.S. Congress, Office of Technology Assessment, 1992).

But the original focus for high-stakes tests—student learning—has shifted to one of *accountability* for teachers and administrators (Smith, 2016). For example, in California in the 1960s, my fellow students and I took a yearly achievement test near the end of the third, fifth, and tenth grades. For these tests, we each received a small test booklet sealed with a tamper-proof sticker. We took the tests during regular class time, and those of us who finished early would simply get to read a book as we patiently waited for others to complete their tests. I don't remember experiencing high levels of stress related to these tests, and I can't recall ever hearing about the results. The expectation of the students and their parents was that these routine tests would provide valuable information to teachers and schools about the students' achievement. Since tests were not administered every year, individual teachers were not held directly responsible for yearly progress. The whole testing process usually took a few days of class time in the spring. It was tedious and almost *boring* for many students, but it didn't create a lot of stress since there were few consequences. (My testing experiences in a middle-class, semi-rural neighborhood school with few minorities did not represent a diverse population. I understand that the stress levels may have been different among various socioeconomic groups.) Then, the 1965 Elementary and Secondary Education Act launched new and increased uses of norm-referenced tests to evaluate student achievement and school programs in the United States.

In 1983, the release of "A Nation at Risk: The Imperative for Educational Reform," a report by President Ronald Reagan's National Commission on Excellence in Education, warned of a crisis in U.S. education and an urgent need to raise academic standards. Reform advocates pressed for stricter accountability measures, including increased testing (Strauss, 2021). As I taught school in the 1980s and 1990s, the tests became more frequent and comprehensive. The test results carried a greater impact on a school's recognition as well as its funding. Teachers were provided more in-depth training in test preparation to ensure that they readied their students with the skills and knowledge that the tests demanded. Schools' test scores were published in the local newspaper, and education funding began to be tied to results. At the time, my mom was a local real-estate agent, and she often reported about new buyers who requested to see the three neighborhood schools' test scores so they might select in which area to live. People wanted to buy houses nearest the highest-performing school because they believed the test scores were crucial, and the best ones represented significantly better teachers and even smarter students.

Testing practices worldwide have continued to evolve over the last few decades. In England, Dylan Wiliam, professor emeritus of educational assessment at the University of London, notes, that by the age of sixteen, students will have taken fifteen to twenty high-stakes exams that determine whether they'll graduate from high school (as cited in Turner, 2014). In Japan, students take high-stakes exams just to get into high school (Turner, 2014). India's high school completion exams, called *board exams*, have become so high stakes that nearly five hundred students were expelled from the tests in 2015, after parents climbed a wall to help them pass. Not only do these students take tests to graduate from high school but they also take dozens of exams to get into college (Lakshmi, 2015; Salaky, 2018). In the United States and Canada, standardized tests vary by state or province, but most students are required to take at least one test per school year (Salaky, 2018), and U.S. students will take over one hundred standardized tests between preK and twelfth grade (Council of the Great City Schools, 2015).

What was once an instrument to assess specific course-content mastery or grade-level achievement has morphed into a tool that federal, state, provincial, and local administrators could wield to reward, punish, evaluate, and represent an entire school, district, state, or province. For example, in 2009, U.S. President Barack Obama signed the $4.35 billion Race to the Top program into law, in which school funding could be "won," inviting states to compete for extra funding based on student test scores (Council of the Great City Schools, 2015). Tests have become mandatory, longer, more comprehensive, more efficient to grade, and less expensive to administer. Consider the following quote following the release of the Common Core State Standards (www.corestandards.org) in the United States:

> The arrival of *Common Core standards–based tests*, marketed as more "rigorous" and consistent than existing state exams, is yielding a new generation of testing nightmares, for students, teachers, parents and administrators. In states that have yet to begin Common Core testing, horror stories based on existing testing misuses and abuses continue. A Federal requirement that every state receiving a waiver from No Child Left Behind must make *student scores a "significant part" of teacher evaluations compounds the problem*, leading to a huge escalation in testing. (FairTest Examiner, 2013)

Although my work has mainly occurred outside the classroom in the 21st century, in 2015, I was a part-time teacher at a charter school when the Common Core State Standards were first implemented, and when the first round of the Smarter Balanced tests (https://smarterbalanced.org) were administered in California. I had a responsibility in preparing students well in advance for these high-stakes tests administered in the spring.

The classes I was teaching usually included science, technology, engineering, arts, and mathematics (STEAM) and project-based curriculum. Throughout the year, my colleagues and I maintained brain-friendly classroom environments and fostered growth mindsets with our students. Students were taught social-emotional skills and participated in daily mindfulness practices. While other schools were lamenting about the extreme test stress that students were experiencing, I discovered that with this type of preparation over the course of the year, students approached the new tests with more confidence and a willingness to persevere. I quickly recognized how other teachers could use these strategies to help prepare students for rigorous standardized tests and minimize students' stress levels so they might do their personal best. That experience led to me writing this book.

About This Book

As a veteran educator, author, and brain research *interpreter*, I offer you, the reader, powerful information about how teachers might help prevent students from experiencing an inordinate amount of stress and anxiety as they anticipate the administration of high-stakes tests. I also provide a variety of suggestions on how we can help our students learn strategies to manage stress when it inevitably does happen. This book comes together in three parts to provide key background information and research on the biology of stress and how educators and parents can help students prepare for and navigate high-stakes tests.

- Part 1: "High-Stakes Tests and Stress"
- Part 2: "Stress Prevention and Management Strategies"
- Part 3: "Ways to Prepare Students for High-Stakes Tests"

Part 1: "High-Stakes Tests and Stress"

Chapter 1 takes an in-depth look at "The Meaning of High-Stakes Tests" and the evolution of testing practices. Proponents believe that by attaching rewards and punishments to test scores, students, teachers, and school administrators will take the tests more seriously, make the necessary instructional adjustments, and put in more effort to improve scores. Critics suggest the push for common standards and high-stakes tests has actually hampered reform efforts and even perpetuates inequality. When teachers are pressured to "teach to the test," instruction in other non-tested subject areas may be reduced. When the threat of the high-stakes exams permeates the classroom culture, the joy of learning may be lost and student engagement may be diminished.

Chapter 2 examines how "The Stress of High-Stakes Testing" can trigger the brain's fight-flight-or-freeze response system. When stress and anxiety are present, the brain's capabilities are minimized. Understanding what happens to students' brains when they perceive a threat, experience confusion and chaos, or feel helpless can provide important foundational knowledge when trying to *de-stress* their test experiences. In 2018, Jennifer Heissel and her team from Northwestern University published an important first-of-its-kind research study on the effects of stress on students' performance when taking standardized tests. Understanding the biology of the brain's stress response is key to creating stress *prevention and management* strategies.

Part 2: "Stress Prevention and Management Strategies"

Chapter 3 investigates how educators can use the knowledge of how brains learn best to orchestrate "Body- and Brain-Friendly Classrooms and Testing Environments," learning environments that are orchestrated around optimizing young brains. *Brain-friendly learning* refers to a safe and secure climate and environment that align with how human brains learn naturally and most efficiently. It includes differentiated teaching methods, curriculum choices, classroom designs, and school programs that are based on the latest neuroscientific research about how brains learn best, including such factors as cognitive development, engagement, movement, play, and social-emotional needs. This chapter provides a variety of design and organizational suggestions that can help teachers orchestrate a classroom environment that is compatible with how human brains can be most successful.

Chapter 4 explores how "The Development of Student Agency Through Self-Efficacy, Growth Mindset, and Perseverance" is key to students' confidence and stress reduction. Camille A. Farrington and colleagues (2012) from the University of Chicago Consortium on School Research refer to these additional skills, attitudes, and the like as *soft skills* or *noncognitive factors*, and Carol S. Dweck, Gregory M. Walton, and Geoffrey L. Cohen (2014) argue that these noncognitive factors "can matter even more than cognitive factors for students' academic performance" and "may include students' beliefs about themselves, their feelings about school, or their habits of self-control" (p. 2). This chapter provides concrete examples of how to explicitly integrate these noncognitive factors into daily instruction to help students develop a healthy growth mindset.

Chapter 5 provides a variety of "Mindfulness Practices for the Classroom," strategies to calm and focus the body and mind. Practicing mindfulness means maintaining a moment-by-moment awareness of one's thoughts, emotions, bodily sensations, and surrounding environment with openness and curiosity. These mindful, in-the-moment practices are important life skills for students to know and use on a daily basis in class. Helping students understand ways to manage their anxiety when it occurs may be one of the best ways to de-stress the test.

Part 3: "Ways to Prepare Students for High-Stakes Tests"

Chapter 6 introduces how frequent "Feedback and Formative Assessments" throughout the learning process can prepare students for upcoming summative assessments. A high-stakes test is a summative assessment *of* learning in which teachers use the results as an evaluation at the completion of a designated time frame. Formative assessments can be informal or formal and occur while a student is in the process of learning new skills and concepts. Maintaining frequent formative assessments *during* the learning process, providing specific feedback, and then orchestrating opportunities to try again can help students develop a greater sense of mastery, confidence, and self-efficacy when presented with similar tasks on high-stakes tests.

Chapter 7 explores the importance of integrating explicit "Academic Vocabulary Instruction." Learning the language of tests will help students as they encounter the specific evaluative or task words one can expect to find in many test questions. Academic vocabulary is also referred to as *tier two* words (Beck, McKeown, & Kucan, 2013). They are words that are crucial to success on tests because they often appear in test directions and questions. *Tier one* vocabulary refers to general everyday discourse. *Tier three* vocabulary is more specific to each academic domain; for example, science and mathematics terms. Students who have learned tier two vocabulary will have a greater advantage during high-stakes tests (Beck et al., 2013; Marzano, 2020).

Chapter 8 takes a deep dive into "Test Prep for Students and Teachers." Preparing students to do well on high-stakes exams is an ongoing process. Developing good study habits, taking care of basic needs, learning how to integrate stress-management techniques, and understanding basic test-taking tips and tricks are all important tasks for test preparation. Teachers can also help prepare students for exams by making sure students have experiences navigating the test technology. This chapter provides dozens of strategies for how teachers can help de-stress the test while promoting successful performance.

A Look Ahead

The messages shared in this book are clear: in order for students to feel capable, focused, and calm when experiencing test pressure, they must have an understanding of stress and stress-reduction strategies. High-stakes exams, in some form or another, are here to stay, and students will inevitably encounter them at various times during their education and in their career paths.

If the test event is right around the corner, don't fret. This book includes dozens of strategies that you can implement immediately. I invite you to help de-stress the test and allow students to flourish even when they are taking high-stakes exams.

PART 1

High-Stakes Tests and Stress

As we explored in the introduction, schools administer a lot of tests to students. There is a test for almost everything. However, standardized tests designed to measure proficiency and achievement don't tell us everything that is important to know about a student. Test scores also provide additional information about how socioeconomic and situational conditions can impact test performance. One factor that has emerged is how test anxiety can greatly impact a student's performance on the test, especially if the assessment carries possible consequences for poor performance. According to a thirty-year meta-analysis, "Test Anxiety Effects, Predictors, and Correlates," from researchers Nathaniel von der Embse, Dane Jester, Devlina Roy, and James Post (2018), "Test anxiety, exam stress, or test stress are often synonymous with the fear or worry of negative evaluation that results in negative behavioral, physiological, or emotional responses" (p. 483). Their research also shows that a student's test anxiety is higher on high-stakes exams when compared with typical classroom assessments. The analyses indicate that between 15 and 22 percent of students exhibit high levels of test anxiety. The results show a "consistent pattern of relationships with higher levels of test anxiety and lower levels of performance, across various testing formats" (von der Embse et al., 2018, p. 490).

Test stress can be triggered by the anticipation of an upcoming exam, the location of the test setting (a classroom), the process of taking the test itself (written, computer based), and time constraints. The specific subject of the test (such as mathematics or reading) and the degree of perceived difficulty can exacerbate anxiety (von der Embse et al., 2018). According to an analysis of several research studies, there are various factors that contribute to an increase in test stress (Fulton, 2016).

- Increased number of administrated tests
- The test's perceived importance (high-stakes value)
- The student's current socioeconomic conditions
- The student's perception of inadequate knowledge and preparation
- Various biological factors (sex, age, genetics, and learning disabilities)

Understanding how our brains react to perceived threats such as a high-stakes tests can provide teachers, students, and parents with important information. When the brain has a *reflex response* (fight or flight), there are physiological, psychological, emotional, and behavioral reactions. Knowing how the biology of the stress response works, and is triggered, can help teachers (and parents) design prevention strategies for students *before* any testing events. Learning about how their brains work—and don't work—under stress can help students learn how to manage their responses. The following chapters in part 1 investigate the two culprits in the *stress mess*: (1) high-stakes tests and (2) the brain's stress response system.

THE MEANING OF HIGH-STAKES TESTS

We live in a test-conscious, test-giving culture in which the lives of people are in part determined by their test performance.

—SARASON, DAVIDSON, LIGHTHALL, WAITE, AND RUEBUSH

T*he New Art and Science of Classroom Assessment* reminds us that, "A major aspect of effective classroom pedagogy is assessment" (Marzano, Norford, & Ruyle, 2019, p. vii). Teachers conduct frequent formative classroom assessments *for* learning during the learning process throughout the year. These assessments are low pressure and can provide valuable feedback to both the students and the teacher. (These important assessments, and how they can help prepare students for a final, high-stakes exam, are discussed in chapter 6, page 119.)

But assessments become *high stakes* when they have greater consequences. According to the Glossary of Education Reform (2014), the term *high-stakes test* refers to any exam that federal, state, provincial, or local government agencies and school administrators use to make decisions that impact students, educators, schools, or districts, usually for the sake of accountability. Teachers use summative assessments *of* learning, usually at the end of a year, to provide data about how well schools and their students are performing with respect to mastering the state or provincial standards. To ensure that the test results represent a specific level of achievement they are *standardized*:

> A standardized test is a test that is given to students in a very consistent manner; meaning that the questions on the test are all the same, the time

given to each student is the same, and the way in which the test is scored is the same for all students. (Burrows, 2020)

W. James Popham (2005), emeritus professor in the UCLA Graduate School of Education and Information Studies, explains that a standardized test is any test that's administered, scored, and interpreted in a standard, predetermined manner. Standardized *aptitude tests* are designed to make predictions about how a student will perform at the next level. For example, the SAT and the ACT predict the grades that U.S. high school students might earn in college classes. Standardized *achievement tests* are designed to indicate how well a student has acquired knowledge and mastered certain skills.

Worldwide, 84 million teachers try to prepare 260 million students to take mandated (and costly) high-stakes exams (a shortage of more than 68 million teachers, according to the United Nations; Roser, 2017; UNESCO, 2020). To prepare for these mandated tests, students spend weeks in test preparation, constituting a major investment in classroom time.

Teachers use tests to assess students' achievement and make predictions about how successful they might be in the future. Schools use the data to make decisions about curriculum design and classroom instruction. The public have faith that these tests are reliable and valid. But the tests have taken on power, and now are used as currency to make many critical decisions about funding, sanctions, teacher evaluations, and school performance.

How did schools get here? This chapter will explore just that.

The Evolution of Standardized and High-Stakes Tests

As explored in the introduction, in the United States and other developed countries around the world, high-stakes tests are an integral component of education systems. In the United States, the 2002 No Child Left Behind Act, meant to hold schools more *accountable*, launched the modern U.S. school reform movement where high-stakes, standardized tests became the hallmark. Seventy-six percent of high school students worldwide take standardized tests (Briggs, 2013).

Various rationales support the use of these high-stakes exams (Churchill, 2015; Gandy, 2016; Meador, 2019).

- **School reform:** One of the most controversial issues is the belief that the promise of rewards or the threat of punishment will actually *motivate* teachers to improve instructional effectiveness, student achievement, and ultimately the overall school performance. The rewards might mean compensation for staff, such as salary increases; bonuses for teachers or administrators; and increased classroom budgets for furniture, supplies, and so forth. The consequences of poor test scores might trigger a variety of possible punishments, such as penalties, funding reductions, sanctions, and even negative publicity.

- **Grade promotion and graduation:** To guarantee that students are not simply advanced without the necessary and required skills (*social promotion*), schools may use test results to determine whether students will be promoted to the next grade level. Secondary schools may use a high-stakes test to determine graduation eligibility. (To address equity issues, many states have modified the policies. In May 2019, only eleven states still had required graduation tests scheduled for the high school class of 2020: Florida, Louisiana, Maryland, Massachusetts, Mississippi, New Jersey, New Mexico, New York, Ohio, Texas, and Virginia [FairTest, 2019]. Pennsylvania had also requested a moratorium on an exit exam. However, due to the COVID-19 pandemic during the 2020–2021 school year, several states issued emergency waivers. For example, in Florida, the state legislature eliminated sanctions against schools with declining scores and declared a ban for the year on using test scores to determine third graders' status or high school seniors' ability to graduate [Solochek, 2021]. Students might be able to retake tests, and students with disabilities may have alternate ways to demonstrate proficiency.)
- **Teacher evaluation:** This rationale contends that teachers should be accountable for ensuring that all students learn what they are expected to learn and that test scores will reflect that students have mastered the standards. Teachers may be encouraged to "teach to the test," which may reduce instructional time on subjects not included on the test, such as the arts, social studies, health, and physical education. Schools and districts then use test results in teacher evaluations, to possibly reward "effective" teachers and to either support or penalize "ineffective" teachers.
- **Student motivation:** Some proponents believe that the threat of possible retention motivates students to work harder and learn more. For example, in 2001, when U.S. lawmakers established the No Child Left Behind Act, they used an unproven assumption that the importance of the new testing requirements would raise student achievement as well as student

motivation and bring accolades, such as awards, public recognitions, celebrations, and positive publicity, for the students or the school. (Further research continues to indicate that high-stakes tests can actually decrease student motivation and contribute to more frequent retention and increases in drop-out rates; Amrein & Berliner, 2003; Briggs, 2013).

- **Equity and accessibility:** Another major rationale for high-stakes tests is to be able to examine the achievement gaps among historically underserved student populations. By making the test scores public, schools can identify and address the results of low-income, minority, and limited–English language students. Schools and districts must be able to show that they are making progress toward proficiency of all students and close these achievement gaps.

  In his book *Catching Up or Leading the Way*, Yong Zhao (2009) describes two achievement gaps. One gap within U.S. schools includes the huge disparities and performance gaps among minorities, English learners (ELs), and low-income subgroups. Black and Latino students are often referenced when it comes to the U.S. achievement gap, especially when looking at results from the National Assessment of Educational Progress (NAEP), an annual high-stakes test given to students in grades 4, 8, and 12 (Muhammad, 2015). The other achievement gap is between the United States and other countries, as seen on international assessments, like the PISA, PIRLS, and TIMSS.

Diane Ravitch, historian and former assistant secretary of education, and critic of the modern *accountability* movement, notes:

> Politicians and the general public assume that tests are good because they provide valuable information. They think that the tests are necessary for equity among racial and ethnic groups. This is wrong. The tests are a measure, not a remedy. (as cited in Strauss, 2021)

Further, standardized tests introduce achievement gaps among minorities, English learners, and low-income subgroups (Muhammad, 2015; Zhao, 2009). As Ravitch notes in the article "What You Need to Know About Standardized Testing":

> Standardized test scores are highly correlated with family income and education. The students from affluent families get the highest scores. Those from poor families get the lowest scores. This is the case on every standardized test, whether it is state, national, international, SAT, or ACT. Sometimes poor kids get high scores, and sometimes kids from wealthy families get low scores, but they are outliers. (as cited in Strauss, 2021)

Additionally, these tests offer little value to teachers or students. Further, because most tests are administered in the spring, schools do not receive results until late summer or fall. Therefore, students have new teachers who cannot see students' answers so are unable to provide additional support for students (as cited in Strauss, 2021). High-stakes tests (Abeles, 2015; Glossary of Education Reform, 2014):

- Are neither fair nor objective
- May promote negative stereotypes about the intelligence and academic ability of minority students and those living in poverty
- Promote a narrow curriculum and drill-like "teaching to the test"
- May unintentionally increase failure rates and graduation rates
- Have created a stress epidemic impacting our students' health and well-being

The emotional and psychological toll on students from high-stakes test will be explored next.

Testing Culture Taking a Toll on Our Students

After the completion of the new testing practices connected to the implementation of the Common Core State Standards in 2013, a group of eight New York State principals published a letter to the public about their observations and concerns for students related to these tests, writing, "We know that many children cried during or after testing, and others vomited or lost control of their bowels or bladders. Others simply gave up" (Strauss, 2013). They cited one teacher's report that a student kept banging his head on the desk during a high-stakes test. The student wrote "This is too hard" and "I can't do this" throughout his test booklet (Strauss, 2013).

Many people have blamed failures in the U.S. education system on the United States' pervasive use of standardized tests, in addition to rising poverty levels, poor teacher quality, and tenure policies. In their book *Collateral Damage: How High-Stakes Testing Corrupts America's Schools*, Sharon L. Nichols and David C. Berliner (2007) report how the United States relies on ability and achievement testing for making important decisions about individuals and schools more than most other nations do. Standardized tests were intended to bring about changes in the education system and then detect whether changes in the system actually occur. But the zealous testing culture has perhaps gone too far.

In 2015, the Association for Supervision and Curriculum Development (ASCD, a network of dedicated empowered educators) called on Congress and the Obama administration to address five legislative recommendations to support the needs of students and educators. The third recommendation addressed high-stakes tests:

> The existing state testing requirements are woefully inadequate to determine whether students possess the knowledge, skills, and traits needed for school and career success. State test scores provide an incomplete appraisal of student achievement and by themselves often offer a misleading depiction of student performance and school quality. Standardized tests alone should never be used for high-stakes purposes, and neither students nor educators nor schools should be ranked or rated based on test scores. (ASCD, 2015)

No matter the specific structural changes that high-stakes assessments undergo over the years, the stress of impending tests affects students of all ages, and in all countries.

In her book *Beyond Measure*, Vicki Abeles (2015) makes the case that although standardized tests have been a part of education for over 150 years, in the past, the stakes weren't so high, the tests weren't so frequent, and relatively little time was devoted to specific test preparation. She documents the inordinate amount of stress that has been put on students and their teachers in her two films: *Race to Nowhere* (Abeles & Congdon, 2009) and *Beyond Measure* (Abeles, 2014). Abeles (2015) shares that her own daughters in middle school went from being happy, confident students who loved school to sleepless and anxious as they anticipated upcoming tests. As she related these experiences with doctors, educators, and other parents, she discovered that there was a silent stress epidemic spreading among our students, and "its source is an education culture gone crazy with competition, and a society so obsessed with one narrow vision of success that it's making our children sick" (Abeles, 2015, p. xii).

Studying for upcoming high-stakes tests, worrying about them, and ultimately trying to show what they know during them creates an incredible amount of anxiety and stress for students. They may feel they lack academic preparation but may also be afraid of letting others down, especially their parents and teachers.

Likewise, teachers feel great pressure for their students to perform well, both to reflect student achievement and to demonstrate their own teacher competence. In desperation, many teachers end up assigning seemingly endless practice with items similar to those expected to be on an approaching test. According to Popham (2005), this dreary drilling often ends up stamping out any actual joy students might experience while they are learning. This testing-stress mess has impacted student performance and, quite possibly, rendered the test results a less-than-accurate representation. As Abeles (2015) puts it:

> We are suffering from a slavish devotion to numbers—tests, and the scores and rankings they produce—that's dehumanizing our schools, increasing homework loads, and enshrining the belief that canned questions asked on paper are the ultimate measure of educational "success." (pp. 97–98)

A Slight Shift in the Testing Culture

Writing for the National Center for Fair and Open Testing, Monty Neill and Lisa Guisbond (2017) report that various test-reform victories are occurring around the United States: "Widespread opposition to the overuse and misuse of standardized testing is producing a marked shift in attitudes about high-stakes assessments and, increasingly, state and district practices" (p. 1). For example:

- Many districts have decreased the amount of state or district testing or their time spent on testing. For instance, Maryland's legislature capped the amount of time permitted to be used for testing purposes.
- Many states allow parents to opt their children out of testing.
- Many districts are joining with local unions to promote the development of assessments at the local level.
- Many states have ended or reduced the use of student test scores to judge teachers.

There are incredible models for assessments for mastery learning that are being used with great success. International educational psychology journalist, and managing editor of *InformEd*, Saga Briggs (2015) outlines several alternatives to standardized testing that high-stakes test critics, like NPR Education Correspondent Anya Kamenetz and even education organizations like Khan Academy, are in favor of. The following alternatives can help lessen the pressure and anxiety that can impact students' performance as well as their mental health.

- Frequent online low-stakes tests and quizzes
- More technology-based assessments that provide on-demand opportunities
- Frequent formative assessments that provide immediate feedback to students and teachers
- Performance or portfolio-based assessments that incorporate direct demonstrations of student learning including projects, individual and group presentations, and reports and portfolios of work

Further, during the COVID-19 pandemic, 188 countries implemented countrywide closures of schools. Due to this, seventy-three countries postponed or rescheduled high-stakes exams, twenty-three replaced the exams with alternative approaches (like research projects), and eleven canceled them altogether (UNESCO, 2020). In the United States, SAT and ACT tests were suspended during lockdown. But even before the pandemic struck, many universities had debated eliminating SAT and ACT scores from their application processes, making those test scores optional. Since March 2020, more than five hundred U.S. colleges, including every school in the Ivy League, have joined the "test optional" movement (Adams, 2020). In a *Forbes* investigation, "How the SAT Failed America," it states that these tests can be harmful especially to disadvantaged students and that requiring the test for admissions "perpetuates class and race hierarchies" (Adams, 2020). (See more about this possible shift in the epilogue on page 167.)

Not only does a harmful high-stakes testing culture affect students' stress levels and ultimately their achievement, but teachers and administrators experience extreme pressure to prepare their students to excel. Preparing students for high-stakes tests can take its toll on students and educators. Addressing this stress mess requires an urgent call to action.

Conclusion

When high-stakes and standardized tests are used for making big decisions, such as student promotion or graduation, teacher evaluations, or the assessment of an entire school or district, the pressure put on students and teachers is massive. Preparing students for high-stakes exams becomes a central focus throughout the year. The intensity regarding test prep in some schools and districts dominates the conversations, classroom instruction, parent communications, and even the signage in the hallways. Schools create contests, incentives, and competitions to try to motivate disinterested students to try harder. Parents begin to feel the pressure and engage in the rat race, pushing their children to do more, achieve more, and get higher test scores.

The discussion here isn't about accountability or whether or not students should take any kind of test. The goal is to find authentic information regarding a student's acquisition of skills, concepts, and understanding.

In the next chapter, we'll look deeper into the brain and how its amazing response system is key to knowing how teachers can help students manage test stress.

THE STRESS OF HIGH-STAKES TESTING

What happens in an exam: Tick tock, mind block, pen stop, eye pop, full shock, jaw drop, time up, no luck.

—ANONYMOUS

On the day of a big test at school, it's not uncommon for many students to feel awful (Cherry, 2020). They may experience stomachaches, headaches, and general fatigue. Almost as if they have the flu, their muscles may feel tense, and their bodies might be shaky and sweaty. They may have dry mouths and feel the need to use the bathroom frequently. Often, they will try to stay home from school. These types of jitters can affect a person's whole body (Cherry, 2020). Test anxiety is one of the biggest challenges students face in school. According to the American Test Anxieties Association (n.d.), students report that schoolwork and tests stress them more than anything else in their lives. About 16 to 20 percent of students report that they experience *high* test anxiety. An additional 18 percent report that they have moderately high test anxiety. Thirty-five percent of all students have moderate, high, or severe test anxiety (Tornio, 2019). Test stress may be the most prevalent learning impairment in schools (American Test Anxieties Association, n.d.).

According to the Anxiety and Stress Management Institute (n.d.), "Stress is how the human body reacts physically, emotionally, cognitively, and behaviorally to change in our everyday lives. Positive change, negative change, and even imagined change may cause stress on our mental, physical, and emotional self." Stress is the brain's response to change and to real or perceived threats that originate from the physical environment or even from emotional or psychological events. Stress is an ordinary, usually temporary, part of our day-to-day lives, and good levels of stress, known as *eustress*, can nurture our brains' growth and development and keep us motivated, engaged, and even excited. But when stress becomes chronic or excessive, referred to as *distress*, it negatively affects our bodies, minds, behaviors, and emotions (Boys & Girls Club of America, 2020).

According to the Mental Health Foundation (n.d.), contributors to what we experience as distress "can vary hugely from person to person" and differ "according to our social and economic circumstances, the environment we live in and our genetic makeup." Some common causes of stress include:

- Experiencing something new or unexpected (facing a lockdown order during the pandemic, taking a pop quiz, or paying an unexpectedly large bill)
- Experiencing a change in routine, relationships with people, or environment (having a substitute teacher, working from home, or moving into a new house)
- Encountering something that threatens our sense of safety (having a ferocious dog chase us, driving with the gas tank on empty in a traffic jam, or giving an oral presentation)
- Feeling little control over a situation (experiencing food insecurity, having a schedule made for us by someone else, or having no choices in school)

Distress can create dramatic physical and emotional responses that may interfere with one's ability to think logically, react reasonably, and interact with others appropriately. Understanding this amazing response system and the long-term effects of chronic stress will be key to knowing how teachers might help students manage distress and use prevention strategies to avoid triggering it. To guide you to this understanding, this chapter will investigate the survival response and the effects of stress on the body, mind, and emotions and behaviors.

The Survival Response

Worrying about an upcoming exam, standardized test, presentation, or performance at school can trigger a student's survival response. The *survival response* is a complex, sophisticated, and powerful defense system through which all the body's major systems coordinate to trigger a fight-flight-or-freeze response to a real danger, a perceived threat, anticipatory anxiety, excess pressure, confusion, or even an unexpected change (Gregory & Kaufeldt, 2015). In the blink of an eye, our multisensory perceptions can trigger our brains to begin a surge of hormones that will alert our hearts, muscles, lungs, and immune systems to prepare a strong defense (Gregory & Kaufeldt, 2015). Teachers can easily observe a variety of fight, flight, and freeze responses in a classroom. The student behaviors listed in table 2.1 may alert teachers to students' stress levels. These behaviors might appear separately, sequentially, or in various combinations. Teachers can explain and make sense of these behaviors when they understand the physiology of the body's reflex response.

TABLE 2.1: Fight-Flight-or-Freeze Responses

Fight	Flight	Freeze
Crying Clenching hands into fists Flexing or tightening jaws Giving glaring, intimidating looks Stomping or kicking Expressing feelings of anger or rage Complaining of an upset stomach or nausea	Having restless leg or foot movements Having rapid or shallow breathing Darting their eyes Fidgeting Expressing a feeling of being trapped and wanting to leave Avoiding or hiding Exhibiting excessive movement and a need to exercise or run	Being unable to move Expressing feeling cold Being pale Exhibiting a sense of stiffness Holding their breath Having a locked stare toward a possible threat (such as the door, a person, or the test) Having difficulty speaking

Source: Gregory & Kaufeldt, 2015; Kaufeldt, 2019.

Several brain regions work together on this survival response (see figure 2.1, page 22). The brain vigilantly scans the environment for potential threats. The *reticular activating system* (RAS) is a netlike bundle of nerve cells located between the brain and the spinal cord that monitors incoming sensory information from the skin, ears, nose, eyes, and so on. The RAS is involved in almost everything we do. The system doesn't take time to interpret the quality or type of sensory input; its primary function is to filter the incoming sensory messages and wake up various brain centers when it receives important messages. Changes in the immediate environment—particularly changes that indicate a threat or possible danger—get our immediate attention and the RAS triggers the *reflex response*. When the RAS doesn't pick up on any threatening conditions to attend to, it can shift focuses on stimuli that might bring opportunities, pleasure, fun, and novelty, arousing curiosity (Kaufeldt, 2019).

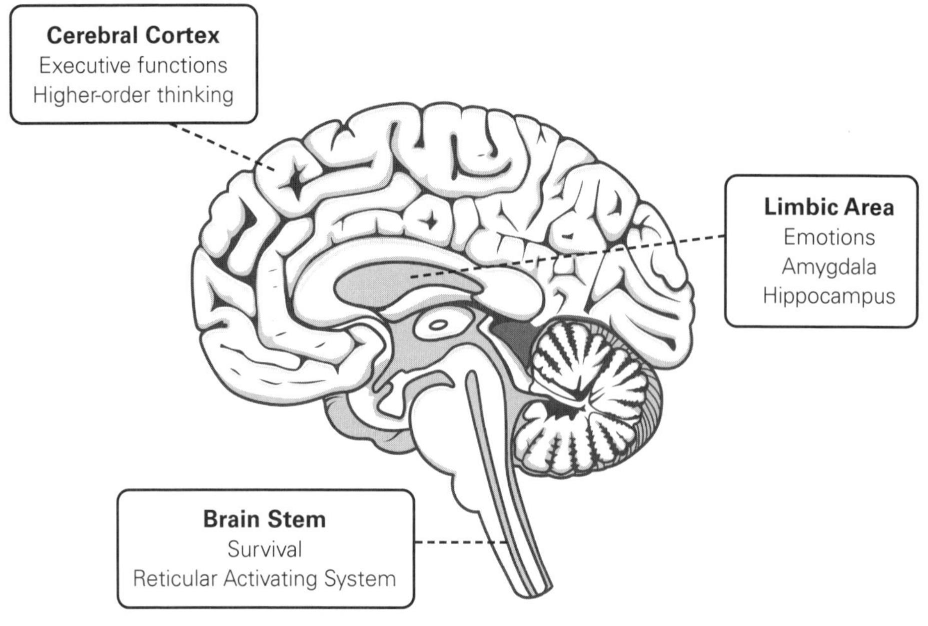

Figure 2.1: Survival response brain regions.

Taking a test isn't inherently a threat to one's survival. There is no physical danger present, and it doesn't keep students from meeting any basic needs. However, the brain may perceive a test as an imminent threat because it interprets perceived emotional and psychological threats as true danger. For example, students might question:

- "Will I know the answers?" (Anticipatory anxiety)
- "What kind of test will it be?" (The unknown)
- "How long will the test be?" (Physical discomfort)
- "Will there be consequences for a poor test performance?" (Psychological or emotional anxiety)
- "Will I have to read directions? Use a computer? Use only English?" (Chaos or confusion)

During the days preceding a high-stakes exam, a student's sensory system may pick up on a variety of alerts. Frequent mentions of the upcoming test and its importance prime the RAS to be on high alert for the important challenge ahead. When schools begin a series of test-preparation activities and even fill the halls with banners and signage to promote the seriousness of the impending test, students' brains are already seeing the signs of a possibly threatening situation. Strategies that are meant to prepare students for success may in fact be creating more stress.

The *amygdala*, an almond-shaped structure embedded deep within our midbrain behind the temporal lobes, receives the filtered sensory input from the RAS. It begins scanning to identify the threat and directs our attention to the possible danger at hand. When this automatic, reflexive action takes over, it triggers the automatic systems in the brain and body to react with the fight-flight-or-freeze response. The amygdala immediately triggers the adrenal glands to release high levels of stress hormones, such as adrenaline (also known as *epinephrine*) and cortisol, alerting the body to get ready to defend, flee, or shut down (Kaufeldt, 2019).

In this survival state, the amygdala acts as a gatekeeper to the *hippocampus*. The hippocampus is part of the limbic area in the midbrain region, important for regulating our emotional responses. As a conduit to the cerebral cortex, the hippocampus helps make connections to prior learning, retrieves long-term memories, and is involved in storing new learning. It is a lightning-fast retrieval system. If the incoming sensory information either matches a negative memory or doesn't connect with any prior experiences, then the amygdala will likely send a signal to the hippocampus, or the "911 operator." If the sensory input is not too alarming, then the hippocampus integrates the new information into known patterns and binds the experience into storable relational memories. It files valuable new learning into the appropriate storage areas of the brain (Kaufeldt, 2019).

If the amygdala triggers the reflex response, all complex cognitive processes are suspended. Little new learning may be processed and stored in long-term memory if we are experiencing perceived threats, stress, or emotional upsets. A student who is experiencing a lot of anxiety and stress following the reflex response may not be very productive while trying to study for an upcoming test. A student's attempts to remember answers during a test may become futile if a reflex response blocks all nonsurvival input from accessing the hippocampus (the "seat of memory"). As neurologist and teacher Judy Willis (2009) describes:

> During stress, any sensory input that is not vital to survival is blocked by the hyperactive amygdala from getting to the higher cortical processing areas. Instead, during high stress states, information input is deflected to a more automatic, reflexive brain response system. (p. 67)

When the amygdala triggers a distress alert, the *hypothalamus*, a very small structure located at the base of the brain near the pituitary gland, activates the sympathetic nervous system and sends signals to the adrenal glands, attached to the kidneys. These glands respond by rapidly pumping the hormones adrenaline and cortisol into the body. This adrenaline rush can make one feel excited and pumped up if no danger or threat is apparent. When the threat is gone, the hypothalamus should tell all systems to go back to normal. The body should relax, and blood pressure, heart rate, respiratory rate, body temperature, and so forth should return to a calm, regulated state of *homeostasis*, maintaining internal stability and making compensations if needed based on environmental and sensory input (Kaufeldt, 2019).

The survival response system can be triggered at various times throughout the day as we navigate our daily lives. Our bodies are designed to recover quickly after an upset or stressful situation. Sometimes there is too much stress and frequent upsets become routine. This can lead to chronic stress.

Effects of Stress

Not all stressful events are harmful or unhealthy. Our unique life experiences and genetics determine the severity of the stressor and our immediate reaction to it. Stress events that happen frequently can lead to a variety of physical and mental health issues. According to the American Psychological Association there are three types of stress (as cited in Freshwater, 2018).

1. **Acute stress:** Acute stress is the most common and usually the least damaging. This momentary stress happens to everyone multiple times throughout our day. It's the brain's immediate reaction to a new or challenging situation that is interpreted as a possible *perceived threat*. This kind of stress occurs when you narrowly escape a dangerous situation, like almost getting in a fender bender or rushing to get to class on time. Doing something fun could also trigger it, like the somewhat frightening yet thrilling feeling you get on an amusement park ride or singing a solo in front of the school. Severe acute stress can happen when you've faced a life-threatening situation such as a car accident, a severe medical event, or lived through a tornado (Scott, 2021). At school, acute stress events might include:
    - Taking a pop quiz
    - Having a substitute teacher
    - Trying to complete a timed activity
    - Being called on to answer or perform without volunteering
    - Getting selected to participate in an assembly
    - Anticipating giving an oral presentation or performance
    - Putting the final touches on an experiment, project, or display
    - Playing in a competitive team sport

2. **Episodic acute stress:** When you are subjected to frequent episodes of acute stress, your brain and body endure intense reactions on a regular basis. Children and adults may have this kind of repeated stress if they are exposed to family or work situations in which acute stress events just keep happening. Certain professionals, such as law enforcement officers and firefighters, often have frequent exposure to high-stress situations that can eventually lead to post-traumatic stress disorder (PTSD) or other mental health problems. Episodic acute stress might happen if you're often anxious and worried about things you suspect may happen. Students in struggling homes or with dysfunctional families may routinely experience traumatic physically and emotionally stressful events in their homes or neighborhoods, such as the following adverse childhood experiences.
    - Physical or sexual abuse
    - Neighborhood violence
    - Mentally unstable or addicted caregivers
    - Death or severe illness episodes of family members

   Students may begin to feel that their lives are chaotic as they go from one crisis to the next. This may elicit a constant state of anxiety as they begin to worry about things they suspect *might* happen.
3. **Chronic or toxic stress:** Adults and children can develop chronic (toxic) stress when they are dealing with acute stressors day after day and even year after year. Acute stress events from our past may become internalized and cause chronic stress even into adulthood. Feelings of anxiety can begin to develop from demands and pressures that just don't let up. It becomes almost impossible to see a way out of the situation. Individuals may begin to feel hopeless and give up searching for solutions. One might actually get used to the chronic stress and ignore physical symptoms. Chronic stress often comes from:
    - Living in poverty
    - Being in a dysfunctional family
    - Living with community or family violence
    - Bullying
    - Experiencing racial and social injustices

> Long-term stress is the most harmful and may contribute to a variety of physical ailments for both adults and children: high blood pressure, headaches, stomachaches, sleep difficulties, acne, chronic pain, memory problems, brain fog, and a weakened immune system. Chronic stress often affects your mood, motivation, thoughts, self-esteem, and energy.

Just how much stress is too much differs from person to person. Some people seem to be able to deal with lots of stress and roll with life's punches, while others tend to fall apart in the face of even minor frustrations. Life being what it is, it's not possible to eliminate stress completely. But people can learn to avoid it when that's possible and manage it when it's unavoidable. The following sections will explore the effects of stress on the body, mind, and emotions and behavior (see figure 2.2).

Source: Adapted from Segal, Smith, Segal, & Robinson, 2020.

Figure 2.2: Effects of stress on the body, mind, and emotions and behaviors.

Effects on the Body

Chronic stress can have negative effects on a person's long-term health. The brain isn't very good at distinguishing between a routine daily stressor and an actual physical life-or-death threat. When the stress response is triggered, many physical signs occur in various systems of the body. Designed to provide strength and stamina to fight or flee the danger at hand, over time, these physical responses can remain engaged and contribute to long-term health problems. Chronic stress can affect nearly every system in the body (Freshwater, 2018; Segal et al., 2020).

- **Respiratory system:** Stress hormones affect your respiratory system. They cause you to breathe faster to quickly distribute oxygen-rich blood to your body. If you already have a breathing problem like asthma or emphysema, stress can make it even harder to breathe. In addition, stress can cause rapid breathing—or hyperventilation—leaving you short of breath. That can also bring on panic attacks in someone prone to panic attacks.
- **Cardiovascular system:** Your heart pumps faster when you are stressed. Stress hormones cause your blood vessels to constrict and divert more oxygen to your muscles so you'll have more strength to take action. The blood vessels that direct blood to the large muscles and the heart dilate, thereby increasing the amount of blood pumped to these parts of the body and elevating blood pressure. Acute stress causes an increase in heart rate and stronger contractions of the heart muscle.
- **Digestive system:** Under stress, your liver produces extra blood sugar to give you a boost of energy. The rush of hormones, rapid breathing, and increased heart rate can also upset your digestive system. You're more likely to have heartburn thanks to an increase in stomach acid. Stress doesn't cause ulcers, but it can increase your risk for them and cause existing ulcers to act up. Stress can also affect the way food moves through your body, leading to nausea, vomiting, or intestinal upsets.
- **Muscular system:** Muscle tension is a reflex reaction to stress—the body's way of guarding against injury and pain. A modest amount of adrenaline will energize your large muscles, such as your hips, thighs, and calves—preparing you to flee if needed. (This is helpful when getting ready to participate in an athletic event, for example.) However, too much adrenaline can cause dizziness, insomnia, and even heart damage. Tight muscles can cause headaches, shoulder pain, and body aches. One area of the muscular system that greatly suffers due to stress is the trapezius muscle group. These muscles over the neck and shoulders tighten up in response to fright or anger. *Raising your hackles* is the body's way of attempting to threaten opponents by helping you appear larger and more

intimidating. In animals, it causes the hair, fur, or feathers to stand up. The "hackles" should release once you relax, but if you're constantly under stress, your muscles may not get the chance to relax—your hackles are in constant tension.

- **Immune system:** When we're stressed, our immune system's ability to fight off antigens (viruses and bacteria) is weakened. That is why over time we are more susceptible to diseases, infections, and injuries. Stress can also increase the time it takes to recover from an illness or injury.

You may easily observe some of these physical symptoms in students during testing, as well as over the days leading up to the exam. Helping students understand how and why their bodies are reacting to stressors can get them ready to manage the stress.

Students' Physiological Response to High-Stakes Tests and Stress Bias

As one might expect, there are many factors that contribute to a poor performance on a high-stakes test. Socioeconomic disparities, student health, and the degree of stress experienced outside of school are all important factors. One study targeted students' stress levels when anticipating and completing high-stakes tests.

The study, "Testing, Stress, and Performance: How Students Respond Physiologically to High-Stakes Testing," was conducted in Louisiana in 2017 with low-income elementary students (Heissel, Adam, Doleac, Figlio, & Meer, 2018). It examined whether students responded *physiologically* to high-stakes testing in the regular classroom and how that impacted their performance on the test. Using a daily saliva sample, the researchers were able to measure how student cortisol levels (the stress hormone) changed during high-stakes testing weeks. Student stress levels were determined to be *elevated* by an average of 15 percent compared to a baseline set the week before. This resulted in a 0.4 standard deviation *decrease* in test scores. (This is equivalent to approximately 80 points on the 1,600-point SAT scale.) Boys had bigger changes than girls, and students who were determined to be the most-disadvantaged had the biggest deficits. Tests that were determined to have the greatest consequences for the schools (high-stakes tests) also influenced the students' poorer performance (Heissel et al., 2018).

Children displayed a statistically significant increase in cortisol level in anticipation of high-stakes testing; this pattern was driven by males. We also find some evidence that, among a sample of disadvantaged students, the most-disadvantaged students had the largest increase in cortisol in anticipation of the high-stakes test. These changes were driven by the occurrence of a test that mattered for schools but had limited consequence for individual students. (Heissel et al., 2018, p. 23)

Heissel et al.'s (2018) research study also describes several other contributing factors. For instance, students who are identified as experiencing chronic stress, trauma, and adversity on a daily basis at home have a much higher *test reactivity*. In other words, if a student's daily life is routinely stressful, that student's systems are pumped and primed to overreact to a trigger more so than other students.

In an interview, Heissel notes that large cortisol (stress) responses were regularly associated with worse test performances, and she contends that perhaps this *stress bias* actually makes these high-stakes tests less reliable indicators of student learning than thought before. This research questions whether or not a standardized test is a valid measure of students' actual abilities—something that many educators have long believed. Heissel believes that if tests unfairly penalize students who respond poorly to stress, that might suggest that "tests aren't fully capturing what we want and perhaps what we think that they capture" (J. Heissel, personal communication, December 27, 2018).

Effects on the Mind

The stress response is meant to protect your body in an emergency by preparing you to quickly react. Sometimes, though, the response becomes about something other than survival. Stress can also lead to high levels of worry, unease, or fear that just won't stop even when there's nothing really threatening or bothering you at that moment, otherwise known as *anxiety*.

Oxford University Press (2021) defines *stress* as "a state of mental or emotional strain or tension resulting from adverse or very demanding circumstances" that "causes strong feelings of worry or *anxiety*." According to the Anxiety and Depression Association of America (n.d.), "Stress is a response to a threat in a situation. Anxiety is a reaction to the stress." Table 2.2 (page 30) features some differences between stress and anxiety.

Often, the main causes of stress are external and caused by people, threatening situations, and dangerous events, but stress can also develop internally. Our own thoughts can make us experience feelings of agitation, anger, anxiousness, guilt, nervousness, or worry in *anticipation* of a possible stressful event. Even when a stressful trigger has passed, with anxiety, the physical responses may remain with additional feelings of anticipation, excessive worry, and even fear. It is fear that can pervade all other emotions felt when anxiety sets in.

TABLE 2.2: Differences Between Stress and Anxiety

Stress	Anxiety
Is a response to a threat (real or perceived)	Is a reaction to stress
Is temporary (varies by individual)	Is sustained beyond the immediate stress
Has external causes and events	Has an internal origin
Happens in the present moment	Focuses on what might happen in the future
Diminishes when the stressor is gone	May remain long after stressor is gone

Some students who are stressed may show mild outward signs of anxiety such as fidgeting; biting their fingernails; tapping their fingers, feet, and so on; playing with their hair or jewelry; needing to use the restroom frequently; or expressing feelings of hunger. For some students, stress hormones can contribute to severe feelings of helplessness, a sense of impending doom, or habitual patterns of negative thoughts.

Anticipatory anxiety or feelings of dread that persist for an extended period of time cause students to worry excessively about upcoming situations such as a test. This may lead to avoidance and cause students to have difficulty coping with everyday situations leading up to the event.

Effects on Emotions and Behaviors

Teachers expect students to be nervous and a little anxious when faced with new situations, such as a new teacher or school. It is perfectly normal to feel some anxiety when performing in a concert, a school play, or a sports event. Moderate anxiety can help students push themselves and persevere when things get tough in order to succeed at home and in school. Test anxiety is a variation of performance anxiety. Nervousness and worry are perfectly normal reactions to an upcoming exam. As Heissel et al.'s (2018) research demonstrates, for many students, however, the fear resulting from test anxiety can become so intense that it can interfere with their ability to perform well on a test.

As school standardized tests have increased in number, length, and rigor, more teachers have reported students who show signs of stress and anxiety (American Psychological Association [APA], 2019). Typical causes of test anxiety in students include the following.

- Poor study skills or underpreparedness
- A fixed mindset about their capabilities due to poor past test performance
- A known learning disability or a shortage in yet reaching the reading or development level of the test
- Negative thought loops about the consequences of the test

- Awareness of the high stakes attached to exams (Many students understand the huge consequences connected to test results. They know that doing poorly could ultimately cause a school to close or a teacher to lose a job.)
- Pressure caused by an inner drive to succeed or a quest for perfection
- Fear of failure, especially if they are unfamiliar with the English language

Negative Thought Loops

A common stressor for many students—especially teenage ones—is when specific thoughts come up over and over, and it seems impossible to get rid of them. These negative thought loops, such as the following, can trigger feelings of fear and insecurity (HeartMath Institute, 2002).

- "I'll never pass the test!"
- "I'll never get a date—I'm not good at talking to people."
- "I'll never get all of this done!"
- "I can't possibly learn all I need to know for the test."
- "I can't believe I said that. I feel so stupid."

In addition to triggering anticipatory anxiety, recurring stress may contribute to depression, personality changes, and other unhealthy behaviors.

Being stressed out can frequently lead to behaviors and patterns that can in turn increase the risk of major depression (Freshwater, 2018). Repeated stress events disrupt many healthy habits, resulting in a lack of sleep, poor diet, limited exercise, and little downtime because of multitasking. Depression can increase worry and negative thought loops that can perpetuate the stress response. This creates a vicious cycle. Symptoms of depression teachers might observe in students include:

- Low motivation
- Lack of engagement
- Feelings of helplessness
- Signs of fatigue
- Loss of interest in things that are usually fun

Stress may not be the only cause of depression; other potential contributors to depression include genetics and family history, hormone levels (especially during puberty), and even certain medications. Loss of any type is a major risk factor for depression; experiencing the loss of a family member, or the loss of a home during a move, might trigger depression in students.

People's personalities are thought to be influenced both by an inherited genetic component (usually called *temperament*) and by interactions with their environment (Saudino, 2005; Schimelpfening, 2020). Some people experience personality changes in response to a flood of stress hormones. Some people may even catastrophize in response to minor stressors. How a person reacts to a stressful event is based on his, her, or their appraisal of the situation, past experiences, temperament, and coping abilities. The following changes in personality are commonly observed in adults, teens, and children who are stressed (Freshwater, 2018).

- Irritability
- Hostility
- Frustration
- Anger
- Aggressive behavior
- Decreased interest in one's appearance
- Obsessive-compulsive behavior
- Defensiveness
- Isolation and social withdrawal
- Attention disorders
- Impulsivity

According to Jodi Ashbrook, founder and CEO of ZenLeader, stress challenges us at an emotional level, making us feel frustrated, overwhelmed, angry, and often helpless (as cited in Stinson, 2018). Stress can affect someone's personality and how that person might react in certain situations. Stress creates a lot of negative energy that can make students more irritable and less patient. Within a classroom or workplace, the negative energy that comes from stress can be contagious.

Conclusion

Teachers already know many students—from elementary school to high school—experience stress every day at home and school. Knowing how the brain reacts to stress and perceived threats can help us design brain-friendly environments to maximize student engagement and learning and ultimately de-stress the test. Teaching students how to better manage school stressors helps them experience less stress, allowing them to perform to their fullest potential during learning and exams.

PART 2

Stress Prevention and Management Strategies

To maximize learning, schools and classrooms need to create environments that maintain a low-threat atmosphere and promote experiences that elicit pleasure and joyfulness for students. When the classroom design emphasizes physical safety as well as emotional and psychological security, teachers can optimize learning. Knowing the kinds of things that can trigger a reflexive response in students allows teachers to design instruction with the brain in mind. As Kagan (2014) emphasizes:

> Whenever there is a perceived threat, the brain's ability to think, plan, problem solve, and control impulses is inhibited or shut down. Learning becomes more difficult or impossible. (p. 27)

A pioneer in the field of brain-compatible teaching, Leslie A. Hart (2002), likens brain-compatible learning to the fit of a glove. She describes that to design a glove to fit perfectly, one must have studied hands and have a good understanding of the mechanics of how they work. Likewise, Hart (2002) believes that educators must study how *brains* learn best in order to be great designers of curriculum, instruction, and learning environments. Understanding what events, systems, procedures, and tasks are likely to upset students can guide teachers to anticipate the stressors and create *prevention* strategies.

There are a variety of *noncognitive factors* that can help students develop self-efficacy and perseverance. Helping students develop a positive outlook on their skills and abilities is a key to their success on a high-stakes test. Building a *growth mindset* takes a variety of experiences over time. Teachers who integrate tasks and activities that allow for failures, feedback, and do-overs can help their students build the confidence and mindset that will begin to minimize test stress. Layous, Chancellor, and Lyubomirsky (2014) describe the many benefits of implementing positive protective activities such as helping students develop positive patterns of emotions, thoughts, behaviors, and tasks that focus on their well-being: "positive emotions—the hallmark of well-being—can serve as antidotes to negative emotions like sadness and anxiety" (p. 3). When we understand how students might even interpret certain subtle movements, gestures, and voice tone as threats, teachers can modify their behavior.

When educators orchestrate their classrooms and instruction with more brain-friendly strategies, they will naturally eliminate many of the most common perceived threats. Designing management strategies that promote student self-regulation will create systems to maximize student engagement. The following three chapters focus on designing and focusing on positive protective factors to prevent stress and strategies for how to manage stress.

BODY- AND BRAIN-FRIENDLY CLASSROOMS AND TESTING ENVIRONMENTS

The brain is designed to attend to, process, retain, and recall certain kinds of information and, information presented in specific ways. When we understand how brains best function, we can align how we teach with how brains best learn.

—KAGAN

The classroom environment can produce positive or negative effects on the learning process and ultimately on testing events. When a classroom includes a healthy level of stress and pressure, it energizes students' brains for engagement, enhances learning, and improves memory. The brain is motivated to engage in learning with appropriate challenges (within one's reach), novelty, and things that are intriguing. But when a classroom has too many perceived threats or distractions, is disorganized or unsafe, has unhealthy elements, and lacks inclusion, and the instructional strategies are designed with a one-size-fits-all approach, it can minimize the capabilities of students' brains.

To create an optimal, safe, and secure climate and environment for learning, educators must keep the brain in mind and consider how to manage possible student stressors. Well-designed and well-maintained classroom environments might actually be able to *prevent* stress responses by reducing perceived threats, and therefore, maximize learning throughout the year. During testing, the classroom environment can also have an impact on students' stress levels and ultimately affect their performance.

As previously discussed, many students arrive to school already operating in a reflex response. Just getting up in the morning, getting ready for school, getting to school, and getting into learning mode can be stressful for many students. When students arrive to school emotionally upset, hungry, tired, and sleepy, everything may seem stressful. This is when teachers must consider what I refer to as the *stressberg* model. Just as an iceberg has massive amounts of ice hidden below the surface of the water, underneath the tip of the iceberg that's visible, students may also have additional stressors that aren't easily apparent to their teachers. Like the ice hidden beneath the surface of the water of a real iceberg, students' thoughts and experiences can be difficult to detect. The students may not even be consciously aware of events and situations they have experienced that are causing trauma and stress. But they are there. Some students are particularly good at keeping the stress they are experiencing quite hidden from their teachers.

When students arrive at school, they may show us a calm and motivated attitude, but make no mistake, some students might have a huge mountain of stressors building up just below the surface. Any additional perception of threats may easily trigger a survival response in them. Students who have had adverse childhood experiences (ACEs) may also have an immediate reaction to classroom events that appear threatening. A test might trigger their *reflex response*, causing them to shut down and avoid interactions, or they may act out. It may take very little to trigger a stress response at school.

Adverse Childhood Experiences

Stress and traumatic events can have negative and lasting effects on children's health and well-being. Such traumatic events may include psychological, emotional, physical, or sexual abuse; domestic abuse; or household members who were substance abusers, mentally ill, suicidal, criminal, or imprisoned. In 1995, a groundbreaking study of over 17,000 participants from the Centers for Disease Control [CDC] and the Kaiser Permanente health care organization in California reported that over two-thirds of U.S children experienced at least one traumatic event before the age of sixteen (CDC, n.d.).

In 2009, the World Health Organization (WHO) along with the U.S. Centers for Disease Control and Prevention began the ACE Global Research Network to help countries identify the prevalence of childhood stressors and understand how ACEs can cause serious, long-lasting consequences. The WHO (n.d.) estimates that in some countries as much as half of the entire population is exposed to at least one adverse childhood experience. The long-term damage due to ACEs is high, especially in settings and communities that have been affected by war, famine, and displacement. The network recommends an ACEs assessment to be included in health data collection around the world (WHO, n.d.).

The Globally Reduce Adverse Childhood Experience (GRACE) Initiatives at the University of California, San Francisco (UCSF) Institute for Global Health Sciences, "aims to advance and translate the science of adverse childhood experiences (ACEs) to improve the lives of children and families worldwide." The initiative directly focuses on those who have been exposed to or are at risk of ACEs, especially in countries affected by war, forced displacement, or ongoing social and economic injustices worldwide (UCSF Institute for Global Health Sciences, n.d.).

Teachers often don't know which students have experienced trauma and extreme stress and which haven't. Some may have experienced an adverse childhood experience but not told anyone. If they are living in traumatic family situations, they may not want to share with anyone for their own safety. To maximize their learning, students who have been impacted by trauma need a safe and secure environment. Becoming *trauma informed* (or *trauma sensitive*) is an essential component of a successful education system. When educators use trauma-informed practices, they ensure all students are supported, even if they don't ask for it (National Child Traumatic Stress Network [NCTSN], n.d.). Schools and classrooms that fail to maintain a positive climate and healthy environment will no doubt see multiple stress-related incidents among their students.

Educators' goal is for powerful learning to take place throughout the year for all their students. To make reaching this goal possible, educators must understand how their students might react to certain school situations, events, and scenarios that are likely to trigger a stress response. Brain-friendly, trauma-sensitive practices can help prevent stress during learning *and* during a high-stakes test.

Even for students who are not experiencing adverse childhood experiences or chronic stress, many school situations may trigger the reflex response. Students can become anxious when they don't know what will happen next or what the expectations are. Lack of inclusion in social situations, limited language abilities, pressure to perform in front of the whole class, and of course tests are all classic stressors. Teachers must do everything within their control to keep their students' brains clear, present, and focused every day to ensure long-term retention and application.

Basic stressors that might trigger a reflex response at school fall into one of six broad categories.

1. Physical environment
2. Schedules, time pressures, and constraints
3. Chaos and confusion
4. Basic needs
5. Social-emotional culture
6. Challenging academics

These everyday stressors may not be triggers for everyone, yet some students may react to them so strongly that their ability to think logically and continue with the learning process is minimized. Every person is unique and comes wired to react to an individual set of potential stressors. Unfortunately, many traditional classrooms still maintain environments and routines that often produce stress for many students *during* the learning process. If our goal is to help students be as prepared as possible for any assessment, teachers need to address these basic stressors.

The following sections provide brief looks at the six potential stressor categories to help teachers identify situations in their classroom that may cause problems for some students. Each section includes suggestions for ways to modify and reduce the perceived threats. These brain-friendly prevention strategies will be particularly important when administering tests.

Physical Environment

The following sections show that *where* learning and testing take place can make a difference. Students' brains and bodies are sensitive to the physical aspects of the learning environment. When conditions are uncomfortable, unhealthy, and distracting and students don't feel safe, their brains are not able to attend and engage as easily. Perceived threats in the classroom keep students from being able to fully concentrate. The following sections will discuss aspects of the physical environment that may trigger stress for students: (1) building condition; (2) school appearance and aesthetics; (3) excess mess; (4) indoor environmental quality; and (5) school dangers, drills, and lockdowns. I will also offer body- and brain-friendly strategies to create healthy environments.

Building Condition

Poor classroom and school-building conditions can cause student stress responses. According to Debbie Alexander and Laurie Lewis (2014) of Westat, more than half of

U.S. public schools in 2012–2013 reported the need to spend money on their school buildings in order to bring them up to a *good* condition. Some of the most commonly reported structural problems include windows, plumbing, temperature regulation, and ventilation. Schools that serve a greater concentration of students who are on free or reduced-price lunch and who live in high-poverty neighborhoods were more likely to report poor-quality buildings.

Inadequate school facilities are related to worse test scores. In 2007, the National Research Council published *Green Schools: Attributes for Health and Learning*, which evaluated twenty studies that investigated the relationship between overall building condition and student achievement. The studies included urban and rural schools in several different states. Several studies concluded that older buildings, or those in substandard condition, contributed to lower achievement and test scores. Nineteen out of twenty studies showed higher test scores for students in buildings that were in better condition.

A meta-analysis of over two hundred scientific studies determined a correlation between building condition and student achievement. According to the 2017 report from Harvard's T. H. Chan School of Public Health's Healthy Buildings Program, environmental exposures in school buildings—air quality, uncomfortable temperatures, inadequate lighting, or ambient noise—can negatively impact student health, thinking, and performance (Eitland et al., 2017).

School Appearance and Aesthetics

When students arrive at the school site, their senses are on high alert. Consciously and unconsciously, they notice how the building appears and feels. When the school looks neglected and is poorly maintained, students may begin to feel fearful, disrespected, or threatened. Whether it be mismatched paint, graffiti, broken stairs and railings, poorly maintained or dead landscaping, or outdated or damaged signage, students' brains alert their bodies that this school *could be* an unsafe place for them to spend time. *The Effect of School Design on Users' Responses* (Manca, Cerina, Tobia, Sacchi, & Fornana, 2020), a long-term analysis of international research findings, reports that a pleasant, warm, and flexible learning environment is key to promoting both the well-being and the performance students. The report notes that pleasant colors and pictures, ergonomic furniture, adequate acoustics, thermal comfort, ventilation, and natural lighting are important features in school designs (Manca et al., 2020).

Excess Mess

Classrooms that engage students in a variety of hands-on projects and activities often have an abundance of supplies readily available for student use but not much room to store them. According to psychologist Sherrie Bourg Carter (2012), messy classrooms and workspaces may leave some students feeling anxious, helpless, and overwhelmed, and excessive clutter and mess can cause student stress in a variety of ways.

- Clutter can bombard students' minds with excessive visual, olfactory, and tactile stimuli, causing their senses to work overtime on stimuli and things that aren't necessary or important.
- Clutter can distract students by drawing their attention away from what their focus should be on.
- The extra stimulation from clutter makes it more difficult for students' brains and bodies to relax, both physically and mentally.
- Clutter constantly signals to students' brains that the work is never done, and it creates a feeling of being buried in disorganization.
- A big mess may make students anxious because they are never sure if they can find what they need. This creates a feeling of being out of control.
- The physical effects of an unclean environment may impact students' health.

Often, our personal tolerance for clutter may relax over time, and we don't even *see* the mess ourselves. Evidence of student projects, materials for problem-solving activities, hands-on science kits, mathematics manipulatives, and lots of art supplies occasionally seem to overwhelm and overcrowd many classrooms. Additional storage is often just not available. I've observed teachers at a school who even rented a small storage locker to get some clutter out of their classrooms.

Indoor Environmental Quality

In addition to noticing the appearance of the school, students' senses may pick up on classroom situations that might be unsafe or unhealthy for them. *Indoor environmental quality* (IEQ) refers to the quality of the conditions inside a building in relation to the comfort, health, and well-being of its occupants. A school's indoor environmental quality can encompass the school's physical buildings and the classroom furniture, maintenance and upkeep, ambient noise, lighting, air quality, and thermal comfort in the buildings (National Center on Safe Supportive Learning Environments, 2018).

According to the Harvard Center for Health and the Global Environment report *Schools for Health* (Eitland et al., 2017), "Improving IEQ can positively affect cognitive function outcomes, such as decision-making, attention, concentration, and memory" (p. 12). Poor IEQ was reported as a factor causing greater fatigue, loss of attention and concentration, and poorer test performances.

Schools that lack adequate heating and cooling systems, or have ones that work intermittently, may have students (and their teachers) worrying about staying warm or cooling off rather than focusing on the curriculum and learning. Schools may not always address mold in a timely fashion; students who have allergies or respiratory issues may be uncomfortable and not even realize what is causing their reactions. Classroom clutter, unemptied recycling collections, old lunches with rotten food, and the odors associated with these things can be found in some classrooms. Students' bodies react to these conditions as possible survival issues. When students are dealing with these kinds of indoor environmental quality stressors, it is likely to minimize their learning. The stressors may inhibit memory and recall, and therefore may also skew testing results.

Additional unhealthy things that may create negative responses in students (and teachers) include nonfunctioning toilets and sinks, trash cans that are not emptied regularly, poor ventilation (plus mold, paint, and sweat odors), rodent or ant infestations, unclean carpets, and questionable food preparation. In one of my own elementary classrooms one year, the sink frequently backed up with sewage. Even when I covered it up with a plastic garbage bag, the smell was disgusting and distracting and upset many students (and parents!). Another school where I was a coach sat adjacent to strawberry fields. On a regular basis, a pesticide-spraying helicopter would pass by, and many students and teachers would feel sick and have headaches. Just hearing the sound of the helicopter arriving would cause students to grab their jackets and put them up over their mouths and noses. Although the school had little control over this particular scenario, after an active campaign from teachers and parents, some changes were eventually made. Local growers agreed to spray on Fridays through Sundays to lessen the impact on students.

School Dangers, Drills, and Lockdowns

A 2019 UNESCO report confirms that school violence and bullying are major problems worldwide. School violence can include shootings, physical attacks, fights, corporal punishment, psychological and emotional abuse, and sexual attacks. According to a RAND Corporation (as cited in Stein et al., 2011) research brief, violence is one of the most significant public health issues. Between 20 percent and 50 percent of U.S. children are exposed to violence. Children exposed to violence frequently have behavioral problems, poorer school performance, more days of school absence, and feelings of depression and anxiety (as cited in Stein et al., 2011). The Educator's School Safety Network (2019) has compiled information on threats and incidents of violence in U.S. schools. The 2018–2019 school year included at least 374 incidents of violence, compared to 279 incidents in the 2017–2018 school year, a 34 percent increase (Educator's School Safety Network, 2019). The continued increase in school violence is of great concern. With more frequent incidents of school violence, schools regularly practice more and more intense drills and shelter-in-place lockdowns in hopes of preventing future tragedies.

Some schools admit students into the building through metal detectors with security guards and place surveillance cameras throughout the building. Some schools have installed bulletproof, automatic-locking doors. Marjory Stoneman Douglas High School in Parkland, Florida, the site of a horrific shooting in 2018, mandated school security measures that include increased security officers on the premises, mandatory ID badges for everyone, locked classrooms, and a new rule that students can only use clear backpacks. Some schools are even recommending that parents buy their children bulletproof backpacks. In 2015, a school district in Oklahoma installed bulletproof shelters, which also protect against tornadoes, inside some classrooms of their elementary and middle schools (Street, 2018).

When students don't believe that their school is a safe place to be, they may be in a constant state of anxiety and worry, unable to fully attend to their lessons. For many, the cumulative effect of this stress will affect their initial acquisition of learning as well as add to the stress of taking high-stakes tests. In her report on *Neighborhood Violence, Peer Effects, and Academic Achievement in Chicago*, John Hopkins's research professor Julia Burdick-Will (2018) states, "Exposure to local neighborhood violence is associated with reductions in test scores and increases in stress, depression, and aggression, all of which can lead to disruptive and distracting behavior in the classroom" (p. 205). A report on international schools from United Nations Office of the Special Representative of the Secretary-General on Violence Against Children (2016) warns that, "The negative impact of violence in schools goes beyond the children who are directly affected by it. It touches the lives of those who witness it, creating an atmosphere of anxiety and insecurity incompatible with learning" (p. 2).

Ninety-five percent of the U.S. states and Washington, DC, have mandated that schools conduct active-shooter drills on a regular basis. In the 2017–2018 school year, more than 4.1 million students endured at least one lockdown (Walker, 2020). Some feel that schools' emphasis on and methods of drills have created excessive fear and stress among many students (Black, 2020). Some districts have been accused of going too far, using starter pistols to simulate gunshots and fake blood smeared on administrators' faces to expose students to the reality of a school shooting.

Gallup senior editor Jeffrey M. Jones (2018) summarizes a poll in which one in five U.S. students express feeling unsafe at school, and 35 percent of parents admit they worry about school safety. In a 2017 report, the National Association of School Psychologists and the National Association of School Resource Officers acknowledge that active-shooter drills have the potential to save lives by increasing preparedness, but warn that if not conducted appropriately, they risk causing physical and psychological harm to students. Psychologists and educators report that frequent realistic drills contribute to anxiety and depression in students and rob students of their belief that schools are in fact extremely safe places. Although meant to provide a feeling of control and empowerment, the increased safety protocols are extremely upsetting and stressful for many students.

Strategies to Create Healthy Physical Environments

The preceding research demonstrates how an unhealthy school environment can add to student stress *during* learning and play a role in students' stress levels when taking tests. There are several ways that teachers, staff, and parents, as well as the students themselves can address their school's physical environment to make it more body and brain friendly.

- Consider creating a school-environment committee to review and report unsafe and unhealthy physical conditions observed on the school campus. Elicit student involvement when appropriate. Video reports and presentations to administration can help bring problem areas to the forefront and demonstrate the need for some repairs and upgrades.
- Create a school-beautification committee of staff, students, and parents to evaluate and address the school's aesthetic appearance. All stakeholders can share this ongoing effort. Parents, community groups, and individual classrooms can help in designing planter boxes, painting murals, adding art installations, and improving lighting.
- Evaluate classroom lighting, temperature, and air quality, and report deficiencies and needed repairs. Investigating, testing, and collecting data for these possible problems are wonderful projects for groups of secondary students to take on.

- Advocate for and insist on timely action and appropriate funding for general maintenance and repairs. Staff members who are aware of issues must be vigilant about reporting and asking for basic maintenance issues.
- Request tables and chairs that allow for flexible seating to enhance student interactions. Classroom furniture should be arranged to meet students' needs rather than the needs of the custodial staff. Teaching staff should ask to be included in selections of new furniture.
- In the classroom, display symbolic objects that remove uncertainty about whether one's social identity will be accepted. These displays can help reduce racial and gender achievement gaps and improve the achievement of students of color and female students of all backgrounds. Teachers can create these safe classroom contexts even with limited resources. Cultural responsiveness, at a very basic level, ensures that all students see their culture reflected in the curriculum and classroom materials.
- Maximize the effectiveness of safety drills by having extensive staff training that results in staff members who inspire calmness and confidence in students. Students model their reactions on adult behaviors.
- Ensure that participation in drills is appropriate to students' individual development levels; take into consideration prior traumatic experiences, special needs, and personalities.
- When conducting safety protocols, make sure school-employed mental health professionals are involved in every stage of drills and lockdowns and they are available to meet with upset students at the completion of the event.

Schedules, Time Pressures, and Constraints

Our brains experience less stress when we know the schedule, routines, and expectations. When daily routines suddenly change without warning, such as a schedule change on the day of a high-stakes test, we might have a reflexive response. Time pressures and constraints can also be stressful enemies. Any disruption to a known pattern or an expectation can trigger an upset. Many students can get quite anxious about time limits when working on a task or when taking a test. Helping students understand what is going on in their brains when there are time changes may relieve some of the anxiety.

The following sections will further discuss how schedules, time pressures, and constraints may trigger stress for students: (1) schedule changes and new routines, (2) time limitations and inflexible schedules, (3) anticipatory anxiety, and (4) unfinished assignments and tasks. I will also offer body- and brain-friendly strategies to reduce stress related to schedules, time pressures, and constraints.

Schedule Changes and New Routines

The brain likes patterns. When a schedule or routine is in place, our brains and bodies get into a comfortable rhythm. A lot of our daily actions are automatic, and our brains like being on autopilot. The brain detects patterns and then creates and stores them as mental programs.

People begin to learn a routine by determining the probability of an event happening after another event. They are learning patterns and developing rules that guide their decisions and next steps (Ohio State University, 2018). Humans find security in being able to recognize a pattern and automatically respond with an appropriate program. We feel more confident when we are able to anticipate the next steps. When students know what the school schedule and the classroom routine are, they feel secure and less anxious and can focus on learning. The brain thrives best with consistency.

When we don't know or are just learning a new routine, we may feel fearful and unsure. When a schedule or routine suddenly changes, it disrupts our brain patterns, and many of us feel off-balance. Frequent schedule changes can be stressful for many students. During test days, students' daily routines are often adjusted. When students arrive at school and discover schedule changes, it can upset them.

Time Limitations and Inflexible Schedules

While consistency is comfortable for their brains, unreasonable time limitations or inflexible schedules can cause students a lot of stress. *Time stress* is a well-known form of stress in the fast-paced, multitasking 21st century environment (Albrecht, 2010). Not making the due date for a school assignment or project can lead to stress—more important, students commonly worry about a lack of time for the expected completion (or possible incompletion) of tasks. Trying and stressing to finish a task on time can have a negative effect on the work's final quality because the assignment was rushed.

Battling to meet even a reasonable deadline or trying to work within a dictated schedule can leave students feeling exhausted and frustrated. Many high-stakes tests have time constraints that contribute to student stress during the exam and may inhibit performance. Time stress is real.

Anticipatory Anxiety

Anticipatory anxiety describes the stress that one feels when thinking about a future event or task. Worrying about an upcoming presentation or test, experiencing anxiety regarding a looming social situation, being fearful of making someone mad or disappointed, and fretting about when something is going to take place are all examples of *anticipatory anxiety*—worrying about what will happen next and when it will happen. Some students are known for arriving to class and immediately asking the teacher about what will happen that day—"When are we going to give our presentations?" or "When will we get to go to the assembly?" Their inquiries may be just needing a simple response, but often these types of questions indicate that the student is experiencing stress.

This type of stress and anxiety can be about specific future events such as upcoming tests, but it can also be an overall sense of dread. Many students anxiously think, *What might go wrong? What will people think? What if I can't do it?* or *What if people find out I'm not smart?* no matter the classroom situation. Many times, the students showing the most anxiety might be some of the brightest and most gifted. They often overthink and get spun out about possibilities. As the Summer Institute for the Gifted (2020) explains:

> Because gifted children experience the world intensely, they may show a heightened level of behaviors that are associated with anxiety. Children who are acutely aware of the world around them may develop anxiety over worrying about global and local problems, perfectionism in themselves, and general fears regarding situations out of their control.

Unfinished Assignments and Tasks

Many students often have difficulty finishing assignments. They may be slow workers, or there simply might not be enough time scheduled. When taking tests, the time limits may really trigger some students as they run out of time. This kind of situational stress may get triggered at the last minute when students realize that they didn't plan ahead and didn't anticipate how much time the task would take, and they begin to panic. This is often a result of a lack of executive function. Making goals, planning the steps needed, and managing time effectively are all relatively higher-level thinking skills. For some students, difficulty completing this process begins with a lack of motivation or relevance. For others, it may be procrastination and an inability to actually start the process. No matter the cause for not getting something done, the body still may react with a stress response.

Everyone reacts to situational stress differently. When taking a test, some students may become angry and show their frustration (fight). Others may try to avoid the confrontation and hide or withdraw (flight and freeze; Gregory & Kaufeldt, 2015). For some, it is the perfect opportunity to blame the limited time allotment as the reason for their lack of success. During class assignments, when students realize that they are not going to make a deadline, some will claim that the teacher didn't give correct directions or didn't provide enough time or materials. Others will blame their partners or teammates for ruining everything. The response becomes "I could have done this, *but* . . . ."

Strategies to Reduce Stress Related to Schedules, Time Pressures, and Constraints

Students will feel less stressed when they can count on schedules and routines. If changes occur, there are some prevention strategies teachers can employ that will help ease the disruption.

- If there will be schedule changes during the test day, rehearse the changes several days in advance. Post, review, and practice the new routine that will be used on test day. Multiple rehearsals will create mental programs of expected protocols.
- In the weeks leading up to the test, orchestrate some classroom tasks that students complete independently and with a time limitation. Give students opportunities to experience what forty minutes of quiet work time feels like. Elementary students, who may be used to a flexible schedule, can especially benefit from practicing with a limited chunk of time to get a sense of how much time it is.
- If the test will be conducted in a different location, practice going there with students and setting up where they will be sitting. Check seating and desks for correct adjustments ahead of the test day. (Desk and chair height should be measured to optimize comfort.)
- Throughout the year, start classes with a daily agenda to help students understand the game plan for the day or class. Post and review a calendar to provide a visual of when big events, such as tests, will be happening.

Chaos and Confusion

Surprises. Not the brain's favorite thing. Although the brain positively responds to *novelty*—something interesting, curious, or fun—new changes that may appear as confusing can trigger the reflex response (Kaufeldt, 2019; Willis, 2009). Our brains also can become stressed when there are too many new things introduced at once.

The following sections will further discuss how chaos and confusion may trigger stress for students: (1) new school, new class, or new teacher; (2) unclear goals and expectations; and (3) student disorganization. I will also offer body- and brain-friendly strategies to reduce stress related to chaos and confusion.

New School, New Class, or New Teacher

Benchmark transitions for students include moving to a new school, leaving kindergarten, going into middle or high school, and so on. Going into a new class or school for the first time can be exciting and intimidating for students, and even for new or experienced teachers. Many students have a nervous excitement that manifests as hyperactivity, silliness, and talkativeness. For other students, the stress of going to a new place, meeting new people, and figuring out the new systems may be quite paralyzing. These students are often worried, quiet, and emotional and may even try to avoid the new situation.

New schools and classrooms pose the possibility of unknown perceived threats. Much anxiety stems from *encounter stress* (Albrecht, 2010), which keeps students worrying about the people they will need to interact with in the new classroom or at the new school. To alleviate this encounter stress, some teachers start the school year very seriously to establish a no-nonsense tone in an attempt to tamper down the excited students. (My master teacher in 1977 unfortunately advised me to not smile until Christmas. He said that if I let the students see that I was "fun" or too friendly, they would try to take advantage of me.) On the other hand, some teachers may try to be exciting and upbeat, hoping to engage students and distract them from their stress.

Encounter stress may also develop as students anticipate their seat locations, various group designations, and the inevitable getting-to-know-you activities. If the first days of the class include lots of planned student interactions, some students may begin to experience contact overload. Common symptoms for contact overload include crankiness; fatigue; and an impersonal, disrespectful, or rude demeanor (Albrecht, 2010). Recovery is one of the most important aspects of the stress cycle. Being able to bounce back from a stressful period and being able to return to a state of equilibrium are essential. Many students who experience stress may take many hours to reboot. Parents may encounter evidence of the stress and contact overload when students get home from school (USQ Social Hub, 2019).

Unclear Goals and Expectations

The brain works most efficiently, and learning is optimized, when it understands the expectations and recognizes clear patterns for how to achieve those goals. Professor of Education John Hattie (2009), through his research and meta-analysis of extensive data, uses *effect sizes* to identify what works and what doesn't with regard to education strategies and initiatives. (An effect size is a measure of the contribution an education intervention makes to student learning.) He determines that the benchmark or standard that represents an average or typical effect size of one year of schooling is 0.40 and calls this the *hinge point*, which means the typical student made one year's academic growth in one year of class time. Any effect size lower than 0.40 indicates a poor strategy generating low achievement. Strategies with effect sizes of 0.50 and above are strong indicators of successful methods. In *Visible Learning: Feedback*, John Hattie and Shirley Clarke (2019) offer an updated list of factors for achievement, noting:

- The effect size for high expectations is 0.40. Teachers develop and maintain a culture of high expectations for all students by setting challenging learning goals.
- The effect size for setting learning goals is 0.68. Lessons have clear learning intentions with goals that clarify what success looks like.
- The effect size for teacher clarity is 0.75. Learning goals are presented clearly so students know what they are intended to learn.

When students don't know the game plan, don't get their questions answered in a timely fashion, and are unclear of the desired outcomes, many will experience stress (Hattie & Shirley, 2019). When teachers aren't crystal clear about the purpose of a lesson, with whom students may work, what materials students should use, and how much time they have to work, many students may experience anxiety. This generates lots of student questions to clarify the following.

- "How much time will we have?"
- "Can we use the computers?"
- "Can we work with a partner?"
- "What if my book isn't here?"
- "How many points will this be?"
- "What should we do when we're finished?"

In addition to providing clear instructions, teachers simply stating procedures for all expected behaviors (such as the procedures in table 3.1) can help reduce students' anxiety. Positive prompts will help students understand with whom they can work, where they can go, what materials they can use, and what they can do if they need help.

TABLE 3.1: Procedures for Small-Group Work and Presentations

Procedures for Small-Group Work	Procedures for Presentations
Stay in your group's area.	Listen and watch.
Do your part of the task.	Stay in your seat.
Offer to help others.	Raise your hand to share or ask questions.
Share materials and resources.	Participate when asked.

Student Disorganization

Teachers know that organization is a key to success. Students who continually lose books, assignments, and the like can get quite frustrated and stressed. Organization and management skills should be integrated into every lesson. Many teachers may assume that students learn these skills at home or in earlier grades. Just as classroom clutter can influence students' stress levels, so can messy desks, lockers, backpacks, and so on (National Center on Safe Supportive Learning Environments, 2018).

Students who struggle because of a lack of organization often experience failure and frustration. Students' disorganization can lead to poor performance because students are missing out on valuable instructional time. Rather than participating in class activities, taking notes, or contributing to class discussions, students are often searching for their lost assignments or missing materials. Students can get into a cycle of always trying to catch up. When students lack organizational skills, they are at a disadvantage because they are often late, unprepared, and seem to be behind the rest of the class. Mental clutter can be just as stressful for students, maybe even more stressful than physical clutter. When students are attempting to multitask and juggle many different assignments and responsibilities in and out of school, their brains may begin to experience high degrees of mental stress.

Strategies to Reduce Chaos and Confusion

When teachers do a little organizational work ahead of instruction, their students will benefit. Positive protection strategies, such as daily agendas and clear procedures, will help all students know what to expect and reduce confusion.

- Consider how you will begin the class. First impressions count! Limit new information, review of classroom procedures, and introductions to just a few minutes to avoid overload. Setting up daily patterns and procedures will create a routine and promote a feeling of consistency.
- Include simple student-to-student interactions to build students' confidence and reduce encounter stress. Clear procedures for social interactions will encourage polite conversations and discussions.
- Use daily agendas to help students know the goals and game plan for the day. Teacher clarity about the schedule for the class and the expectations gives students a clear vision of what they need to do and complete.
- Create and use clear procedures to reduce anticipatory anxiety and promote student self-regulation. Students will benefit when teachers take the time to develop procedures for routine tasks and maintain consistent patterns of behaviors.
- Take five minutes to sit in a student desk after the class leaves and look around the classroom. It might give you a new perspective and inspire some cleanup and organization. We often get oblivious to the clutter build up.
- Integrate organizational skills into every lesson. Help students develop strategies to save and file assignments, manage books, and review research materials. Teachers who teach organizational strategies really are providing valuable life skills for their students.
- Make sure you review testing goals, expectations, and procedures during the days leading up to testing events. Anticipate student questions and worries. The added anxiety that high-stakes tests bring means that students may need to be reminded more often and instructions may need to be especially clear.

Basic Needs

In 1943, Abraham Maslow first developed the hierarchy of basic needs and described how people are driven to get these needs met (Maslow, 1968). These basic needs are biological and can be overwhelming. Students cannot help but seek to meet their needs because "the brain is wired to maintain homeostasis. Hungry, thirsty, and tired brains will set aside opportunities to learn, seeking out food, water, and rest in order to feel satisfied and calm" (Kaufeldt, 2010, p. 67). In classrooms that have tight restrictions, students may be in a constant reflex response. During stressful events such as testing, these basic needs may be exacerbated.

The following sections will further discuss how factors related to basic needs may trigger stress for students: (1) hunger and thirst, (2) restricted movement and physical activity, (3) lack of downtime or playtime, and (4) language fluency. I will also offer body- and brain-friendly strategies to reduce stress related to basic needs.

Hunger and Thirst

Our brains always monitor our survival needs of food, water, sleep, and shelter. We must first meet these needs before we can really pay attention to learning or have fun. In classrooms, there are often strict rules about eating, drinking, and using the restroom. Students who arrive to school hungry will think about their hunger until they can get something to eat. A feeling of thirst can happen at any time, yet at school, students are often not allowed to hydrate as needed. The stress of being hungry or thirsty can be a huge factor in a student's ability to have success.

Another basic need—getting rid of bodily waste—can be a huge stressor for many students. Many students may have anxiety associated with bathroom access, possible accidents, menstrual issues, and gastrointestinal upsets.

Restricted Movement and Physical Activity

For many students, having to sit still in an uncomfortable chair and having their movement restricted for up to an hour at a time can be very stressful. Unfortunately, many classrooms still rely on an inordinate amount of sitting. The time schools have dedicated to physical education and recess has steadily decreased. In the era of increased rigorous instruction, many teachers have been pushed into thinking that movement and play are frivolous and a waste of time (Abdelbary, 2017). Students who frequently feel the need to get up and move may become frustrated and anxious, and that may lead to behavioral issues and disciplinary actions. Some students report feeling dread when they must go to a classroom that severely restricts movement of any kind.

Even with curriculum that includes more project-based and hands-on learning, movement in the classroom is often quite restricted. Students spend much more time in a passive learning setting. In "Promoting Physical Activity in Schools," the World Health Organization (2007) states, "Public health officials are becoming increasingly concerned that young people in both developed and developing countries are becoming increasingly inactive" (p. 1). The report cites benefits of physical activity, including helping students stay alert in class, which improves their academic achievements, as well as helping to relieve tension, restlessness, and lack of concentration resulting from continuous sitting, which leads to high academic achievement.

The lack of physical activity among people of all ages is so critical that it is considered to be a major health risk. The *Physical Activity Guidelines for Americans* recommends that children and adolescents ages six to seventeen years do sixty minutes or more of moderate-to-vigorous physical activity daily (U.S. Department of Health and Human Services, 2018). For many students, the idea of having to participate in physical education creates lots of anxiety and stress. Many students worry and experience stress over the reactions the other students might have about their physical skill abilities (or lack of skills). Also, in grades 4–8, students' attitude about physical education participation can change significantly and cause psychological and emotional stress. So many biological, psychological, and social changes occur during adolescence and are often associated with a decline in their self-esteem. This transition time has much to do with physical changes and body image for teens, and participating in physical education makes these new changes apparent to the other students.

Lack of Downtime or Playtime

The absence of downtime can be a stressor for many students. The need for constant engagement and focused attention can create overload in the brain and body. When teachers don't find ways to orchestrate opportunities for a little rest and relaxation within the class, they may find a number of students begin to have meltdowns and behavioral issues. Downtime may be a simple, quiet activity of reading or drawing. For some students, downtime is having a chance to play vigorously outside. Even brief opportunities to play can help the brain get ready for more serious learning activities (Brown, 2009).

Play, as described by affective neuroscientist Jaak Panksepp (1998), is a primary emotion. His research indicates that opportunities for play set in motion many brain systems that not only facilitate learning but also promote happiness (Davis & Panksepp, 2018; Panksepp, 1998; Panksepp & Biven, 2012). In his foreword for *The Motivated Brain: Improving Student Attention, Engagement, and Perseverance* (Gregory & Kaufeldt, 2015), Panksepp explains:

> The many benefits of play should alert educators to the problems that may emerge when children are deprived of this vital resource for mental health. Without a regular diet of fun social engagements, children become hungry for play and begin to "act out," potentially disrupting the flow of classroom instructional activities. (p. xi)

Research indicates that, in the 21st century, many children never get sufficient amounts of natural, self-generated play. This may be a reason that children develop hyperactivity and attention disorders and lack impulse control—all issues that have a connection to anxiety and stress (Panksepp & Biven, 2012). Several researchers have gathered data suggesting that kids are being overdiagnosed with attention deficit hyperactivity disorder (ADHD) and other attention disorders because 6.4 million children in the United States (over 9 percent), ranging from age six to age seventeen, are diagnosed with ADHD each year (Hamed, Kauer, & Stevens, 2015); see also www.cdc.gov/ncbddd/adhd/data.html for more data. Many of the referrals come from teachers with students who have difficulty sitting still and paying attention. According to a 2003 report, ADHD is not purely a U.S. disorder. The rate of identification in many countries is in the same range as that in the United States (Faraone, Sergeant, Gillberg, & Biederman, 2003), with a global rate of 5.29 percent, or 116 million children being diagnosed worldwide (Smith, 2017).

Language Fluency

Language is an instinct that is driven by evolutionary adaptations. Being able to use language to ask for help, get food, and express wants and needs is an important basic need. One's ability to communicate involves both receptive and productive language skills. *Receptive language* allows us to comprehend and understand others. *Productive language* allows us to generate ideas and use words to ask questions (MacWhinney, n.d.). Not being able to communicate in your native language can generate a lot of stress.

Diverse 21st century classrooms commonly include English learners at various levels of fluency. For some English learners, it is very stressful to begin speaking English in class. They have thoughts like these: *What will the other students think? What if I make a huge flub? My thoughts are much faster than I can express them verbally.* Foreign-language anxiety is a real thing. Translator Huong Tran (2016) explains that *xenoglossophobia*, as it's also known, is an extreme "feeling of unease, worry, nervousness, and apprehension experienced when learning or using a second or foreign language."

Learning English within the regular classroom can be inherently stressful. When learning a new language that operates with different grammar, vocabulary, and pronunciation, students can have extreme anxiety about trying to speak out loud. Students who are not yet fluent in the new language may be in a constant state of stress about written and oral communication. For those who are deemed ready to take exams in English, there may be a lot of test anxiety, which can trigger the reflex response. The levels of foreign-language anxiety can be so extreme that the anxiety can hamper performance and productive learning. Teachers who understand their ELs' anxieties will be able to adjust tasks to minimize stress:

> Three closely related cognitive factors are said to cause [foreign-language anxiety]. First is communication apprehension, which is the fear of speaking, whether in front of the class, to the teacher or with a native speaker. Second is test anxiety, which is the fear of being tested and being put on the spot. And last, which is very much related to the second one, is the fear of negative evaluation—the fear of the judgment of others, including us teachers. Nobody wants to look stupid, but in [foreign-language anxiety], that fear reaches feverish heights. These three are self-sustaining and can easily snowball to the point of the student not being able to acquire the target language. (FluentU, n.d.)

Some students experiencing foreign-language anxiety might try to become invisible and avoid having to participate, and others might appear shy and even try to avoid coming to class.

Strategies to Meet Students' Basic Needs

Consider the following strategies to reduce stress related to students' basic needs.

- Determine whether students are getting their basic nutritional needs met. Create ways to provide simple healthy snacks for those students who come to school without a morning meal. School meal programs may be able to supply individually packaged snacks such as granola bars or dried fruit snacks. Parent support groups might also help provide these handy snacks that can be given to students as needed in the classroom.
- Work with the school's food services, the administration, and your colleagues to address hunger issues if they are impacting student learning. Investigate the success of the current food program at your school. Are all students who qualify able to get the meals they deserve? If hunger is an ongoing issue that is keeping students from engaging and being successful, this basic need must be addressed.
- Provide students with opportunities for hydrating and using the restroom as needed. Allow students to bring a water bottle with them to class, and have scheduled bathroom breaks, for example.
- Integrate opportunities for students to get up and move *during class*. Regularly take a few minutes for stretching and simple exercises. In the classroom, *brain breaks* are quick, structured breaks using physical

movement or sensory activities. Teachers can use them as a transition from one activity to another. Brain breaks take only a few minutes of time and give students a little break from what they're doing to help their brains and bodies get energized and ready to return to learning. For example, at the start of the day, the teacher can incorporate some stretching; or to refocus after lunch, the teacher might play a game like *Simon Says*. There are lots of great free online resources to get started. Visit https://bit.ly/3gpZBFT for a brain breaks bank.

- Be aware of English learners' needs. Avoid unnecessary reasons for students to have to speak in front of large groups of their peers. Working with a partner or in a small group might feel more comfortable at first.
- Orchestrate study and process partners to support English learners. When students can get to know a partner, there will be less anxiety about speaking English aloud. Staying with the same study buddy will feel safer.
- Notice student stress levels, and work in opportunities for some playful tasks or quiet downtime to reduce anxiety and fatigue. The brain loves novelty so playing a quick game of *Charades* or *Four Corners* can be energizing and a great distraction if stress levels are high. For *Four Corners*, label each corner as 1, 2, 3, 4 or A, B, C, D. Give students a choice prompt, and have them go to the corner that corresponds with their opinion or selection.
- Be aware of students' fears and stress levels around physical education tasks. Orchestrate ways for students to participate that support their abilities without embarrassing or humiliating them. Team selections can be devastating. Create random team selections or design teams ahead of time. Again, working in small groups or with a partner will feel less intimidating than participating all alone.

Social-Emotional Culture

Body- and brain-friendly classrooms promote a healthy social-emotional culture. *Social-emotional learning* (SEL) refers to the process through which students learn and apply a set of social, emotional, and character skills that are necessary to succeed in school, in the workplace, in relationships, and ultimately as citizens. Further:

> Social-emotional learning, then, is the first step toward developing a positive school climate, which can lead to fewer behavior problems, stronger social-emotional health, and higher academic motivation and achievement, especially for those populations that are more likely to struggle in school. (Thorton, 2018)

The following sections will discuss how to promote a social-emotional culture when certain elements may trigger stress for students: (1) lack of social and emotional skills; (2) lack of inclusion; (3) bullying, teasing, or put-downs; (4) self-esteem; and (5) cultural unresponsiveness, implicit bias, and stereotype threat. I will also offer body- and-brain-friendly strategies to reduce stress related to a social-emotional culture.

Lack of Social-Emotional Skills

When students haven't yet developed core social-emotional competencies such as self-awareness, responsible decision making, relationship skills, social awareness, and self-management (see figure 3.1), they may experience frequent stress in classroom situations and lack the skills needed to navigate through the stressors (Collaborative for Academic, Social, and Emotional Learning [CASEL], 2015).

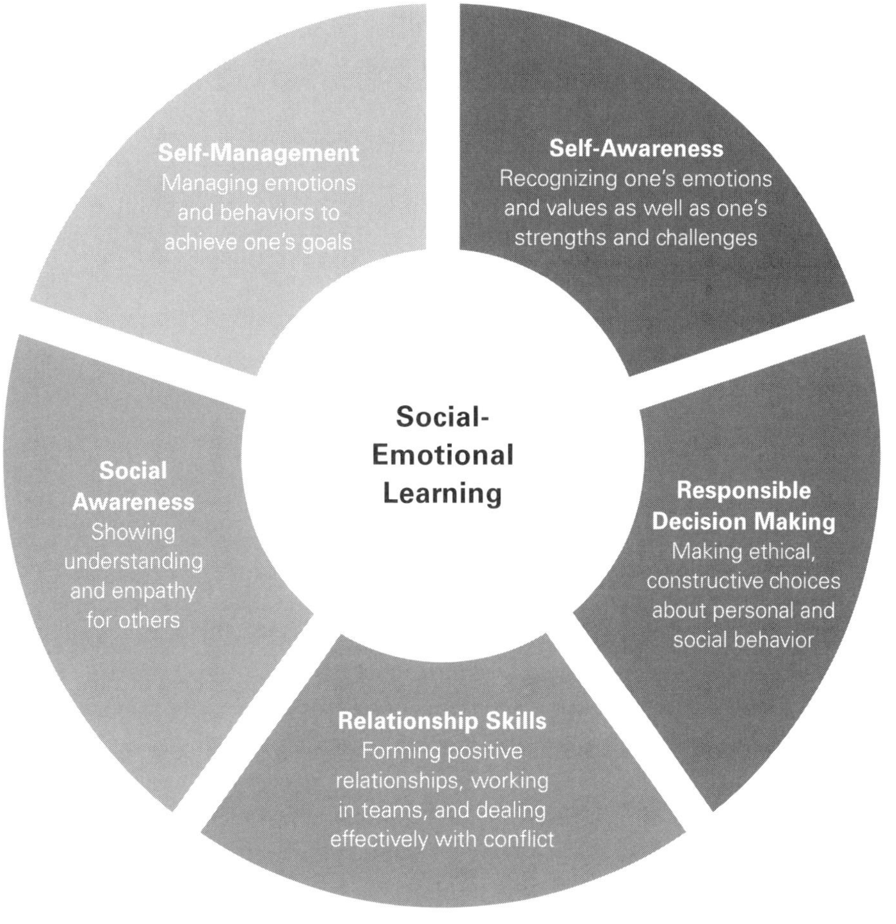

Source: Adapted with permission from CASEL, 2015.

Figure 3.1: Five core competency clusters of SEL.

Developing social-emotional learning plays a critical role in promoting student success. Cognitive-regulation and executive-function skills required to focus, plan, and control one's behavior in order to reach a goal are also included in the core competencies of social-emotional learning. The CASEL guide for middle school and high school adds that social-emotional learning is the "process through which children and adults acquire skills necessary to understand and manage emotions, set and achieve positive goals, feel and show empathy for others, establish and maintain positive relationships, and make responsible decisions" (CASEL, 2015, p. 5).

Orchestrating a positive social-emotional climate and culture in a classroom can help prepare students with the necessary skills to understand and manage their emotions, behaviors, and relationships. Schools and classrooms that integrate social-emotional learning play an important role in helping students build a repertoire of skills for success.

Developing social-emotional learning skills and practices can help alleviate some stress from students who experience test anxiety. Research shows that when social-emotional skills are taught, it not only improves achievement by an average of 11 percentile points but also improves student attitudes toward school and reduces depression and stress among students (Durlak, Weissberg, Dymnicki, Taylor, & Schellinger, 2011). Social-emotional learning also increases prosocial behaviors (such as kindness, sharing, and empathy).

Lack of Inclusion

The term *inclusion* can mean many different things in today's classrooms. Referring to student interactions, *inclusion* is when one feels a sense of belonging to a small or large group. There can be a sense of inclusion within a project group, and there can be a feeling of inclusion within the classroom community. When students don't feel respected, included, heard, or acknowledged, they may experience a high degree of stress. Humans are social beings and seek to be in the company of others. Professors Alison Gopnik, Andrew N. Meltzoff, and Patricia K. Kuhl (1999) state that everyone is born with a *contact urge*. We are a social species with an innate desire to communicate and connect with each other.

We crave inclusion. Robert M. Sapolsky (1998, 2004), a neuroendocrinologist and professor at Stanford University, observed primates and how they reacted in group situations. If a group was experiencing a high-stress situation, a primate's stress was lessened if the primate had friends around and the group was inclusive and supportive.

If the primate was in a threatening, unsupportive group, its stress was magnified. Social support is key to reducing stress. This is true in classrooms as well.

I have been greatly influenced by Jeanne Gibbs and the Tribes Learning Community (TLC), a process that was first developed in the 1970s (see https://tribes.com). The Tribes books and trainings have been a terrific resource for brain-friendly group processing and cooperative learning strategies. The Tribes TLC process believes that creating a positive school or classroom environment is the most effective way to improve behavior and learning. Based on neuroscience research, the model includes learning systems that develop *positive protective factors* such as resiliency, problem solving, and social skills. A key factor is making sure everyone feels included in a caring and supportive community. Numerous school districts have reported that their standardized test scores have improved when the schools adopted the Tribes TLC model (Gibbs, 2006).

Gibbs (2006) explains the stress and anxiety of being new to a group and working with others:

> All newcomers to any group feel an initial anxiety and have many unspoken questions.
>
> - I wonder if I'll like this classroom.
> - Will the teacher and other kids like me?
> - How will they get to know me? I feel scared.
> - Why am I nervous?
> - What will we be doing?
> - I wish this were the end of the day, not the beginning. (p. 73)

Inclusion is a basic human need. Not feeling included can cause students to feel shy, vulnerable, and possibly defensive. Lack of inclusion may also trigger stress-related physical symptoms such as headaches and upset stomachs.

Bullying, Teasing, or Put-Downs

Students frequently experience stress at school from a wide spectrum of teasing to bullying, from so-called jokes and put-downs, to flat-out harassment. *Put-downs* are when students treat others unkindly by saying negative remarks, calling them names, teasing them, making hurtful gestures, or behaving disrespectfully. According to the National Center for Injury Prevention and Control, the Centers for Disease Control and Prevention, and the U.S. Department of Education (Gladden, Vivolo-Kantor, Hamburger, & Lumpkin, 2014):

> Bullying is any unwanted aggressive behavior(s) by another youth or group of youths who are not siblings or current dating partners that involves an observed or perceived power imbalance and is repeated multiple times or is highly likely to be repeated. Bullying may inflict harm or distress on the targeted youth including physical, psychological, social, or educational harm. (p. 7)

The damage that bullying, teasing, or put-downs can do to a student's self-image, social interactions, or school performance can be severe and long lasting.

Frequent aggressive or disrespectful behavior in the classroom interferes with creating a positive learning environment. A classroom atmosphere that fails to vigorously prevent and address teasing and bullying can become quite toxic. The bullied students experience stress and trauma, and students who are bystanders and witnesses of bullying behaviors can also be affected.

Teachers dealing with frequent teasing, bullying, and other behavior issues have found that using *restorative justice* can be an effective way to handle conflicts. "Restorative justice is a theory of justice that focuses on mediation and agreement rather than punishment" (We Are Teachers, 2019). Community building is considered a powerful preventive measure and daily circles of sharing help the class develop a sense of inclusion and respect. Classroom rules and agreements are co-created with students and to promote respect, accountability, and harmony. When agreements are broken, the students use discussions, mediation, and conflict resolution strategies to see if the damage can be fixed without disciplinary actions. Schools that have invested in establishing restorative discipline practices report that classroom behavior improves dramatically, and it keeps students on track with their education (We Are Teachers, 2019).

Self-Esteem

In my many years of teaching, I've had a variety of K–12 students who have celebrated their uniqueness and have made sure they stand out in a crowd. I remember a fifth grader who wore an assortment of wacky hats every day; a sixth grader who always had some kind of battery-powered toy or tool that he had built and wanted to show everyone; and my seventh-grade student who morphed during the year into a pretty intimidating goth character. They were each unique individuals. They had relatively high self-esteem and confidence and were not afraid to make a statement through their dress, actions, or quirky behaviors. However, there are also students who would *like* to be noticed but have lower self-esteem and confidence. They often struggle with making it happen and may act inappropriately and display attention-getting behaviors. Dealing with anonymity and being overlooked can be constant sources of stress. Then there are students who dread the idea of standing out in a crowd. Students' self-esteem plays an important role in how they experience stress. In general, students who have developed higher self-esteem can better manage stress and, therefore, have better academic performance (Galanakis, Palaiologou, Patsi, Velegraki, & Darviri, 2016): "Self-esteem is a psychological trait related to a person's image of self-value and self-confidence in total aspects of human activity. Studies all over the world have associated self-esteem with human health and psychological well-being" (p. 688).

Stress and self-esteem have a strong relationship. A stressful environment or encounter can contribute to low self-esteem. Low self-esteem can generate negative looping thoughts, which in turn bring on more anxiety and stress, which can lead to poor performance and failure. It can be a vicious cycle for many students (see figure 3.2).

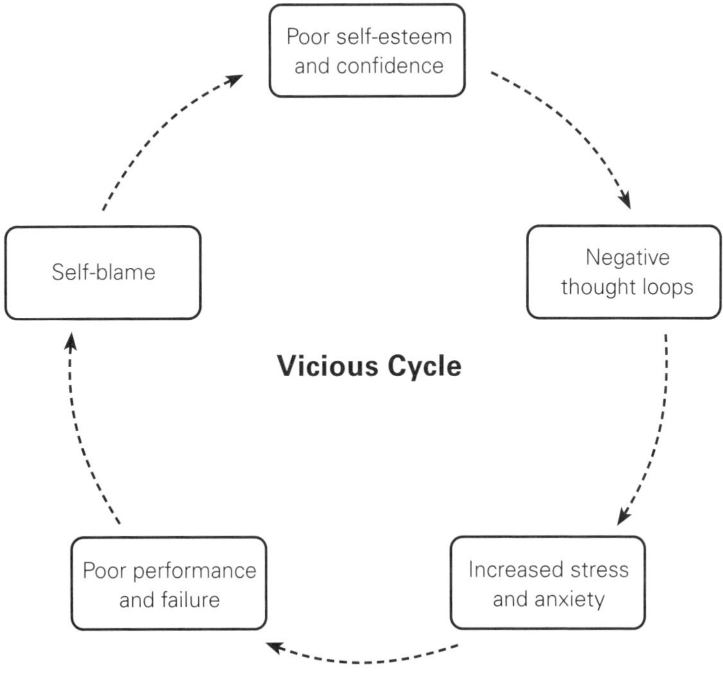

Figure 3.2: The vicious cycle of stress and low self-esteem.

Especially as puberty begins, the rapid and often overwhelming changes in one's body create concern and worry and may contribute to low self-esteem (Galanakis et al., 2016). Students in their teen years have unique vulnerabilities. Middle and high school students often fear getting ridiculed or being judged. The teenage brain has difficulty handling perceived or real peer rejection. Fortunately, as teenage students become young adults, they will usually become less susceptible to issues of peer approval and rejection. The more developed young-adult brain is better equipped to handle these sensitive issues.

Cultural Unresponsiveness, Implicit Bias, and Stereotype Threat

Students who have an ethnic or racial background different from that of the teacher or most other students at a school may experience many forms of stress and frustration in their classroom—if the teacher does not orchestrate a culturally responsive learning environment (Hammond, 2015). Being culturally responsive in the classroom consists of using cultural knowledge, prior experiences, and frames of reference to make learning more effective and relevant for *all* students. The United States is quickly becoming more racially and ethnically diverse. D'Vera Cohn and Andrea Caumont (2016) of the Pew Research Center estimate that by 2055, the United States will not have a single racial or ethnic majority. In Canada, by 2036, people of color are projected to be one-third of the population (Catalyst, 2020). As our classrooms become increasingly more diverse, a culturally responsive learning environment is essential. In her book, *Culturally Responsive Teaching and the Brain*, Zaretta Hammond (2015) defines *cultural responsiveness* as:

> An educator's ability to recognize students' cultural displays of learning and meaning making and respond positively and constructively with teaching moves that use cultural knowledge as a scaffold to connect what the student knows to new concepts and content in order to promote effective information processing. All the while, the educator understands the importance of being in a relationship and having a social-emotional connection to the student in order to create a safe space for learning. (p. 15)

Zaretta Hammond (2015) also reminds us that dependent learners who feel marginalized or unsupported because of their race, gender, or language may "experience a great deal of stress and anxiety in the classroom as they struggle with certain learning tasks" (p. 50).

At the most basic level, cultural responsiveness requires teachers to:

- Acknowledge the existence of the student's ethnicity and culture
- Show interest in the student's ethnicity and culture
- Demonstrate knowledge of the student's ethnicity and culture
- Express appreciation for the student's ethnicity and culture

Many teachers may still unintentionally demonstrate *implicit bias*—unconscious attitudes and stereotypes that shape our responses to various ethnic and racial groups. Even with lots of training and awareness about cultural bias, our brains have been wired for years with these stereotypes, and on occasion, even a well-intentioned teacher may demonstrate bias. A cultural divide between a teacher and his or her students can lead students to develop a poor self-concept, feel disrespected and not understood, and ultimately have poor achievement results (Louisiana State University Shreveport, 2017). *Stereotype threat* is a phenomenon in which a student's anxiety about possibly confirming a negative stereotype actually leads that student to underperform on a challenging assessment or test (Center for Teaching and Learning at Washington University in St. Louis, n.d.). This worry about performance increases a student's likelihood of experiencing a stress response.

Strategies to Build a Positive Social-Emotional Culture

Consider the following body- and brain-friendly strategies to build a positive social-emotional classroom culture.

- Integrate social-emotional learning opportunities every day to help students build a repertoire of skills for success. Establish daily check-ins, reflection journal prompts, and class meetings as established routines.
- Use daily partner and group processing activities to build inclusion and classroom community. Assign study buddies, reading pairs, lab partners, and so on to make sure students can develop personal connections with other classmates.
- Emphasize cooperative group learning tasks, and explicitly teach social skills. Establish group agreements. For example:
    - *Attentive listening*—We pay close attention to others and let them know they have been heard.
    - *Participate fully*—We have the right to share or the right to pass while participating.
    - *Appreciation*—We show kindness and respect. We avoid negative and hurtful comments. (We don't use put-downs, even as a joke!)
    - *Mutual respect*—We recognize and appreciate our differences and similarities. Show respect for yourself, others, property, and the environment.

- Celebrate students' uniqueness. Create positive ways for students to express themselves and demonstrate talents and expertise.
- Maintain a non-negotiable norm of mutual respect to affirm and value the individuality of each student in the classroom community.
- Immediately address put-downs and bullying of any kind. Orchestrate opportunities for restorative justice practices such as mediation and sharing circles.
- Reflect on your own implicit biases. Use cultural knowledge and frames of reference to make learning more effective and relevant for all your diverse students.
- Discuss with students in middle school and high school the phenomenon of stereotype threat, and acknowledge circumstances where it may manifest in classroom instruction.

Challenging Academics

Brain-friendly classrooms reduce the amount of unhealthy stressors and maintain a healthy amount of beneficial stress. Endocrinologist Hans Selye (1974) coined the term *eustress*, or good stress. We experience eustress when a goal is not too far out of reach but is still slightly more than what we think we can handle. When we perceive that a goal is challenging, yet possibly attainable, we become motivated. This kind of stress can keep students engaged in difficult tasks as they work hard to solve a problem or complete a project.

However, when we perceive a big gap between what we know and can do and what is actually expected, we can become overwhelmed. When students lack prior experiences and knowledge, they may not see a new assignment or task as within their realm of capabilities. This awareness of a perceived gap in their learning can be very frightening causing *distress.* When a student's workload becomes overwhelming, he, she, or they can also become frustrated, disengaged, and hopeless. Excessive amounts of homework can trigger the stress response in some students.

Distress from a lack of prior knowledge and a heavy workload can manifest when taking high-stakes tests. Many students become stressed when they encounter test questions that are beyond what they know. When tests are lengthy with few breaks allowed, the workload may become unbearable, and students often become defeated. Preparing students in advance on ways to navigate these two issues with challenging academics can help get them ready for the test.

The following sections will further discuss how challenging academics can trigger stress for students: (1) lack of prior knowledge and (2) heavy workload. I will also offer body- and brain-friendly strategies to reduce stress related to challenging academics.

Lack of Prior Knowledge

Some degree of foundational knowledge is often necessary for students to process and integrate new learning. Helping students access and recall prior knowledge before a new lesson or concept is introduced is key to their understanding and processing the new information. Advance organizers, such as short readings, minilectures, overviews, photos, video clips, and graphics, can help students' brains build a contextual map for the new learning. Cues and questions also prime learners by helping them access prior knowledge and recall experiences. When students can see the big picture, their brains will be more likely to make connections and see where and how the pieces fit.

Preassessment helps teachers determine the degree of prerequisite knowledge students have. If the assessment identifies areas of prior knowledge that are insufficient but necessary for the new lesson, it can really trigger student stress and anxiety. Being aware that they have deficits in their prior knowledge may give students a sense of dread and may make them feel overwhelmed. If during the lesson these students are left in the dust, they may begin to feel hopelessly ignorant and frustrated. When students have nothing to hook new information to, they may not realize their confusion until it is too late (Svinicki, 1993–1994).

Determining students' prior knowledge, or lack of, will help teachers know where to target instruction. Sometimes a student's prior understanding may be incorrect. This can lead to additional stress for the student as they must relearn the new information and change the student's existing concept of understanding. Campbell and Campbell (2009) describe it this way:

> Students, of any age, bring beliefs and life and academic experiences to the classroom that influence what and how they learn. At times, such prior knowledge facilitates learning by creating mental hooks that serve to anchor instructional concepts. Conversely, the acquisition of new content can be thwarted if it conflicts with students' preexisting misinformation. As a result, the role of prior knowledge in learning is paradoxical: it can lead to success and failure in the classroom. (p. 7)

Heavy Workload

Several studies have been conducted in the 21st century to research the effects of too much homework and a heavy workload on student well-being and success. In high-performing middle and high schools, students spend about three hours per night on homework (Pope, Brown, & Miles, 2015). Writer K. J. Dell'Antonia (2014) explains:

> Researchers asked 4,317 students from 10 high-performing high schools in upper-middle-class California communities to describe the impact of homework on their lives, and the results offer a bleak picture that many of us can see reflected around our dining room tables. The students reported averaging 3.1 hours of homework nightly, and they added comments like: "There's never a break. Never." It "takes me away from everything I used to do," says one.

According to Cathy Vatterott (2018) in her book *Rethinking Homework*, the actual amount of homework hasn't increased dramatically in the 21st century for most students. The exception is in the early grades of elementary school. It has been reported that in preparation for standardized tests, more and more teachers are assigning homework to students as young as six years old. In fact, a fifteen-year study at Duke University determined that homework had little or no benefit on achievement for students in elementary grades and "diminished returns" for high school students (as cited in Cooper, Robinson, & Patell, 2006). Further, two student groups indicate that their workload is quite overwhelming and challenging: (1) high school students in rigorous classes, including honors and Advanced Placement courses, and (2) students who are trying to catch up and those needing to take extra classes or tutorials (Vatterott, 2018).

There are also factors that make completing a heavy, difficult workload challenging. Vatterott (2018) explains that it's common for students who live in poverty not to have a quiet place to work. Many students of poverty have lots of additional responsibilities at home, such as taking care of siblings, cooking dinner, doing laundry, and so forth. If they're teenagers, they might also have part-time jobs to contribute to the family's income. English learners may have family members who don't speak English, and thus, these students might not have access to help if they need it.

A heavy and difficult workload can cause students to stress out and disengage. Vatterott (2018) reminds us in her book *Rethinking Homework* that when students repeatedly receive homework tasks that are too hard for them, frustration builds, and students can start to hate learning and going to school—which can shut down learning altogether. Students who spend more time doing homework tend to be more anxious and report more physical symptoms due to stress (Galloway, Conner, & Pope, 2013). Even if students have not experienced an increased homework load, many may experience stress due to overscheduling and overstimulation. Heavy schedules (including out-of-school activities) can stress students' brains and impair their ability to learn. The excess homework and heavy workload can contribute to whether students like school.

Strategies to Reduce Stress Related to Challenging Academics

Consider the following strategies to support students who may be overwhelmed with challenging academics.

- Prior to presenting new learning, encourage students to discuss what they know about the topic and any related information to set a context for the new learning and create curiosity and intrigue. Using a classic K-W-L strategy (What do you already *know*? What do you *want* to know? What have you *learned*?) can help students brainstorm what they already know about an upcoming topic (Ogle, 1986).
- Review students' homework load. In middle and high school, coordinate with other teachers to determine if, collectively, the students are overburdened. Teachers should create opportunities to discuss homework policies and examine the overall workload of their students. Keeping a calendar of when major projects are due across a student's various classes can help teachers from assigning too many things at any given time.
- Collect data from students about their situations and responsibilities after school. Consider modifications for students who may live in poverty. As teachers learn more about students' specific details about their homelife, they can become more sensitive to their unique situations. The inequalities among families may be staggering. Some families have high-speed internet, a quiet place for students to work, and parents who can help with homework and others may not. Making slight adjustments in the homework tasks can accommodate these various limitations.
- Integrate tutorials and homework help for students who need them by implementing a multilevel system of support. A well-designed response to intervention program can provide students with the necessary supports to be successful. Students who have had additional intervention and tutorials will feel more confident.

When students have help and support *during* the learning process, they are less likely to experience a stress event while taking a test. When working to learn new skills and concepts, students who have just the right amount of stress and pressure applied to their unique situation will be able to persevere in the learning process. When learning hasn't been derailed, students will be more inclined to feel prepared when high-stakes tests are administered.

Conclusion

De-stressing the test demands that teachers examine everyday stressors that students might encounter at school. There are at least six areas that teachers can assess and possibly modify to help reduce student stress in the classroom, including: (1) physical environment; (2) schedules, time pressures, and constraints; (3) chaos and confusion; (4) basic needs; (5) social-emotional culture; and (6) challenging academics. Promoting a brain-friendly classroom environment will help create those critical *positive protective factors* that can make a huge difference for students *during* the learning process. This will ultimately help them feel more prepared for high-stakes tests.

THE DEVELOPMENT OF STUDENT AGENCY THROUGH SELF-EFFICACY, GROWTH MINDSET, AND PERSEVERANCE

People's beliefs in their capabilities affect how much stress and depression they experience in threatening or taxing situations, as well as their level of motivation. Such emotional reactions can affect action both directly and indirectly by altering the nature and course of thinking.

—BANDURA

Assessing academic skills in elementary and secondary schools is critically important to document student achievement, but according to researcher Camille A. Farrington and her colleagues at the University of Chicago (2012), there is growing agreement that scores on standardized tests of academic knowledge and skills are incomplete measures of all the valuable things that students actually learn at school. In their report titled *Teaching Adolescents to Become Learners: The Role of Noncognitive Factors in Shaping School Performance*, Farrington and colleagues (2012) state that "in addition to content knowledge and academic skills, students must develop sets of behaviors, skills, attitudes, and strategies that are crucial to academic performance in their classes, but that may not be reflected in their scores on cognitive tests" (p. 2).

When educators nurture these skills among their students, they're promoting students' sense of *agency*. In a report by the Achievement Gap Initiative at Harvard

University, researchers Ronald F. Ferguson, Sarah F. Phillips, Jacob F. S. Rowley, and Jocelyn W. Friedlander (2015) explain:

> Agency is the capacity and propensity to take purposeful initiative—the opposite of helplessness. Young people with high levels of agency do not respond passively to their circumstances; they tend to seek meaning and act with purpose to achieve the conditions they desire in their own and others' lives. The development of agency may be as important an outcome of schooling as the skills we measure with standardized testing. (p. 1)

Developing student agency, then, means orchestrating curricular and instructional opportunities through which students can begin to acquire a sense of voice, ownership, and self-determination in their learning. By taking into account students' interests and what students find meaningful and relevant, educators can help students develop some autonomy with regard to what, how, where, and with whom they learn. Agency can empower students to influence their own path to mastery and enhance their cognitive abilities, and it can contribute to long-term success in school and in life (Darling-Hammond, Flook, Cook-Harvey, Barron, & Osher, 2020). By the same token, students who fail to develop agency will often feel helpless, angry, and frustrated. When students have little to no choice with regard to their learning and how they might demonstrate mastery, the teacher is generally the exclusive planner and decision maker in the classroom. And when decision making is never in the student's control, oppositional and defiant behaviors may manifest. Figure 4.1 lists behaviors that students exhibit in the classroom when they have agency and when they lack it.

So, while teachers may think that high-stakes tests are all about the substance of what students learn in school—those cognitive factors that include content knowledge, academic skills (such as reading, writing, and mathematics), and critical thinking and problem solving—we must prepare students to succeed on high-stakes tests by explicitly integrating noncognitive factors into daily instruction. To do this, we need a more concrete understanding of what characterizes student agency. In her article "What Do You Mean When You Say 'Student Agency'?" researcher Jennifer Davis Poon (2018) concludes that student agency involves four distinct components: (1) setting advantageous goals (future planning), (2) initiating action toward those goals (present effort), (3) reflecting on and regulating progress toward those goals (past reflection), and (4) believing in their ability to succeed (self-efficacy).

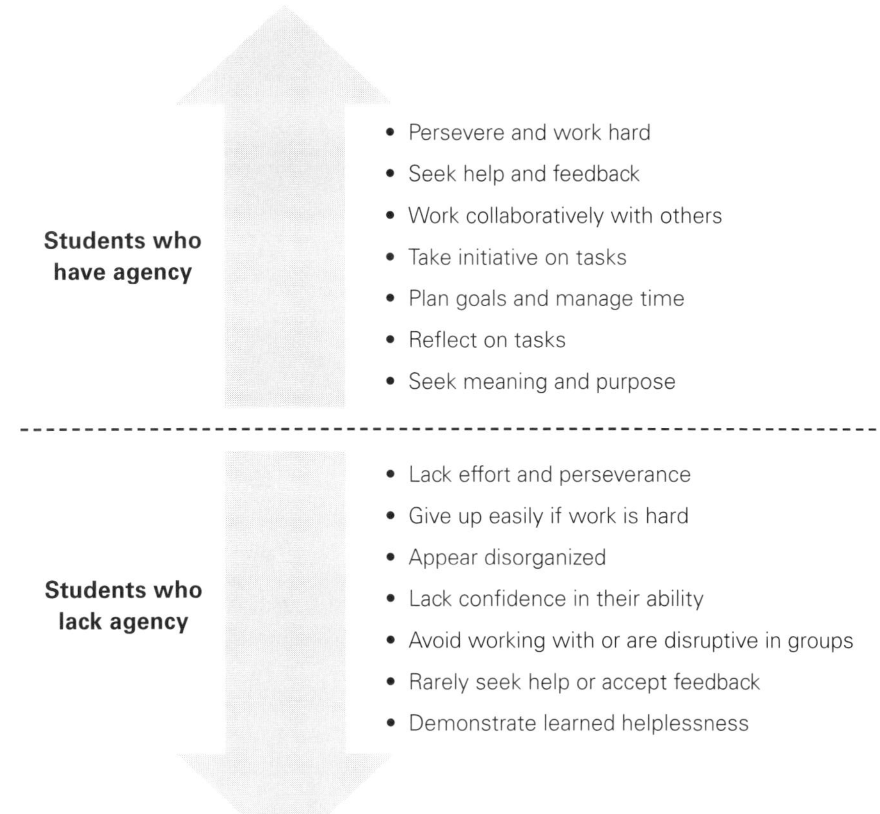

Source: Adapted with permission from Ferguson et al., 2015.

Figure 4.1: Observable evidence of student agency (or a lack thereof) in the classroom.

I propose that educators focus on fostering in students the following skills as agency boosters, which we will explore in this chapter.

- **Self-efficacy:** Believing in one's ability to achieve an outcome or reach a goal and having a realistic expectation that if you use the right strategy and make a good effort, you'll succeed
- **Growth mindset:** Believing that one's abilities can change with time, effort, and perseverance
- **Perseverance:** Demonstrating persistence when experiencing extreme challenges, setbacks, or failures

Self-Efficacy

"I think I can . . . I think I can . . . I know I can!" The famous affirmations from *The Little Engine That Could* (Piper, 1930) represent the attitude students must develop to have a positive outlook on their skills and abilities—an absolutely key attitude for success on a high-stakes test. Introduced by psychologist Albert Bandura (1977), the awareness that success in school and in life requires self-efficacy, as the most crucial mechanism of agency, is not new. According to Bandura's (1977) social cognitive theory, *self-efficacy* is one's *perceived* ability to deal with a task or situation and *agency* is one's *actual* ability to deal with a task or situation.

Developing the belief in one's capability to accomplish a goal or task and the belief in one's power to attain the goal through one's actions are important. But making sure these factors are integrated into school experiences hasn't always been a focus for education policymakers. "Prevention programs and interventions that address self-efficacy and climate may be most effective for reducing test anxiety associated with high-stakes testing in schools" (Segool, von der Embse, Mata, & Gallant, 2013, p. 10).

Students who have developed high self-efficacy demonstrate confidence, easily approach difficult tasks, and are able to sustain effort and persevere in order to achieve goals. They are also more likely to quickly recover from failures and setbacks. Students with undeveloped or low self-efficacy often avoid tasks involving a high degree of challenge—they may in fact consider themselves *incapable* of solving them—and lack confidence in their own abilities (Bandura, 1997b). According to Bandura (as cited in Fertman & Primack, 2009), "Self-efficacy is a central mechanism in the exercise of agency. An individual's belief about her or his capacity to perform a task or overcome difficulties will greatly determine how they actually behave."

Self-esteem denotes our subjective evaluation of our own worth. Self-efficacy isn't about a sense of self-worth; it's about believing we are capable of producing a desired result—that we can achieve our goals. We develop self-efficacy, in part, through experiencing success, and according to Bandura (1997b), our self-efficacy affects how we feel, think, and act; determines whether we stay committed to goals; and informs our social relationships. High self-efficacy has numerous benefits to daily life, such as resilience to adversity, reduced stress, and improved educational achievement (Lopez-Garrido, 2020).

According to researchers Karineh Tahmassian and Niloufar Jalali Moghadam (2011), there is a strong relationship between low self-efficacy and helplessness, avoidance, anxiety, and depression. Fortunately, whether a student's level of self-efficacy is average, robust, or absent, much like physical attributes, self-efficacy can be further developed.

Higher levels of self-efficacy are related to healthy student habits. Students with higher levels of self-efficacy are often more organized, and they set goals, persevere, maintain motivation, and ultimately end up doing better in school (Lopez-Garrido, 2020). Educators who integrate noncognitive factors and social-emotional competencies into their instruction can help students feel more motivated to persist and succeed. Amy S. Gaumer Erickson and Patricia M. Noonan (2012) of the University of Kansas Center for Research on Learning developed the College and Career Competency Framework to support educators in systematically embedding intrapersonal, interpersonal, and cognitive competencies into course content. They identify ten student outcomes teachers achieve when they explicitly teach self-efficacy (Gaumer Erickson & Noonan, 2012).

1. Increased confidence in their own abilities
2. Improved ability to see the areas they need to work on and why
3. Increased willingness to take on and persist in challenging tasks
4. Increased sense of control and awareness of their academics
5. Increased perseverance
6. Increased initiative and motivation
7. Increased ability to see mistakes and constructive criticism as opportunities to learn
8. Improved behavior
9. Improved attitude toward school
10. Increased engagement in the course

How exactly can teachers tailor instruction to promote high self-efficacy? What experiences can be orchestrated to influence the development of one's self-efficacy? Bandura (1997b) describes how individuals can build their *self-efficacy beliefs*—how people feel, think, motivate themselves, and behave—by interpreting information from four main *sources of influence*: (1) performance experiences, (2) vicarious experiences, (3) verbal persuasion, and (4) physiological and emotional states. Psychologist James E. Maddux (2009) contributes a fifth source—(5) imaginal experiences (see figure 4.2, page 76).

Teachers can easily integrate all five sources into classroom instruction to contribute to the development of student self-efficacy. The following sections will elaborate on each source. I'll also suggest a self-efficacy assessment teachers can use to identify students' strengths and areas for improvement.

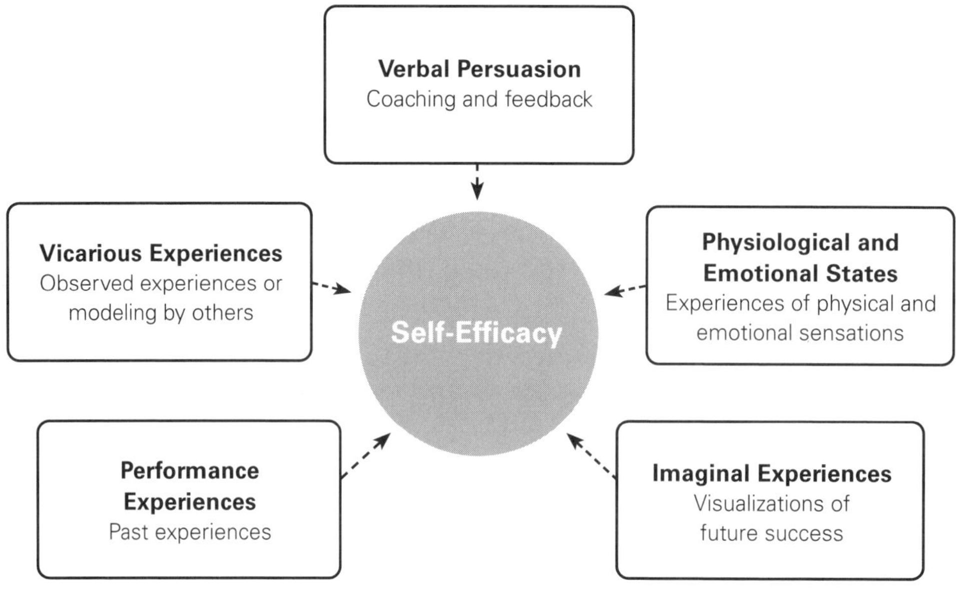

Source: Adapted from Bandura, 1997b; Maddux, 2009.

Figure 4.2: Five sources of self-efficacy beliefs.

Performance Experiences

Our sense of mastery and confidence is likely to increase if we experience ourselves coping effectively with difficult situations. Bandura (1997b) describes *performance* experiences, or mastery experiences as "the most influential source of efficacy information because they provide the most authentic evidence of whether one can muster whatever it takes to succeed. Success builds a robust belief in one's personal efficacy" (p. 80). When goals are clear, concrete, and specific, and when we perceive the task as doable, we are more likely to become motivated to engage.

When students successfully attempt tasks that involve real-world, firsthand experiences, they may attribute the positive outcome to their own efforts, and it will strengthen self-efficacy for that behavior or domain. Self-efficacy is often diminished when students believe their attempts have failed (Lopez-Garrido, 2020).

To provide students with performance experiences in the classroom, do the following.

- Orchestrate frequent hands-on, firsthand multisensory experiences. For example, have students set up and conduct an experiment using the scientific method; construct a model of a bridge or building; plan and cook a meal; or organize and create an art display.

- Make sure that the goals for tasks are concrete, specific, and manageable. Provide detailed and clear rubrics, scales, and performance indicators.
- Allow for do-overs and second chances to correct a failure or mistake. During the learning process, students should have opportunities, and be encouraged, to try again and improve one's results.
- Debrief after activities so students can reflect on the processes and strategies they used and the emotions they felt, and so they can consider, "What might I do differently next time?"

Vicarious Experiences

Our observations of others' experiences and behaviors and the consequences of those behaviors can influence our self-efficacy. When we see others doing a task—either in person or virtually—we use the information to form expectancies about our own abilities. If we believe that we are similar to the person we are observing, it may give us the confidence to give the task a go. Vicarious experiences generally have a weaker effect on the development of self-efficacy than firsthand performance experiences do, but they are an important source of our beliefs: "Seeing people similar to themselves succeed by perseverant effort raises observers' beliefs that they, too, possess the capabilities to master comparable activities" (Bandura, 1997a, p. 3).

To provide students with vicarious experiences in the classroom, do the following.

- Model difficult tasks for students. Anticipate where there may be challenges, and provide a brief demonstration or video clip to show how to complete the activity. Demonstration lessons from sources like Khan Academy (www.khanacademy.org) are excellent resources.
- Have students do demonstrations for one another. Students can demonstrate how to do a complex mathematics problem or something as simple as how to make a sandwich. Watching another do a task is a powerful way to build your own confidence.
- Encourage students to do a web search of videos that others have posted that show successful results of a similar activity or task.
- Arrange for students to work in heterogeneous groups. Have them take turns doing the task, and allow reluctant students to go last, after they have observed others. Using cooperative groups and flexible grouping can provide multiple opportunities for students to observe others completing tasks.

Verbal Persuasion

What others say to us about what they think we can or cannot do influences our self-efficacy. The power of this verbal feedback may depend on whether we feel the source is trustworthy, respected, and an expert. To enhance a student's self-efficacy beliefs, rather than being a sage on the stage, try being a guide on the side, providing feedback and encouraging small steps that may lead to small successes. Verbal feedback is not considered as powerful as firsthand and vicarious experiences, which may be more likely to trigger neuroplasticity, or brain growth and wiring (see page 82 for more on neuroplasticity). However, when students receive positive verbal feedback while undertaking a complex task, it can persuade them to believe that they have the skills and capabilities to succeed. See chapter 6 (page 119) for more on how feedback is an important tool for developing confident students.

To provide students with verbal persuasion in the classroom, consider the following.

- Deliver frequent formative assessments during learning to give students feedback they can use to improve before a summative assessment. Brief, informal low-stakes practice assessments are opportunities for students to show what they know. Teachers can provide immediate feedback that gives specific suggestions for improvement.
- Orchestrate partner and small-group work. Explicitly teach social skills that promote opportunities for positive discussions and feedback. Using basic manners and courteous behaviors show kindness and respect. Create group ground rules for how to work successfully with other students (using active listening, taking turns, staying positive, and so on).
- Provide written and verbal feedback as soon as possible. Avoid waiting multiple days to return student work. Immediate feedback allows students to stay actively engaged and make modifications in a timely moment. We learn faster when we have a clear sense of how well we are doing.
- Consider ways to use technology (for example, Google Classroom, Microsoft Teams, and so forth) to provide immediate feedback. During the 2020–2021 school year, educators all over the world discovered ways to use technology to create collaborative thinking spaces that enhanced instruction. Provide multiple opportunities for students to collaborate using Google Docs, Jamboards, and so on.

Physiological and Emotional States

Physiological and emotional states can influence self-efficacy. Feeling unpleasant physiological arousal or anxiety (such as tight muscles, an upset stomach, or shakiness) when faced with a task may make us doubt our competencies. We may begin to associate physical unease with the possibility of failure or poor performance. When we are able to shift the unpleasant feelings to more comfortable sensations (for example, a relaxed body and calm breathing), we are likely to feel more confident in our abilities. We usually feel more self-efficacious when we are calm than when we are aroused and distressed. Teaching strategies for controlling and reducing emotional arousal such as stress and anxiety should increase students' self-efficacy. Investigate chapter 5 (page 95) for strategies that can help students reduce physiological stress.

To provide students with ways to take control of their physiological and emotional states, consider the following.

- Teach students about the stress response and how to notice cues in one's body.
- Introduce core breathing practices to help reduce stress and anxiety (see mindfulness practices in chapter 5, page 102).
- Explain how to do a body scan to be aware of physical arousal, and instruct students to practice tightening and releasing muscles to reduce the sensation (see mindfulness practices in chapter 5, page 105).

Imaginal Experiences

Imaginal experience refers to the art of visualizing ourselves performing or behaving effectively or successfully in a given situation (Maddux, 2009). Imagining ourselves engaging in a challenging or scary activity and then succeeding by overcoming difficulties can enhance self-efficacy. A student may be able to gain a sense of control over a challenging task by first imagining him- or herself dealing effectively with the situation and succeeding. Visualization can stimulate the same part of the brain as when we actually do that same activity. Using visualization to recall positive experiences and successes can help us imagine the outcome of things that are about to take place. Using our minds to create mental repetitions can help our brains wire the patterns needed to be successful.

To provide students with imaginal experiences in the classroom, do the following.

- Give students opportunities to practice making mental movies—the art of creating visuals in their minds. Listening to stories and read-alouds allows students' brains to create their own mental movies. Taking time to do some reflection after completing a task or project helps students recall the steps and events they did and analyze ways they could have done things differently.
- Use guided visualization with students before stressful tasks or tests to help them imagine being successful. Practice visualizations often with students to help them learn how to visualize color, size, shape, perspective, movement, and various senses, such as smell, touch, and taste. Provide a guided visualization before a test to relieve anxiety (Warren, n.d.).
- Explore various apps or video clips that students can use to visualize their competencies and abilities, helping them achieve success. Visualizing may be one of the most important strategies when it comes to test taking. Visit https://enrichmenttherapies.com/visualize-success-test-taking-101 for test-taking tips and tricks in regard to visualization.

Assessment on Student Self-Efficacy

A brief survey may help students identify areas of self-efficacy that they have already developed as well as shine a light on some ways of thinking that may not positively contribute to their learning. The Research Collaboration Lab at the University of Kansas Center for Research on Learning offers self-efficacy questionnaires (Gaumer Erickson & Noonan, 2021). Visit www.researchcollaborationsurveys.org to access surveys and free lessons and resources on self-efficacy. This companion site to the College and Career Competency Framework supports educators in easily launching, collecting, and analyzing data. Its free assessments help students better understand both their strengths and their areas for improvement related to intrapersonal and interpersonal competencies, as well as provide educators with data to inform instruction and support content.

The Self-Efficacy Formative Questionnaire identifies two components essential for developing self-efficacy. Positive self-efficacy increases when students (1) believe in their ability to meet specific goals and (2) believe that ability can grow with effort (Gaumer Erickson & Noonan, 2018). Responses to the survey are on a 1–5 scale with 1 being "not very like me," and 5 being "very like me." Questions 1–8 are associated with the belief in one's ability to meet goals and include items such as:

1. I can learn what is being taught in class this year.
2. I can figure out anything if I try hard enough.
3. If I practiced every day, I could develop just about any skill.

Questions 9–13 are associated with believing that ability can grow with effort and includes items such as:

10. I believe hard work pays off.
11. My ability grows with effort. (Gaumer Erickson & Noonan, 2018, pp. 175–176)

Students can use the questionnaire results to build an awareness of how their perceptions and beliefs about their abilities contribute to their academic success and performance on exams. As students better understand that they can positively impact outcomes with effort, they build confidence in their ability to take on more challenging tasks. By determining which perceptions impact students' motivation to succeed, teachers can enhance their instructional practices through targeted instruction (Gaumer Erickson & Noonan, 2012).

Students with low self-efficacy who lack confidence in their abilities will approach exams with increased anxiety, reducing the probability that they will perform well. On the other hand, students with high self-efficacy who have strong confidence in their abilities to manage stress and to perform well on exams will approach those exam events with minimal anxiety and will not be thrown by difficulties.

Growth Mindset

Self-efficacy and growth mindset are dynamic components in the development of student agency. Carol S. Dweck (2016), a world-renowned Stanford University psychologist and author, has been gathering data on people's attitudes about failure, motivation, achievement, and success since the 1980s. In *Mindset: The New Psychology of Success*, she shares that people primarily develop one of two predispositions toward their intelligence: (1) a *fixed mindset* or (2) a *growth mindset* (Dweck, 2016). Helping students understand the concepts of fixed and growth mindsets can influence their success in school and in life. Whether students believe they can be successful makes a significant difference in student achievement and performance.

Individuals with a fixed mindset believe that their basic qualities, like their intelligence and talents, are simply inborn traits—they have a certain amount, and that's that. They often spend their time documenting their intelligence instead of working on developing it. In the classroom, students might be consumed with showing how smart they are via grades, test scores, and teacher recognition, always working hard to prove how great they are rather than spending time and effort actually getting better.

By contrast, individuals with a growth mindset believe that they can develop their most basic abilities and intelligence over time through dedication and hard work. They often develop a love of learning and perseverance, and they intuitively understand that the brain can change and grow with experiences. In effect, they believe in the brain's ability to make changes in neural connections—what we call *neuroplasticity* (Cherry, 2021a).

It is estimated that we are born with more than one hundred billion neurons in our brains. Research confirms that throughout life, new neurons may also be created in various regions of the brain (*neurogenesis*)—especially after brain injuries. These new neurons may be prompted to grow by a variety of physiological stimuli including physical exercise and being in an enriched environment (Ming & Song, 2011). Our brains are constantly being shaped by our experiences. In *The Brain That Changes Itself*, Norman Doidge (2007) documents the incredible research on neuroplasticity that began with Paul Bach-y-Rita in the 1960s.

Multisensory experiences in enriched environments can stimulate brain growth and development. The neural circuitry in the brain must reorganize in response to experiences and sensory stimulation. The stimulation triggers neurons to grow dendritic branches. These branches migrate and connect with other neurons to organize neural pathways in the brain. The points of connection are the synapses. When we experience and learn new things, the new connections are restimulated, and they form long-lasting changes in the brain. This is neuroplasticity.

With every repetition of an action, a thought, or an emotion, we reinforce the new neural pathway and create lasting memories. These small changes, repeated frequently, form our neural networks and lead to changes in how our brains grow, develop, and learn. Neuroplasticity is the muscle-building part of the brain. With frequent multisensory experiences, our brains grow and actually become denser. When we do things often, the connections become hardwired and create long-term memories. When newly formed synapses are not restimulated, they are at risk of fading away—*pruning*. "Use it or lose it" is true! That is the physical basis of why having a thought or doing an action over and over again increases its power. In *Human Brain and Human Learning*, Leslie A. Hart (2002) describes this as *patterns* becoming *programs* in our brains. Over time, the thought or action becomes automatic—a part of us. We literally become what we think and do, and this can continue throughout our lifetimes. Neuroplasticity is the biology of how the growth mindset works. Trying and experiencing new things prompts our brains to grow and develop. We can always create new neural connections and thus grow our intelligence.

Students of all ages should have opportunities to learn about the amazing ability of the brain to change and grow over time with new experiences and practice. This plasticity and the fact that neurons can grow dendrites and continue to make connections are responsible for new learning, even into old age. Spending time discovering and doing things in enriched environments is the key for maximizing the brain's potential.

With opportunities for multiple rehearsals and do-overs, students will begin to understand that it is effort and practice that make one successful. Although we may not immediately—or *not yet*—get a concept or skill, we can improve our abilities and our intelligence with time, effort, and practice (Dweck, 2016). Through multiple rehearsals, persistence, and determination, the brain will produce its own incentive with a release of dopamine, the brain's natural pleasure chemical, as we get closer to the goal and anticipate achievement. Working hard on something can actually bring about pleasure!

However, Dweck's (2016) theory about mindsets is not binary. In fact, most people really don't have a dedicated fixed or growth mindset, but they will be somewhere along a spectrum. In various situations, at different points in your life, or in response to the degree of difficulty in a task, you may find yourself behaving with a fixed or growth mindset. This spectrum of fixed and growth mindsets exists in all of us and where and how we operate may be dynamic.

Students with a growth mindset are committed to persevere and try different strategies to reach a learning target. Students who view learning through a fixed mindset, though, may respond in one of two distinct ways (see table 4.1, page 84). Perhaps the more common response—or the one more plainly attributable to the fixed mindset—is the one in which a student views a struggle or an instance of failure as a confirmation that he, she, or they is not smart: "There's no point in even trying because I've never been any good at mathematics. I will never get better!" These students believe their intelligence has a limit and resign themselves to a probable failure before even attempting to achieve the success they want. The other response is one teachers observe in students who *have* found success but later develop a fixed mindset about their intelligence. A fixed mindset isn't limited to feeling inadequate or lacking intelligence. When students who were always at the top of their class in elementary school reach secondary school, they may experience learning challenges that are quite new to them. The new curriculum may demand some struggle and perseverance to succeed. They may have developed a fixed mindset about how bright they are and, therefore, attribute the struggle to something other than their own level of intelligence or talent: "I've always

TABLE 4.1: Growth- Versus Fixed-Mindset Characteristics

Growth Mindset	**Fixed Mindset**	
The student:	The student doesn't feel smart and:	The student feels quite smart and:
• Keeps trying something until he or she gets better at it • Asks questions to try to figure out the answers • Doesn't immediately give up when experiencing difficulties • Is willing to put in extra time to get better	• Believes that a person's intelligence, talents, and qualities can't be changed • Feels that trying hard and exerting effort is futile • Avoids challenging tasks, preferring low-level, low-risk learning activities	• Believes that success is not about learning but about proving one's abilities • Feels pressure to prove him- or herself over and over • Fears that if he or she is unsuccessful, people will think he or she is unintelligent • May rest on his or her laurels

been super smart in mathematics, but the teacher didn't explain the assignment well enough, so I didn't get a good grade this time. I already know this stuff anyway—I did it last year." Deep down, these students may know that they have hit the limit of their current understanding but are hoping that no one "finds them out." Those students who have fixed-mindset thinking are often concerned with others' perception.

Many factors contribute to the development of students' mindsets. Socioeconomic status, ethnicity, gender, and home environments often inform students' beliefs about school, learning, and their potential. Dweck (2016) points out that most experts agree it's not nature *or* nurture, genes *or* our environment, but it's "the view you adopt for yourself profoundly affects the way you lead your life" (p. 6). But teachers at all grade levels can cultivate growth mindsets within their students, which will allow students to approach academic challenges with a positive attitude, a willingness to persevere, and a genuine belief in their capabilities. A growth-mindset way of thinking can help students prepare for high-stakes tests and maintain motivation during actual testing. Teachers can nurture a growth mindset and set students up for test success by providing process praise, rather than personal praise, throughout their learning and by helping students understand the power of mistakes.

To examine fixed- and growth-mindset language, provide students with common statements for fixed and growth mindsets; either list the statements on a single handout or record them individually on small strips of paper. Various statements might include the following.

- "Mathematics is not my thing."
- "I'm not there . . . yet."

- "People can always change."
- "A good attitude is important in learning."
- "Playing my hardest with dignity is more important than winning."
- "Rankings aren't set in stone. If I work hard, I could be number one."
- "It's better to look smart than to take risks."
- "Playing against tough competitors helps me grow my ability."
- "My hard work and effort have paid off."
- "This is really too hard."
- "People who care about me will support me no matter what."
- "Everyone is going to think I'm a loser."
- "I'll work hard to try to win the game."
- "There's no way I'm going to beat her."
- "I'm going to feel so bad when I lose."
- "I feel dumb if someone corrects me."
- "I'm a problem solver."
- "I need to change my strategy."
- "Beth is the smart kid in our class."
- "Grades mean more than learning."
- "I can prompt my brain to grow."
- "I will never be that smart."
- "I'm just not good at this."
- "I might as well quit now; I'm never going to win."

On a separate sheet of paper, have students create a T-chart with *fixed mindset* and *growth mindset* at the top of either column. Working with partners, students list or place the statements in the most appropriate column. Ask students how they might change a fixed-mindset statement to a growth-mindset statement. Visit **go.SolutionTree.com/assessment** for a reproducible version of this activity.

In the following two sections, we'll explore two powerful ways to encourage a growth mindset in students: (1) process praise and (2) mistakes.

The Power of Process Praise

Praising students for working hard, applying what they learned in the past, and persevering even when a task is difficult contributes to development of a growth mindset. In *Mindset: The New Psychology of Success*, Dweck (2016) describes a New York experiment in which teachers told one group of students that they were smart and complimented another group of students on their effort as they completed a puzzle. Given an opportunity to do a second, more difficult puzzle, many students in the first group avoided doing a more challenging task and chose to stay with an easier one, whereas the group of students who were praised for their efforts appeared to have enjoyed the challenge, with 90 percent of them choosing to do a more challenging puzzle in the next round.

Dweck (2016) theorizes that students who get *personal praise* about their abilities—in this case, that they are smart—often give up more easily, reasoning that if you have to work too hard, you are not clever. When teachers tell students they are smart, those students are less likely to try challenging tasks, as they don't want to risk losing their smart status. When they encounter failures, many are often defensive and blame others. But students who receive *process praise* for the efforts that they demonstrate gain an understanding of the specific strategies and actions that contribute to their success. They don't feel that their intelligence is being threatened. They appear to be more resilient and are willing to take more risks to solve problems. They develop perseverance (see page 90).

How teachers and parents give praise and feedback to students will contribute to the development of their fixed or growth mindsets. In his article "How Not to Talk to Your Kids," Po Bronson (2007) summarizes Dweck's (1999) research and her conclusions about praise:

> Dweck had suspected that praise could backfire, but even she was surprised by the magnitude of the effect. "Emphasizing effort gives a child a variable that they can control," she explains. "They come to see themselves as in control of their success. Emphasizing natural intelligence takes it out of the child's control, and it provides no good recipe for responding to a failure."

This is because personal praise focuses on students' personal traits and qualities. It convinces students that there is an inborn intelligence and suggests that perseverance and effort aren't really factors in success—which contributes to the development of a fixed mindset. Process praise, on the other hand, focuses on the specific efforts students make, strategies they use, and actions they take as they work on a task. It contributes to building a growth mindset by helping them understand that success takes time and perseverance.

For years, educators were encouraged to praise a student's success, believing it would boost self-esteem and achievement, but praising students for their abilities can often backfire. Alfie Kohn (1999), in his book *Punished by Rewards*, contends that praise can become a form of manipulation. Teachers often praise students to get them to do what *we* want them to do. Many teachers believe that when we praise our students for what they did, we are motivating them. However, it's much closer to manipulation (Kohn, 1999). Kohn (1999) cites research that makes it quite clear that praise comments such as, "You're the best in the class" and "You're so smart!" undermine intrinsic motivation.

Dweck's (1999, 2016, 2017; Dweck et al., 2014) work indicates that it is more powerful to provide feedback on qualities that students can control, like their effort. Consider the remarks in table 4.2 to help you avoid personal-praise statements and build up a repertoire of process-praise examples. See page 172 for a reproducible version of this table. For more ways to provide specific process praise, see chapter 6 (page 119) on feedback and formative assessment.

TABLE 4.2: Personal-Praise Statements and Process-Praise Statements

Personal-Praise Statements	Process-Praise Statements
To discourage a fixed mindset, avoid personal-praise statements such as these. • "You're so smart." • "You are a talented athlete." • "You are a born artist." • "You are such a good boy."	To encourage a growth mindset, offer process-praise statements such as these. • "Your paper shows that you put a lot of effort into the research." • "I noticed that you redid several problems—way to go!" • "This story shows me that you are really expanding your use of descriptive words." • "I noticed you showed initiative and got started right away."

As you encourage a growth mindset through specific process praise, be sure to also do the following to support your students.

- Encourage risk taking and outside-the-box thinking without the threat of getting a low grade. Orchestrate more open-ended tasks that allow students to try different strategies.
- Encourage students to try new and difficult things. Have students discuss famous quotes, such as this one from the Roman philosopher Seneca: "It is not because things are difficult that we do not dare, it is because we do not dare that they are difficult" (as cited in BrainyQuote, n.d.).

- Provide opportunities for feedback about the process and effort students are using. Use formative assessments and cooperative group work to provide frequent, specific feedback.
- Help students learn from failures. Orchestrate time to reflect on any failures or mistakes and determine what you might do differently next time.
- Promote positive self-talk. Help students notice when negative thoughts enter their brains. Be aware of fixed-mindset phrases. (See the reproducible "Activity to Evaluate Inner Thoughts," page 173.)
- Encourage students to keep persevering even if things don't go as planned. Learning is sloppy; expect it to take time. Things don't always come easily.
- Encourage do-overs, and invite students to propose a redo if they think it will help them be more successful.

The Power of Mistakes

A key factor in the development of a growth mindset is learning to deal with setbacks and failures. Mistakes are part of learning. Some even say, "If you are not struggling, you are not learning!" When students are learning new skills and concepts, they may have multiple challenges and setbacks. If the new learning is too far beyond the student's current capabilities, he, she, or they could experience a lot of frustration. Psychologist Lev Vygotsky (1978) introduced the *zone of proximal development* (ZPD) model of learning theory. His model includes three main layers, as illustrated in figure 4.3. The innermost ring represents what a student can already do independently, or his, her, or their current level of achievement. The outermost ring is the frustrational zone. This is currently beyond the student's reach—even with lots of help. The middle layer ring is the learner's sweet spot. This instructional zone is where the content and skills are a little beyond the student's current level of understanding and where new learning can occur.

Vygotsky's (1978) model suggests that in their ZPD, students will need some help, feedback, and opportunities to explore and even redo tasks as needed. Mistakes are welcome in the ZPD, and educators should encourage and coach students to try again until they reach mastery. However, as it is in classrooms, the emphasis tends to be on *mistake avoidance*, in which students feel pressure to get answers correct on the first attempt and they have few opportunities to redo an assignment or test.

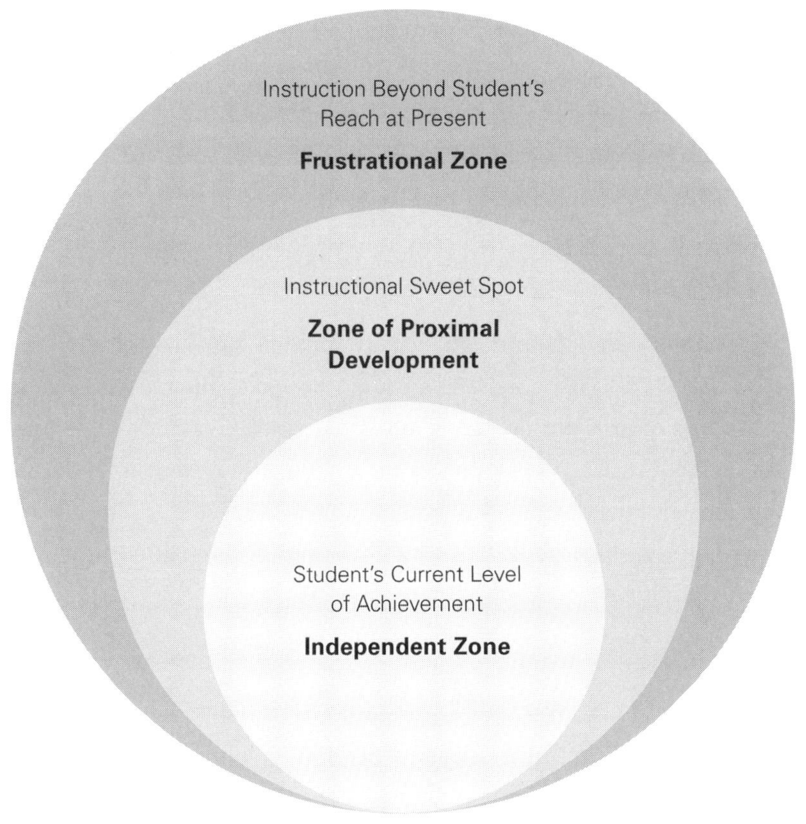

Source: Adapted from Vygotsky, 1978.

Figure 4.3: Vygotsky's zone of proximal development.

Janet Metcalf (2017), in her paper *Learning From Errors*, suggests that teachers and learners alike should be encouraged to be open to mistakes and to actively use them in becoming prepared for a test. People view mistakes and failures in different ways. Those who have already developed a growth mindset believe that challenges and obstacles are inevitable and not an indication of personal failure. They view failures as learning opportunities. They understand that learning often involves a struggle but keep going anyway. They persist. Those who maintain a fixed mindset view making a mistake as a confirmation that they are not smart, and they are reluctant to try again.

When I have discussed failures with my students, I have asked them, "When you fail at something, what do you usually do?" Think about it for yourself. When you fail at a task at work, for example, how do you react? Common responses I've heard are "I get mad at myself," "I feel like a loser," "I blame someone else," "I act like it doesn't bother me," "I try not to let anyone know about it," and "I try to forget it ever happened." But the preferred, growth-mindset responses to failure are "I think about what happened,"

"I explore other possibilities," "I decide what I can do better next time," and "I try again." Students must learn to understand why they made a mistake or had a failure and then take corrective actions. That's what people with a growth mindset do. Making errors can greatly facilitate new learning and if mistakes are investigated and corrected, learners will begin to develop a growth mindset about their learning.

Perseverance

Findings from researchers and journalists such as Paul Tough (2012), Angela Duckworth (2016), and Carol S. Dweck (2016) provide valuable information about our understanding of grit, perseverance, and tenacity. When students recognize mistakes and failures as learning opportunities and no longer see them as horrible, defining events, students can begin to develop perseverance. As teachers focus on supporting students through productive struggle, we may use several different terms. *Grit, tenacity,* and *perseverance* each have a slightly different definition.

- ***Grit***: Having passion to work hard toward long-term goals; telling yourself, "Push yourself to the limit!" but knowing when to take a break
- ***Tenacity***: Holding firm and persisting; telling yourself, "Never give up!"
- ***Perseverance***: Continuing in spite of difficulty or obstacles; telling yourself, "Don't get discouraged!"

Perseverance is the ability and self-control that pushes us to work through challenges; this means that teachers must allow for struggle time. Students learn to persevere in solving challenging tasks or problems by having time to struggle with the challenging tasks or problems. Teachers can and should support them *through* struggle rather than *around* it. Students will begin to understand that many problems do not have a quick, easy solution.

According to Merriam-Webster (n.d.a), the definition of *perseverance* is "continued effort to do or achieve something despite difficulties, failure, or opposition." Every classroom has students who tend to give up quickly or ask for help when they encounter any kind of problem. Even if the task is within a student's ZPD, some students may show reluctance to even begin and choose to sit and wait for the teacher to come and help. Students may need some specific ideas when learning how to transition from thinking "This is too hard," and "I give up," to "This is going to take some time and effort, but I can do it!" Parenting guru and motivational speaker Brené Brown says, "Hope is a function of struggle" (as cited Flintoff, 2013). She believes that the two key factors in developing perseverance are to show courage and be vulnerable (as cited in Flintoff, 2013).

Consider suggesting the following to students to help them develop a perseverance mindset.

- Set reasonable goals, and make a plan. Break down a task into smaller goals if needed. ("Is this task doable? What parts do I think I can complete today?")
- Before beginning, brainstorm some things that might go awry during the progress toward the goal. ("What might go wrong? Where might I have a problem? Do I need any other directions or materials to be successful?")
- Consider removing anything that might cause a distraction, get you off track, and keep you from reaching the goal. ("Is my work area set up? Are other distractions [screens, phones, and so on] put away? Do I need to get a drink or use the restroom before I start?")
- Know what to do first if there is a problem or you get stuck. ("What can I do first, before asking for help? Should I reread the instructions? Can I skip this problem and return to it later? Is there a different way I can solve this? Can I turn the problem into a drawing or work it out on a piece of paper?")
- Understand the procedures and protocols are set up in the classroom to get help if needed. ("Did I ask three other students first before going to the teacher? Is there a student helper designated who I can ask for help? Can I look up some help online?")
- Discuss a reasonable amount of time to keep trying. ("At what point should I ask for help? How can good effort and perseverance still be celebrated even if there is still a roadblock?")

Students tend not to persevere in a learning experience when:

- They feel excluded
- The learning environment makes them feel stupid
- The material they are learning is culturally exclusionary
- They do not believe they will be successful
- They are lacking the necessary skills and haven't been taught the skills necessary to achieve

- They are given insufficient voice and choice in how they learn
- The relationships with their teachers are strained or nonexistent

However, there are many low-prep activities that can help students begin to develop perseverance. Consider the following activities. You can use any of these activities to generate a class discussion about feeling frustrated, experiencing do-overs, trying alternative strategies, having patience, and getting feedback and help from others.

- **Drops on a penny:** Working alone or with a partner, have students use a dropper or pipette to see how many drops of water they can put on a penny. They begin by making a prediction regarding the number of drops, and then carry out the experiment. Place the penny on a piece of paper towel. Then, slowly drop water onto the surface of the penny, and see how many drops can be added before the surface tension gives way and the water spills onto the towel. Repeat at least five times, trying various techniques to improve the results. They'll discuss strategies with other students. For example:
    - Can you get about the same amount of water on the heads side of the coin and on the tails side?
    - Would how you hold the dropper make a difference?
    - What would happen if you wiped the coin with a little hand sanitizer first?
- **Card houses:** Using a standard deck of cards (or *UNO* or flash cards), students try to balance and stack the cards to build a two- or three-story house. They can try various base configurations—triangles versus rectangles, for example. If the house falls down, start again.
- **Tongue twisters:** Students can learn and practice saying some tongue twisters, such as this one: "Betty bought a bit of butter, but the butter Betty bought was bitter, so Betty beat a bit of butter to make the bitter butter better" (Wells, 1899). Students should say them over and over until they have them, and see how fast they can repeat them.
- **Paper and book challenge:** Students can try to balance a not-too-heavy book on a single sheet of paper. They must suspend the book off a surface by at least four inches using no other materials. The book must stay balanced on the paper for at least ten seconds without the student touching the book or the paper. (Hint: Rolling the paper into a cylinder or folding it into a triangle will create a strong base.)

Conclusion

Preparing students to be successful on and less stressed for high-stakes tests requires more than teaching content and skills. Students need to have multiple opportunities throughout the year to build self-efficacy, a growth mindset, and perseverance. These noncognitive psychological factors comprise the skills that prepare students to persevere and demonstrate confidence as they take high-stakes tests. As the Bandura (1989) quote states at the beginning of this chapter, "People's beliefs in their capabilities affect how much stress and depression they experience in threatening or taxing situations, as well as their level of motivation" (p. 1177). Helping students understand their capabilities and giving them opportunities to learn more about their personal challenges will help them build agency. Remember, according to Poon (2018), there are four components to address when helping students develop agency: (1) future planning, (2) present effort, (3) past reflection, and (4) self-efficacy (see page 72). Helping students develop self-efficacy, a growth mindset, and perseverance will help them in all aspects of learning and life. When students take a high-stakes test, these elements of agency will be crucial.

MINDFULNESS PRACTICES FOR THE CLASSROOM

True happiness is to enjoy the present, without anxious dependence upon the future, not to amuse ourselves with either hopes or fears but to rest satisfied with what we have, which is sufficient, for he that is so wants nothing.

—SENECA

Daily-life stressors, rigorous school expectations, puberty, social-media interactions, and the pressure of high-stakes tests are all possible triggers that can derail students' brains. Moderate stress (eustress) can be beneficial and motivate students to perform well. High levels of stress can occur when we perceive that a situation is dangerous or threatening, either physically or psychologically. Stressful situations such as taking a high-stakes test may trigger the reflex response and minimize the brain's abilities to recall important information. Understanding the stress response and what it feels like is key, but perhaps more important is learning coping strategies for how to reduce stress *before* it becomes overwhelming. While students from families of low socioeconomic status may have more frequent and more intense stress events, no one is immune to the reflex response (Jennings, 2015).

When students report that they are feeling stressed, it is often because they are either thinking about things that *already happened* (rumination) or worrying about things that *might happen* in the future. Their brains rarely get to experience calm and settle in the present moment in a nonjudgmental way. Learning how to focus and attend to our thoughts, sensations, and emotions that are happening *right now* can provide benefits to one's physical and emotional health (Parmentier et al., 2019).

When we are attending to the *present* moment, we are in control of our sensory awareness and we are paying attention *on purpose.* When we can direct our thoughts and sensations to the present moment, we can interrupt the ruminations of what has already happened or the anxious thoughts of what may occur in the future. We can give our stressed-out brains a little break. To be fair, most of us rarely stay in the present moment, as several factors compromise our ability to do so. When we do things automatically, without much thought or awareness, we are quite mindless. When we attempt to multitask, we actually demand our brains stay in a state of continuous partial attention. This state can mentally exhaust us and add to our stress. It can reduce our ability to focus and feel satisfied. Endless distractions and the stress of information overload can affect students' ability to concentrate and even make them feel inadequate. When they feel they have reduced mental capacity, they feel less able to think clearly, problem solve, and generate creative ideas. Such a social or emotional event in the classroom can derail learning. Therefore, managing emotions and self-regulating are key skills for success in school and in life (Goleman, 2019). But how do we help students develop them in classrooms? We can do so by teaching students about *mindfulness*—"the awareness that arises through paying attention on purpose, in the present moment, and nonjudgmentally" (Kabat-Zinn, 2003). Mindful practice can teach students a way of *being* rather than always *doing* or *thinking about doing.*

Mindfulness is not new. In 1979, Jon Kabat-Zinn, considered the father of the mindfulness movement, founded the Stress Reduction Clinic at the University of Massachusetts Medical School, which was further developed into the Mindfulness-Based Stress Reduction training program. He created the approach to help reduce stress, basing his work in traditional Buddhist principles of mindfulness and meditation (Kabat-Zinn, 2003). Research Linda E. Carlson and Sheila N. Garland (2005) have since conducted at the program confirms that mindfulness practices can improve how well our brains counteract depression and process information, improve our sleep patterns, strengthen our immune systems, lift our moods, and reduce stress. Taking time to do a mindfulness strategy can help us step back from our automatic thought patterns and behaviors and see things more clearly.

Through mindfulness, students can become more aware by being able to pay attention to their body and thoughts, here and now, with kindness and curiosity. To help our students avoid the deleterious effects of continuous partial attention, let's take a closer look at the causes of an inability to concentrate, mindful self-regulation strategies, and social-emotional vocabulary.

Mindfulness* Versus *Meditation

Mindfulness and meditation are often interchangeable, but there is a clear distinction between them. Mindfulness is the practice of purposely focusing your attention on the present moment and accepting it without judgment; the purpose of which is to relax and calm the mind and body (Harvard Health Publishing, 2019). It can be done anywhere, anytime, with anyone, and with whatever you are doing.

Mindfulness practices teach you how to focus on something—your breath, your pulse, your hearing, or so on—to help you notice the present moment. Meditation is a little different in that the goal is to think about nothing. Creating a way to open your heart or clear your mind of everything, meditation is usually practiced for a specific amount of time on your own (Shapiro & Shapiro, 2017).

The Causes of an Inability to Concentrate

Without mindful coping strategies, the stress of mindlessness, multitasking, continuous partial attention, and information overload can diminish students' attention, focus, and concentration (Mason, Rivers Murphy, & Jackson, 2018, 2020). This can happen to any of us, but it can be particularly devastating to students. Helping students develop a mindfulness routine in the classroom can have amazing benefits. Learning how to practice mindfulness techniques on a regular basis can bring improvements and positive changes in one's physical and mental health, attitudes, and even behaviors. According to Harvard Health Publishing (2019), "Some experts believe that mindfulness works, in part, by helping people to accept their experiences—including painful emotions—rather than react to them with aversion and avoidance."

The following sections take a closer look at some causes of an inability to concentrate: (1) mindlessness, (2) multitasking, (3) continuous partial attention, and (4) information overload.

Mindlessness

As discussed in chapter 4 (page 71), our brains grow and make connections when we are learning through the process of neuroplasticity. Rehearsing or practicing can help us strengthen the connections and streamline many of our everyday routines, allowing us to complete various tasks efficiently and without much attention. We're often doing things that are automatic or require very little cognitive processing. These programs of behavior are helpful; they let us get dressed, cook, exercise, complete routine mathematical computations, and even drive without taxing ourselves too much or demanding an inordinate amount of focus.

Humans are bundles of habits and are often unaware of what we are doing. Psychologist Ellen J. Langer (2016) refers to this state as *mindlessness*. It is like we are on autopilot. When we are mindless, we are trapped in routines for how we do things, and we are fairly oblivious to events going on around us. Our inner rules and routines determine our behavior. We may be quite disconnected from our surroundings, our relationships, and our health and well-being. We are not *aware*.

Multitasking

In the 21st century, aided by technology, people often attempt to do several things at once. David Yang (2019) reports in his article "The Myth of Multitasking" that we frequently overestimate our ability to handle multiple tasks. His report indicates that "individuals have the propensity to overrate their abilities and lack the metacognitive ability to realize that the decisions they have made are incorrect." We may actually be the worst judges of our own abilities. This phenomenon could prove dangerous when taking a high-stakes test. Earl Miller (as cited in Hamilton, 2008), a professor of neuroscience at the Massachusetts Institute of Technology, says that we *think* we are multitasking, but for the most part, our brains can't focus on more than one thing at a time. Instead, he explains, we actually switch our attention from task to task extremely quickly. When we are cooking a meal, we multitask. We move from one thing to the next. We are trying to get as many things done as we possibly can, thinking we are being more efficient and more productive. Attempting to complete a variety of tasks that demand more cognitive load than cooking a meal (or, for students, completing assignments) all at the same time is mentally exhausting, and it may diminish the quality of the finished tasks. When we attempt to multitask, there is often a high error rate (Makhlouf, 2015).

High-stakes tests are often administered around the same time every year. The stress of finals week finds many students doing their best to finish assignments and study for upcoming exams. A simple solution to improve performance would be to systematically arrange the testing schedule to only focus on *one* test subject each week. This would allow students to focus on the test at hand and not try to juggle lots of different study sessions, readings, and research on a variety of topics.

Continuous Partial Attention

When we multitask, we have a desire to be more productive and more efficient. Since the late 1990s, former Apple and Microsoft executive Linda Stone (as cited in Fallows, 2013) has referred to the quandary this creates as *continuous partial attention*. Continuous partial attention is motivated by a desire to connect and be connected. In any given moment, we are continuously scanning for the best opportunities, activities, and social connections. "To be busy, to be connected, is to be alive, to be recognized, and to matter," says Stone (n.d.). We use continuous partial attention in an effort not to miss anything. It is a state of being always on, anytime, anyplace. When we multitask, we are motivated by a desire to be more efficient and productive. But in the case of continuous partial attention, we're motivated by the desire to not miss anything. When we're engaged in two (or more) activities that demand our thinking and brain power, we are always on high alert! We pay attention to multiple things at once, but we may not *complete* tasks. This way of operating can contribute to over-stimulation and create a sense of constant crisis (Fallows, 2013; Stone, n.d.).

We are always on high alert when we pay continuous partial attention (Stone, n.d.). This vigilance can be very stressful for our brains. In the long term, the stress hormones adrenaline and cortisol create a hyperalert state that is always scanning for stimuli. During a week of scheduled tests, students' brains and bodies may be in a constant hyperalert state as they prepare for multiple exams.

FOMO

In the 21st century, we are also experiencing *infomania*, an "obsessive—and often excessive—consumption of news and information," according to Merriam-Webster (n.d.b). We may feel like we need to be consuming as much as possible because it's out there, and it *might* be important. We want to be sure we are as informed as (we assume) everyone else is. *Fear of missing out* (FOMO) is a specific social anxiety that has grown exponentially with the proliferation of social media. The anxiety comes from the belief that others are having fun or doing something interesting while we are not present. It triggers a desire to stay constantly connected to see what others are doing. Similar to an addiction, a quick check of emails or text messages temporarily relieves our anxiety. Over-achieving students may be sucked into the FOMO mindset, and obsessively check phones, apps, and announcements to make sure they are also included and in the know.

Information Overload

As technology innovations accelerate, we are increasingly experiencing a state of *information overload*. There is a huge amount of information to take in and to shut out. Incessant distractions and interruptions make it hard to concentrate. Edward M. Hallowell (2015), a leading expert on attention deficit disorder and attention deficit hyperactivity disorder, believes that many people are suffering from an *acquired attention deficit trait* (ADT). Rather than a genetic disorder, ADT is an adaptive response to the hyperkinetic environment in which we live and work and the constant barrage of information. As the mind fills with noise and interruptions, the brain gradually loses its capacity to attend fully and thoroughly to anything. Those with ADT begin to feel a constant low level of panic and guilt (Hallowell, 2015).

Students use technology to keep a constant pipeline of knowledge, social connections, and often irrelevant information streaming into their lives. The volume and complexity of information students are expected to handle continues to increase. Simultaneous demands create a feeling of inadequacy for students. They can become more impatient, impulsive, forgetful, and stressed. So, in this age of technology, there are many scenarios that may trigger a stress response. But it is important to examine some everyday attention strategies that may also be contributing to student stress. When someone is functioning on autopilot, he, she, or they may experience mindlessness. Students may lose attention when they are frequently attempting to multitask. Students may also feel the drive to multitask in an effort to become more productive. Students may also begin to operate with a high-alert stress level while they maintain continuous partial attention, so as not to miss out on anything.

Table 5.1 summarizes this section's causes of an inability to concentrate.

Mindful Self-Regulation Strategies

A multitude of things can cause stress in students' daily lives. Over time, chronic stress can derail learning and even affect social relationships. All ages of students can benefit from mindfulness training, from preschool to high school and higher education. Not only does mindfulness training help students lower their stress and manage their emotions, but it can bring about improvements in attention, concentration, conflict resolution, and empathy for others—all huge payoffs for school and life (Mason et al., 2018, 2020). Practicing mindfulness can help build a calm atmosphere and can improve the overall classroom environment. Teachers should introduce and integrate mindfulness strategies into daily classroom practice way before any upcoming testing date. They will help reduce test stress when the time comes.

TABLE 5.1: Learner Behaviors and Drawbacks to Causes of an Inability to Concentrate

	Learner Behaviors	Drawbacks
Mindlessness	• Being on autopilot • Disconnecting from what you are actually doing	Lack of awareness
Multitasking	• Attempting to be efficient and more productive • Quickly switching attention	Diminished attention and contentment
Continuous Partial Attention	• Being on high alert • Scanning surroundings and technological devices • Trying not to miss anything	Inability to be in the present moment (Lots of brain "switching")
Information Overload	• Having difficulty filtering out important information • Feeling inadequate because of simultaneous demands	Difficulty concentrating and focusing

Daily mindfulness practice can help students focus their attention, self-regulate, and de-stress their active brains. Teachers often ask students to "pay attention" dozens of times a day, yet they rarely teach them *how*. Teaching students how to pay attention to be aware of their internal and external worlds can enhance executive function and learning, develop social-emotional awareness, and promote general well-being. Developing a daily mindfulness routine in the classroom can help prevent the reflex response from derailing the learning process. Additionally, mindfulness practices are designed to help calm and focus the body and mind when students face unavoidable stressors, such as high-stakes tests.

There are many low-prep, easy-to-do mindfulness exercises that can help students learn to be more aware of their thoughts and actions. Mindfulness practices include a wide variety of relaxation and focus strategies that can range from traditional meditation and yoga to deep breathing, progressive muscle relaxation, and guided visualization. Four key mindfulness practices that any classroom can incorporate are as follows.

1. Mindful breathing
2. Calming movement
3. Focused attention
4. Healthy distraction

The following sections describe how teachers can integrate each of these practices into the classroom to help with self-regulation.

Mindful Breathing

To begin a mindfulness practice, start with the super stress buster—*mindful breathing*. It is free, requires no preparation, works for all ages, and can be practiced anywhere. The key is learning how to do deep breathing. The American Institute of Stress (2012) reports:

> Deep breathing increases the supply of oxygen to your brain and stimulates the parasympathetic nervous system, which promotes a state of calmness. Breathing techniques can help you feel connected to your body—it brings your awareness away from the worries in your head and quiets your mind.

Most people are not very conscious of their breathing patterns. When people are anxious, stressed, or upset, they tend to take rapid, shallow breaths that come directly from the chest. Chest breathing, also known as *thoracic breathing*, uses the top lobes of the lungs and may create an imbalance in the oxygen and carbon dioxide levels in the blood. This can cause an increased heart rate, dizziness, muscle tension, and other physical sensations. These sensations may trigger a reflex response that can contribute to more anxiety and even launch a panic attack (Ankrom, 2021).

During abdominal breathing, or *diaphragmatic breathing*, the diaphragm drops, pushing the belly out and allowing the lungs to fill deeply and completely. When you are in a deep sleep, you are using abdominal breathing. If you are breathing properly, your abdomen, not your upper chest, should expand and contract with each breath. During stressful and anxious times, you're more likely to breathe from your chest (Ankrom, 2021).

Teaching students to focus on and control their breathing can help them become more reflective and less reactive when feeling anxious or experiencing a stressful event. Begin to practice deep breathing when students are already fairly calm to ensure they focus on and learn the technique. During a breathing exercise, ask students to notice their breath, their body, and their mind chatter to become more aware of themselves in the present moment. Shifting to deep breathing for even a few minutes can help regulate their stress and help them become calm. See figure 5.1 for a graphic representation of deep breathing.

The sections that follow describe five deep-breathing practices—(1) belly breathing, (2) flower-candle breathing, (3) 8-4-7 breathing, (4) hummingbird breathing, and (5) mandala breathing—to use in the following classroom situations.

- At the beginning of the day or class period to help students get calm and focused
- During transitions from one activity to another to have students reflect on what they just did and get ready for the next task

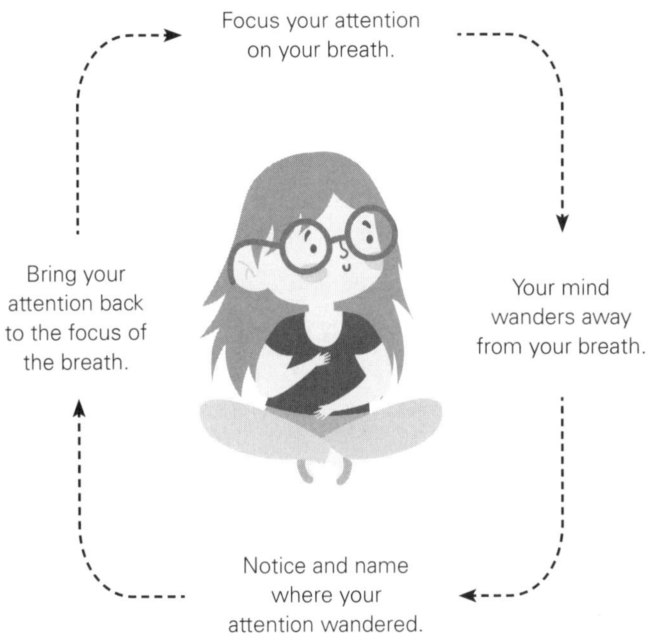

Figure 5.1: Deep breathing.

- Before a stressful event, such as a test or performance, to calm students' nerves
- After a stressful event or emotional upset to calm students down
- At the end of the day or class period to have students reflect on what they completed and note successes

Belly Breathing

Belly breathing has proven to be highly effective as a stress-reduction strategy for both students and adults. According to the American Institute of Stress, twenty to thirty minutes of belly breathing each day will reduce anxiety and stress (as cited in Sharma et al., 2013). Students can try this exercise sitting comfortably in a chair or lying down on the floor. Note, too, that you can dim the classroom lights; play soft, relaxing music; or tell students that instead of looking downward, they may keep their eyes closed if they wish (but avoid insisting that they close their eyes, as some students can find this threatening). Once you've determined those options, begin by asking students to pay attention to their normal breathing, putting one hand on the upper chest and one on the belly—just below the belly button. Ask students to take a deep breath through the nose so that the hand on the chest does not rise up but the hand on the belly does. Have students inhale for a count of five, hold the breath in for a count of five, and exhale slowly through slightly pursed lips, pushing the air all the way out using their belly. Continue for three to five minutes.

Flower-Candle Breathing

Have students sit comfortably in their chairs. Take a moment to review the differences between *chest breathing* (thoracic) and *abdominal breathing* (diaphragmatic). Then ask students to each hold their left hand in a fist and imagine it's holding a beautiful flower. Ask students to simultaneously hold their right hand in a fist and imagine it's holding a lit candle. Alternatively, you could use real or inexpensive artificial flowers and wooden craft sticks to represent the candles. Have students inhale slowly and deeply through their noses, pretending to smell the flower, savoring the beautiful fragrance for a count of four. Have students turn their heads to the right and exhale slowly and completely, pretending to blow out the candle. Repeat this pattern three to five times.

8-4-7 Breathing

Have students sit comfortably in their chairs. Review belly breathing. Have students exhale completely through their mouths for eight seconds as you count. Students should then inhale quietly through their noses for four seconds—making their bellies expand. Students then hold their breath for seven seconds before starting over, exhaling for eight seconds. As you lead this breathing routine, count with a slow cadence and a calm voice. Repeat the pattern for at least four cycles. This serves as a great beginning-of-the-day routine.

Hummingbird Breathing

The unique sensation of this yoga-breathing practice can help create instant calm, relieving frustration, anxiety, and anger. Have students sit in a comfortable position and either close their eyes or look downward and relax their faces. Instruct students to gently place both their index fingers on the cartilage that partially covers their ear canals and get ready to push that in. Begin deep breathing, having students inhale for four counts. As they exhale, have them gently press their fingers into the cartilage to plug their ears. Encourage them to hum loudly (while keeping their mouths closed) as they exhale completely. They should try to produce the humming sound from deep in their bellies. Continue for several minutes. Note that since students will be muffling external sounds, they may have trouble hearing verbal instructions, so try using a visual, such as a video clip, that shows a pattern for rhythmic breathing.

Mandala Breathing (Mindful Minute)

Mindful breathing techniques can have benefits even if only done for a minute or two. In my classrooms, we just referred to this time as a Mindful Minute. Focusing on one's breath can be challenging. After a couple of inhales and exhales, students may find it difficult to stay in a pattern. Watching a mandala expand and contract or using another visual to pace students' breath can help them stay in a steady pace. I've found that this technique is most powerful with middle and high school students, who may at first be self-conscious or embarrassed to try breathing strategies. I use any of the online video resources that follow. Project them on a screen or SMART Board for all to see, and use them with or without the accompanying sounds.

- **One minute of triangle breathing:** https://bit.ly/3ayrh7N (Klassen, 2015)
- **Five-minute breathing exercise:** https://bit.ly/3sHgLRY (Daring Authenticity, 2011)
- **Five minutes of breathing for relaxation:** https://bit.ly/3tMNdni (Marthe Creations, 2015)
- **Ten-minute resonant-breathing exercise:** https://bit.ly/2RMu8n0 (Power You Are, 2015)
- **Five breathing techniques for students:** https://bit.ly/3vbF8c9 (Floyd, 2017)

Calming Movement

Helping students learn breathing techniques is most important as teachers begin to incorporate mindfulness practices into daily classroom routines. For many students, these additional movement and relaxation strategies may also help reduce stress and anxiety. Consider the following calming movement strategies: (1) calming stones or fidget toys, (2) glitter jars, (3) body scan, (4) take-five area, and (5) exercise.

Calming Stones or Fidget Toys

Holding and fidgeting with something in their hands can help calm students' busy minds. Students may hold stones or fidget toys for this purpose. In terms of stones, hematite stones work best. But polished river rocks are easier to find; they are often readily available at dollar stores. Fidget toys that students can hold include small squishy or bendy toys. You may also have students make their own stress balls by filling twelve-inch latex balloons with Play-Doh.

Glitter Jars

Have students each fill a jar to the top with water. Then have them pick three colors of glitter: one to represent their thoughts and worries, one to represent feelings, and one to represent behaviors or urges to do things. They should drop a few pinches of each color of glitter into the water. (Adding a little glycerin to the water will slow down the glitter's settling.) Students then each seal their jar with its lid or duct tape. Once all students have sealed their jars, tell them, "Think of an upsetting event, and swirl the glitter around. To get the glitter to settle and see clearly again, you must be still! When we are still, we can see clearly again."

Body Scan

The body scan is a progressive relaxation technique. Give students the following directions to have them each do a body scan. For the most relaxing results, allow students to lie down on mats on the floor. If they are at home, lying down on their beds would be best. This is a wonderful nighttime ritual that parents can do with their children (Bertin, 2016).

1. Sit comfortably in a chair or lie down flat on your back. Let your legs and your arms relax. If you are sitting, make sure your feet are planted on the floor. Settle yourself in a comfortable position, and close your eyes.
2. Begin by taking two or three gentle, large belly breaths. Place one hand on your belly, and feel it move with each breath. Focus on how it feels as the air moves in and out of your body.
3. Begin to pay attention to the other parts of the body. Start with your feet. Wiggle your toes a bit. Flex your toes and tighten them, then if you can, relax your feet now. Notice how that feels too.
4. Let yourself be still for a full minute. Pay attention as best you can to just your relaxed feet. If your mind gets busy, bring your attention back to your feet again.
5. Now focus your attention to your lower legs. Do they feel heavy, light, warm, cold, or something else? Relax your calf muscles. Give yourself a few moments of rest.
6. Move your attention up to your knees. Tighten your kneecaps and relax them. Notice the front, back, and sides of your knees.
7. After a few more breaths, move your attention to your upper legs. Tighten your muscles, and let them relax. Notice how completely relaxed your legs are.
8. Focus your attention on your belly when you breathe; you can feel it rising and falling, up and down. If you feel hungry, that can make it hard to focus; that's normal.

9. Bring your attention to your chest. Notice how it is rising and falling as you breathe. Gently practice coming back again and again to notice how your chest feels when you breathe.
10. Bring your attention to your hands. Are they touching the bed, the floor, or somewhere on your body? No need to move them or do anything with them. Tighten your hand or wiggle your fingers. Now relax them if you can, and simply pay attention to your hands for another moment.
11. Move your attention up into your arms. Tighten your muscles, and then let them totally relax.
12. Now pay attention to your back. Can you feel it against the back of the chair, bed, or the floor? Notice how it moves slightly with each breath.
13. Now focus your attention on your neck and shoulders. Tighten up the muscles in your shoulders, and then let go and relax them. Roll your head around a couple of times, and then let it settle at the top of your spine and relax. If your mind wanders, that's fine.
14. Bring your attention to your face muscles. What expression do you have right now? What else do you notice in your face? Can you relax your eyebrows, cheeks, and mouth?
15. Now take a few moments to pay attention to your whole body. Remain still and relaxed, and continue to pay attention to your breath and your relaxed body.
16. Now open your eyes and sit for a few moments before deciding to move.

Students can do a shorter version of the body scan on their own in less than five minutes by taking these steps.

1. Find a quiet place with no disturbances.
2. Get comfortable. Lie down if possible, or sit in a chair.
3. Close your eyes.
4. Breathe deeply—five counts in and five counts out.
5. Notice when you are feeling calmer.
6. Relax your muscles from head to toe.
7. Tense your muscles, and then relax them.
8. When you reach your toes, take a few minutes to just relax.

9. Slowly open your eyes.
10. Notice the feeling, and enjoy it!

Take-Five Area

Create a small space within the classroom that can be a place for quiet reflection. Set up clear procedures and reasonable time limits. (I always have allowed five minutes, with no questions asked. Students can go there without having to ask for permission, although I do ask them to wait if the teacher is in the middle of giving instructions.) Include a comfortable chair, a lava lamp, a timer, fidget toys, stuffed animals, pictures, headphones for music, and so forth.

Exercise

Virtually any form of exercise, from aerobics to yoga, can act as a stress reliever. Even if you're not very athletic, or even if you're out of shape, you can still make a little exercise go a long way toward stress reduction. Exercise can increase your overall health, improve your sense of well-being, and provide some major stress-busting benefits (Penn State, 2018).

- Aerobic exercise reduces the body's levels of stress hormones, such as adrenaline and cortisol.
- Movement pumps up your production of endorphins—your brain's feel-good neurotransmitters. Running, a game of tennis, or a nature walk can contribute to this same feeling.
- Exercise distracts you from your daily stress as you keep your focus on the movement. It's sometimes called *meditation in motion* (Maree, 2020).
- Regular exercise can increase your self-confidence, relax you, and improve your mood. It can also improve your sleep, which stress can disrupt.
- Some simple stretches can be helpful. Focus on the muscles in the neck and shoulders. Your hackles can be quite triggered when dealing with stressors.

Focused Attention

A very basic form of mindful awareness is often called *focused attention*. It involves intentionally directing and maintaining attention on a target. Activities that use the senses, such as the following, can allow teachers to help students develop the skills to focus their attention in a variety of ways: (1) picture-to-picture partner activity, (2) raisin-eating activity, and (3) minute guess activity.

Picture-to-Picture Partner Activity

To complete this activity, students pair up with a partner. One partner looks at a given picture and orally describes that picture in detail to the other partner, thus creating a picture in the mind of the listener. (Use pictures with few details, little background, and only one or a few central figures.) The listener can check for details by asking questions that feature *gross* and *fine* structure words. *Gross* structure words relate to the *what* and *where* of the picture; the listener may ask questions involving size, color, number, and so on. ("Is there more than one? What is the main color?") *Fine* structure words relate to the *when* of the picture; the listener may ask questions involving mood, movement, emotions, and sounds. ("Is anything moving in the picture? What sounds were probably going on?") The listener should then describe the picture he, she, or they visualized back to the partner. Then the listeners can look at the picture to see how closely their visualization matched the photo.

Raisin-Eating Activity

Give each student a raisin. Then, guide students through the following steps, which require that they use their senses to focus their attention on the raisin.

1. **Holding:** Take a single raisin, and hold it in the palm of your hand or between your finger and thumb.
2. **Seeing:** Take time to really focus on it. Let your eyes explore every part of it.
3. **Touching:** Turn the raisin over between your fingers, exploring its texture.
4. **Smelling:** Hold the raisin beneath your nose.
5. **Placing:** Bring the raisin up to your lips, and gently place the raisin in your mouth—without chewing.
6. **Tasting:** Chew the raisin, noticing how and where it needs to be for chewing—without swallowing.
7. **Swallowing:** Swallow the raisin, and notice what parts of your mouth you are using.
8. **Following:** Try to feel what is left of the raisin moving down into your stomach.

Minute Guess Activity

Have all students stand (or sit with one hand raised) and close their eyes. On your *go* signal upon starting a timer (or starting a countdown on your screen), students should each try to estimate when one minute has elapsed while keeping their eyes closed. When they think it has been a minute, they sit down or lower their hand.

Healthy Distraction

A very easy way to quickly reduce stress involves finding ways to distract yourself from whatever it is that is bothering you. A healthy distraction works by interrupting the stress so that we stop thinking about what is bothering us for a while and instead think about something else. As the saying goes, "Out of sight, out of mind." There are many ways people might distract themselves away from stressful thoughts. Some distractions include doing chores, engaging in hobbies, seeking out sources of entertainment such as movies or games (including video games), reading books, and getting together with friends. It helps if the activities are interesting; otherwise, the activity may fail to distract people from their stress and worry for very long (Mills, Reiss, & Dombeck, n.d.).

When students are able to notice that something is consuming their thoughts and energy, they can choose a purposeful alternative activity to interrupt their thought pattern and distract themselves. By shifting focus away from the stress, they can give their busy minds a much-needed break. You might introduce students to these five alternative activities so that they have several to choose from when they need a healthy distraction from a tough task or situation.

1. **Laugh it up:** Students can shift their perspective by seeing something funny about the situation. Having a good laugh does some great things.
    - It gets the brain's attention.
    - It releases endorphins, which makes us feel good.
    - It bonds us with others, which gives us feelings of inclusion.
    - It enhances retention of new learning.
    - It relieves stress and tension.
2. **Organize something:** Sometimes, it can be a great distraction to get external things organized. Making a plan to reduce clutter and sort through things can make the task at hand seem easier and doable. Organizing one's work area prior to taking a high-stakes test can be a

healthy distraction and also get materials ready to go. Starting with one area—a drawer, a notebook, a backpack, or a desktop—can distract students from the stress at hand as well as help get things organized for when they are ready to return to the task.

3. **Let it go, and get away:** Move away from the source of the stress; do something else for a while, and try to ignore the source of the stress. Changing the environment through one of the following methods is a quick way to get distracted from a stressful situation or thought pattern.
    - Get outside. Go for a walk with your dog. Researchers Margaret M. Hansen, Reo Jones, and Kirsten Tocchini (2017) explain that the Japanese practice of *shinrin-yoku* (forest bathing), or nature therapy in green spaces, can be a restorative activity. Humans have an inner biological attraction to nature and its importance in our overall health. We intuitively know the relaxing and soothing effects of forests, plants, flowers, urban green spaces, parks, and our own gardens.
    - Escape into a book, movie, or video game. Listen to music. Students can allow themselves to take a break that takes their mind off current stressors.
    - Communicate with a friend. Talk with someone about an unrelated topic. Students can distract themselves from their own stress by listening to another person and hearing what he or she is going through.
4. **Play:** Playing is good for your brain. Take time out for enjoyable activities that are mentally restful and fun!
    - Create and build something.
    - Get together with friends to relax and hang out.
    - Play cards or a board game with someone.
    - Play with a pet or visit with an animal.
    - Engage in your hobby.
5. **Be of service to others:** Offer some help to someone else. Research indicates that helping others boosts well-being (Curry et al., 2018). When we help someone else, we increase our own positive emotions.
    - Attending to someone else's needs has been linked to decreased stress levels.

- When you do good deeds for others, it makes you feel good too.
- The more daily acts of kindness you do, the less likely you'll feel stressed.
- Even if you don't have a lot, sharing whatever you can spare is a simple but generous way to help others.
- Give a little of yourself and your time. Do some chores for someone, perform some random acts of kindness, volunteer in your community, or fix something that is broken.

When students can be their own panic "mechanics," they can learn to use simple, quick fixes in order to calm their bodies and minds. When students learn mindful breathing practices, healthy movements, and simple distractions, they have a wonderful toolbox of strategies from which to draw when they are feeling stressed.

Llamapalooza!

In 2018, to take some pressure off students during finals week, a festival called Llamapalooza was born on the campus of the University of California, Berkeley. Designed to remind students that academic exams are not the entire world, it has become an event that several thousand students look forward to twice a year. This human–llama social occasion, which takes place on a campus lawn, allows students to spend some time petting llamas, helps students relax, and takes the edge off the impending exams. One student said of the festival:

> During finals season, we're always just thinking about all the work we have to do, so, to take our mind off that, even for like a couple minutes just 'cause there's llamas. . . . It's kind of nice just to have our mind off of the stress. (Barber, 2019)

Social-Emotional Vocabulary

In order for students to be mindful about their own and others' feelings, students need to have a working vocabulary for those feelings. Many students say that they are either "happy" or "mad" and miss all the gradations in between because they don't have words and definitions for those subtler emotions (Morin, 2019). Developing a broader and more complex feeling vocabulary allows students to make finer discriminations between feelings, which allows them to better communicate with others. Having a limited emotions vocabulary severely limits our ability to name how we're feeling. Amanda Morin (2019) describes how being able to sense and understand the emotions of others is an important part of children's social development.

Helping students build an accurate, detailed picture of what they are feeling is absolutely key if we want to be able to help them do anything about it through a mindfulness practice. Explicitly teaching student-friendly definitions for social-emotional words, such as the words in table 5.2, can help students develop a strong social-emotional learning vocabulary.

TABLE 5.2: Student-Friendly Definitions of Social-Emotional Words

Social-Emotional Word	Student-Friendly Definition
angry	Feeling strong emotions because you feel that someone has behaved in an unfair way, or that a situation is unacceptable
attention	The power of carefully thinking about, listening to, or watching something
aware	To pay attention through all your senses and thoughts
calm	A still, quiet peacefulness
distraction	Something that makes it difficult to think or pay attention
emotions	Strong feelings (such as love, anger, joy, hate, and fear)
focus	To direct your attention, thoughts, or effort at something specific
gratitude	Showing appreciation for what one has; being thankful
hopeless	Feeling desperation from something unable to be solved or finished
nervous	Being fearful, anxious, or excited
present moment	Things happening right now
relax	To become less tense and anxious
stress	To feel very worried, scared, unsure, or anxious
worry	To feel concern or anxiety

Following are two strategies to help integrate social-emotional vocabulary into mindfulness.

1. **The RULER approach:** Marc Brackett, the founding director of the Yale Center for Emotional Intelligence, and his team have created a phenomenal approach to social-emotional learning that teaches emotional intelligence skills to people of all ages, with the goal of creating a healthier, more equitable, innovative, and compassionate society (RULER, n.d.). *RULER* is an acronym for the five skills of emotional intelligence.

a. Recognizing emotions in oneself and others
b. Understanding the causes and consequences of emotions
c. Labeling emotions with a nuanced vocabulary
d. Expressing emotions in accordance with cultural norms and social context
e. Regulating emotions with helpful strategies

Bracket and his colleagues believe that emotions drive learning, decision making, creativity, relationships, and health (RULER, n.d.). People of all ages can be taught to develop their emotional intelligence. (Visit www.rulerapproach.org to learn more about the RULER approach.)

2. **Healthy mind platter:** Developed by Daniel Siegel (n.d.) and David Rock (2011), the healthy mind platter features seven essential mental activities to do every day to maintain a healthy brain and optimum mental health.

   a. *Focus time*—When we closely focus on tasks in a goal-oriented way, we take on challenges that make deep connections in the brain.
   b. *Playtime*—When we allow ourselves to be spontaneous or creative, playfully enjoying novel experiences, we help make new connections in the brain.
   c. *Connecting time*—When we connect with other people, ideally in person, and when we take time to appreciate our connection to the natural world around us, we activate and reinforce the brain's relational circuitry.
   d. *Physical time*—When we move our bodies, aerobically if medically possible, we strengthen the brain in many ways.
   e. *Time in*—When we quietly reflect internally, focusing on sensations, images, feelings, and thoughts, we help to better integrate the brain.
   f. *Downtime*—When we are unfocused, without any specific goal, and let our mind wander or simply relax, we help the brain recharge.
   g. *Sleep time*—When we give the brain the rest it needs, we consolidate learning and recover from the experiences of the day.

According to Siegel (n.d.), by integrating these seven daily activities every day, "you promote integration in your life and enable your brain . . . to strengthen [its] internal connections and your connections with other people and the world around you." (Visit https://bit.ly/3citsgw for an introduction to the healthy mind platter.)

Conclusion

Preparing for high-stakes exams can be challenging and can make many students feel overwhelmed. Developing a repertoire of mindfulness practices will help students manage the test stress more easily. Mindfulness can help students think more clearly and avoid just reacting to high-stress situations. It is a skill that can help students deal with stress and pressure, both in and out of the classroom.

PART 3

Ways to Prepare Students for High-Stakes Tests

Students want to do well on high-stakes tests. But if they don't feel well-prepared, they are likely to have test anxiety. If they know they're unprepared, they'll be worried about doing poorly. There are a variety of reasons for why students might feel unprepared for an upcoming test. The subject matter and content of the test might have been particularly challenging, or they may know that they simply have not studied enough and didn't put in the effort needed. They might feel exhausted because they have been overwhelmed with lots of schoolwork or personal matters and consequently didn't get enough sleep the night before.

Students can gain a lot of confidence and peace of mind going into the test when they have had lots of formative assessments and feedback *during* the learning process, which is why it's the topic of chapter 6 (page 119). Formative assessments and frequent feedback enable students to identify what they already know and what they don't yet fully understand. It helps determine the next steps in the learning process. The use of grading is optional in formative assessment, since the objective is not to *evaluate* the progress of the students yet but to identify their challenges and avoid the teaching-learning process ending without mastering the learning objectives.

Another important way that educators can prepare students for tests is with an emphasis on vocabulary development, particularly tier two words (Beck et al., 2013). Tier two words are referred to as *academic vocabulary.* Academic vocabulary is defined as "words that are traditionally used in academic dialogue and text. Specifically, it refers to words that are not necessarily common or frequently encountered in informal conversation" (Learning A-Z, n.d.). Tier two words might include *distinguish*, *elaborate*, *summarize*, and *contradict*. Students, including English learners, arrive to school with a wide range of vocabulary development. In the elementary years, much of the oral language development and reading comprehension focuses on tier one vocabulary—common everyday words used in the course of general conversations: *warm*, *jump*, *farm*, *factory*, *storm*, and *celebration*. Tier three vocabulary consists of words that are domain or discipline specific. Students must learn and study these words in particular classes in order to master the concepts and pass the tests: *photosynthesis*, *equilateral*, *filibuster*, or *alliteration*.

When students have had explicit instruction in tier two academic vocabulary, they will be better able to understand test directions and reading passages. They are often considered the most high-leverage words for improving a student's overall vocabulary (Beck et al., 2013). Chapter 7 (page 135) will go further into this discussion of academic vocabulary instruction.

Lastly, chapter 8 (page 147) will discuss test prep and things that teachers and students really do have control over when it comes to high-stakes testing. We'll discuss having good study habits, meeting students' basic needs, preparing for the stress mess, and more. When students understand how their bodies might react during stressful testing events, there are many ways they can prepare ahead of time.

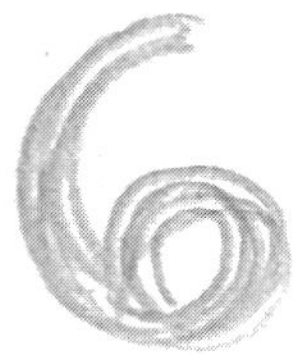

FEEDBACK AND FORMATIVE ASSESSMENTS

Active strategies combined with formative assessment resulted in improved student performance due to increased learning and reductions of stress and anxiety.

—CARDOZO ET AL.

According to educational researcher John Hattie (2015), educators shouldn't just use tests and assessments to determine how much students know about a specific subject on a particular day after a lesson occurs. Educators need to use them to find out what students *already know* at the beginning of a lesson and what they will need to know to progress in their learning. These informative assessments should be an integral part of the teaching-learning process. Also integrating low-stakes assessments during learning provides teachers with information about how to adjust their instructional next steps. When students have frequent opportunities to get accurate feedback during the learning process, they can adjust their next efforts accordingly. Many refer to this as *feeding forward* as opposed to just receiving feedback. The concept *feedforward* was originally developed by management expert Marshall Goldsmith (2007). He felt that traditional feedback was limited because it "focuses on past events—not on the infinite possibilities of the future" (Goldsmith, 2007). When teachers can provide students with ideas on how they can be even more successful, they increase students' chances of success in learning the new curriculum.

When students receive ongoing feedback that measures their performance against a concrete, achievable goal, they also must have opportunities to redo the task so that they can use the feedback to modify their next efforts. Frequent formative assessments help students understand that they can practice, make mistakes, receive corrective feedback, and try again until they succeed. Setting goals and providing feedback are crucial to success, as the brain needs to know where it's going and what the destination looks like and then receive time to make the necessary adjustments and corrections. Feedback to feed forward should provide information about how the student can do better on a similar problem or task in the future or ultimately on a high-stakes test. Formative assessments look to the present and future; summative assessments and high-stakes exams are all about the past.

This chapter dives deep into formative assessment and the impact when feedback is frequent, immediate, meaningful, and constructive. It will also explain how opportunities for failures and do-overs allow students' brains to grow, adjust, and strengthen new connections. The chapter will end with helpful formative assessment strategies. Maintaining frequent formative assessments during the learning process, providing specific feedback, and then orchestrating opportunities to try again can help students develop a greater sense of mastery, confidence, and self-efficacy when presented with similar tasks on high-stakes tests.

Frequent Formative Assessments

Different from summative assessment, which typically occurs only at the end of a learning sequence to evaluate the degree to which a student has achieved mastery at a point in time, formative assessment, in its simplest description, includes any strategy that involves checking for understanding before and during the learning process. *Formative assessment* is "a process used by teachers and students during instruction that provides feedback to adjust ongoing teaching and learning to improve students' achievement of intended instructional outcomes" (Wylie, 2008, p. 3). According to Hattie (2009), providing this formative evaluation comes with an effect size of 0.90—more than double the hinge point of 0.40, making it an effective instructional strategy applicable across disciplines and grades. Data and evidence a teacher collect during a lesson or task help both the teacher and the student know how they are doing. When teachers check for understanding and provide feedback, they do so as a means to ensure that students will later be successful on any summative assessment. Teachers may get information in order to decide whether students are ready to move on or they need additional instruction. When provided with constructive feedback, students can find out where they are along the route to the stated goal and learn what next steps need to happen. Frequent formative assessments help both teachers and students know what they should do next.

A GPS is the perfect metaphor for how formative assessments can provide a real-time check-in, supplying meaningful feedback and specific information students need to get to the destination. Formative assessments encompass three key questions: (1) "Where am I going?" (2) "Where am I along the route?" and (3) "How can I close the gap?" (see figure 6.1). With a GPS, when you start your trip, you mark your current position and then plot your goal—where you hope to arrive at the end of your journey. The GPS then plots an efficient route. With guidance from the GPS, you are able to navigate through the step-by-step instructions. At any time along the way, if you stray or make a wrong turn, the GPS will give you constructive feedback. You then use the information to make the necessary corrections and ultimately to reach the goal.

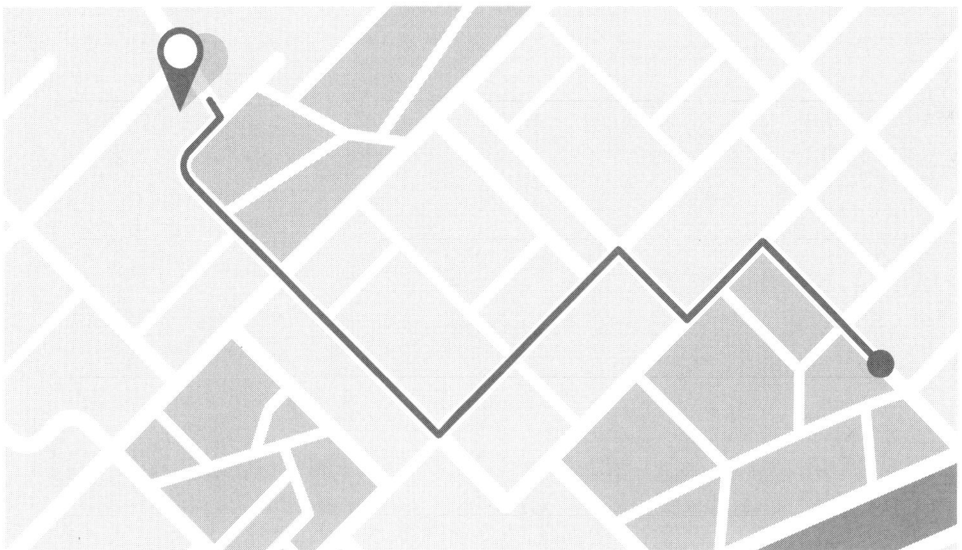

Where am I going?	Establish the learning targets, and communicate to students what mastery will look like—the success criteria.
Where am I along the route?	Establish where the students are in their learning process, and reflect on strengths and areas needing improvement.
How can I close the gap?	Work out how students can meet learning targets, and give them both feedback they can use to improve and opportunities to take action.

Figure 6.1: GPS metaphor for formative assessments.

Generating data and evidence of students' understanding and achievement through a formative assessment helps the teacher and the student (see figure 6.2, page 122).

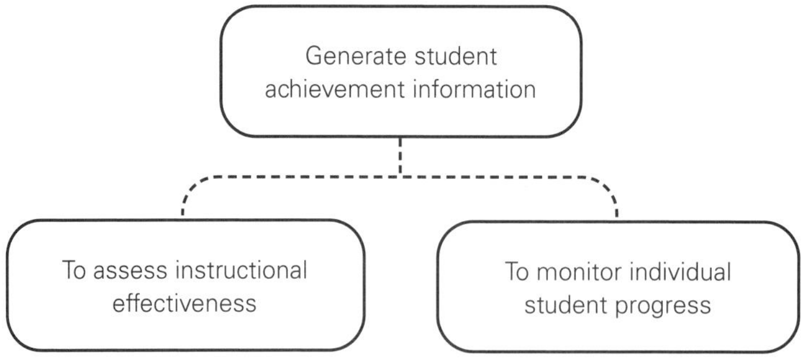

Figure 6.2: Achievement data for teachers and students.

The teacher can assess to what degree the instruction was effective and make decisions about moving on, differentiating instruction, or providing some reteaching. The teacher and the student can use the evidence to determine the individual student's progress toward the success criteria of the learning target. The teacher and the student can gather this evidence using a formative assessment orchestrated by the teacher, such as an exit card, teacher observations, or mini teacher conferences, or the student can begin to use self-assessment strategies, such as referring to a rubric with success criteria, taking an online quizlet, or checking answers with an answer key. Students who have regularly experienced self-assessment strategies may be better prepared to analyze their responses on a test in the future.

The Meaning of Immediate, Meaningful, and Constructive Feedback

In their book *The New One Minute Manager*, Ken Blanchard and Spencer Johnson (2015) contend that "Feedback is the breakfast of champions!" (p. 55). People want to know how they are doing! Feedback keeps us going. Various studies confirm what many teachers have already known: providing students with immediate, meaningful, and constructive feedback can greatly enhance their learning and achievement as measured on high-stakes tests (Hattie, 2015; Hattie & Clarke, 2019; Stenger, 2014). In her article *Five Research-Based Tips for Providing Students With Meaningful Feedback*, Marianne Stenger (2014) notes the following best practices for providing students with feedback they can use.

1. Immediate feedback is the most effective—the sooner the better!
2. Feedback should be specific. What did students do well, and what still needs improvement?

3. Feedback should help students understand where they are in the learning process.
4. Feedback should keep the learner engaged but without rewards, punishments, or competition (Deci & Cascio, 1972).
5. Involving students in the formative assessment allows them to be part the process of collecting and analyzing performance-based data and even providing their own feedback. Hattie (2015) refers to this as *formative interpretation*—"students learning to know what to do next in light of their progress."

If students receive vague feedback or if they receive only a grade, they may not really understand how they performed and what they need to do next. Teachers who use frequent formative assessments during learning can help students find out what next steps they need to take to get better. This feedback cycle builds deep learning and ultimately student confidence.

When teachers make students wait days or weeks to receive a grade or an evaluation of an assignment or project, it usually leaves students with too little time to do anything about it. This may leave students feeling betrayed and hopeless about future assignments. More immediate feedback that guides students to what they need to do to get better is more helpful. Feedback must provide specific information related to the task or learning process that helps learners fill the gap between what they currently know and understand and the goal they are aiming for.

Hattie and Timperley's (2007) research considers feedback one of the most powerful influences on student achievement. Teachers should provide feedback on a task, the process, and students' self-regulation rather than provide just praise, which contains no concrete learning information. Peer feedback, individual feedback from the teacher, and feedback from a computer are all helpful; however, the best feedback from a formative assessment arises when students are able to self-assess, provide their own feedback, and then demonstrate to teachers what they have learned. When feedback originates with students, they can assess their current understanding and see what they need to do to improve through formative interpretation (Hattie, 2015). See Formative Assessment Strategies on page 130 for examples of self-assessment strategies.

In their article on the power of feedback, John Hattie and Helen Timperley (2007) provide several other ideas to keep in mind.

- Praise, punishments, and extrinsic rewards are the least effective feedback for enhancing achievement.

- The average effect size of feedback is 0.79, almost two times the average effect size of one year of schooling (0.40), putting feedback in the top-ten most effective strategies for influencing learning and achievement.
- Master teachers seek feedback about their own effectiveness as they monitor learning and use the data to make important decisions about next instructional steps.
- Feedback is more effective if it provides information about correct rather than incorrect responses, as well as showing growth and progress.

In 1982, Daniel Kirschenbaum, Arnold M. Ordman, Andrew J. Tomarken, and Robert Holtzbauer from the University of Wisconsin researched the impact of focusing on what's correct rather than incorrect—through bowling. They took a group of beginning bowlers and asked them to review their performance after each bowling session (Kirschenbaum et al., 1982). One group of bowlers tracked only what they did right and focused on doing those things more often. Another group of bowlers tracked only the mistakes they made and focused on *not* doing those errors on future tries. Both teams improved, but the bowlers tracking what they did right had 100 percent greater improvement than those who tracked their mistakes.

The study concluded that when people learn new skills, they can benefit from lots of positive feedback that focuses on what they are doing right and what's working, rather than focusing on their errors and mistakes. This type of feedback can increase motivation and reduce stress. The study also noted that once someone has mastered a skill, providing feedback on what needs to be improved can be helpful (Kirschenbaum et al., 1982).

In the same way, in the classroom, formative assessments should generate feedback that is constructive and provide students with guidance about what to do next to get better. Constructive feedback doesn't criticize or tear down the student. Feedback should give the student hope and confidence. If students have received negative feedback in the past or anticipate that the teacher is about to say something critical, their confidence and self-determination may be weak, making the feedback less rewarding (Deci & Cascio, 1972). This may leave the learner unable to fully attend to and comprehend the feedback. Teachers should focus on how to deliver constructive feedback in ways that minimize the threat response. Meaningful, thoughtfully worded, just-in-time feedback given routinely in a safe, inclusive setting will help prevent such a reflex response.

With time and practice, students begin to handle feedback as information rather than criticism. When there is a culture of feedback, students can develop or reinforce a growth mindset. Students are actively involved in their own learning and can self-assess progress they have made to deepen their current understanding. In a culture of feedback, all teachers and students believe that with time, effort, and feedback, all students can improve, encouraging students to give it a go rather than give up.

To enhance student learning, use the following guidelines when providing feedback.

- Focus feedback on the task, not the learner.
- Give unbiased, objective feedback.
- Present elaborated feedback in manageable chunks.
- Be specific and clear with feedback messages.
- Keep feedback as simple as possible.
- Clarify any uncertainty between performance and success criteria.

In *The Motivated Brain*, Gayle Gregory and I (2015) discuss feedback as it relates to the *law of effect*, which suggests that humans and other animals try different behaviors and then assess the outcomes. In simple terms, we repeat behaviors that generate better or more satisfying results and cut down on those behaviors that effect negative or poor results. In this way, the brain is intrinsically motivated to improve, and the process of feedback influences our future decisions and behaviors. Providing students with accurate constructive feedback generates motivation to keep going. A classroom culture of feedback will be apparent when students constantly stop and look at where they've been and what they've done well (using success criteria) and they determine where and how they should move on, asking themselves, "How can I make this better?"

Failures and the Power of Do-Overs

Students may experience some degree of failure during a formative assessment. How they learn to deal with failures can be a significant factor when taking a high-stakes test.

In K–12 classrooms, there is often a culture of avoiding mistakes, instead of looking at failures and struggles as learning experiences (Metcalf, 2017). A mistake-friendly culture of feedback can develop when teachers create a brain-friendly teaching and learning environment that routinely uses positive formative assessment feedback. Students understanding that formative assessments are not graded but, instead, are used to generate constructive feedback is an important point to make. Feedback that only tells students that they failed or passed will often shut down the learning process. Feedback should provide the learner with two types of information: (1) *verification*, which confirms whether an answer is correct; and (2) *elaboration*, which explains why a selected response is wrong, what the correct answer is, and ways the learner can get there. In a mistake-friendly culture, students regularly receive specific information about where to go next and how to do better without being compared to other students. Normalizing mistakes is key and promotes a culture of actionable feedback.

Some students are devastated when they make a mistake or a simple error, yet others are more than willing to examine the problem and make necessary corrections. "I can learn from my mistakes" is the mantra of students who are developing a growth mindset. These learners believe that challenges are inevitable and not an indication of personal failure. They know that with time and effort, they can get better at whatever they put their minds to. But some students start becoming afraid of challenges. In her article "How to Help Kids Overcome Fear of Failure," Vicki Zakrzewski (2013) reminds us that students' fear of failure is directly related to their feelings of self-worth:

> If a person doesn't believe he or she has the ability to succeed—or if repeated failures diminish that belief—then that person will begin, consciously or not, to engage in practices or make excuses in order to preserve his or her self-worth both in his or her own eyes and in the eyes of others.

Students might avoid situations where they might fail, believing failure will confirm they are not very smart. Students might not expect to succeed—they just want to avoid failing. They stop trying to get better. They develop a fixed mindset, giving up easily under pressure, and may even exhibit learned helplessness. If teachers want to instill a growth mindset in students (as discussed in chapter 4, page 71), they must normalize failures. Understanding that it is normal to fail or make mistakes, students can then learn that a mistake is not an ending. It is the beginning of learning and that there is power in failure. Table 6.1 describes how students with growth mindsets and students with fixed mindsets typically react to mistakes and failures.

TABLE 6.1: Student Reactions to Mistakes and Failures

Students With Growth Mindsets	Students With Fixed Mindsets
Are better able to bounce back from mistakes and failures	Divert attention away from the task when faced with a mistake or failure
Pay greater attention to errors, reflect, and analyze	Blame errors on their lack of intelligence or the task itself
Pay careful attention to feedback and take action	Express negative emotions—limiting how they receive feedback
Achieve higher post-error correction and accuracy	Achieve lower post-error correction and accuracy

Source: Schroder et al., 2017.

Performance anxiety (that is, the fear of failure) can trigger the reflex response and leave a student quite paralyzed and unable to correctly respond with known answers.

Learning in an environment that allows for failures—and in fact celebrates them—can shift how the brain views new challenges. New synaptic connections are made in the brain as we experience new learning. These connections are reorganized and strengthened when we persevere and struggle through rigorous tasks. The more actively that we process the new material over time and strengthen those connections, the better that our interconnected neural networks and knowledge structures, or *schemas*, of long-term memory and understanding become. In *Make It Stick: The Science of Successful Learning*, Peter C. Brown, Henry L. Roediger III, and Mark A. McDaniel (2014) explain how building strong, lasting neural connections requires conscious effort to repeatedly pull the newer information from memory, including making mistakes along the way and correcting them through feedback and further practice.

Teachers and parents can create a mistake-friendly culture that will encourage students to endure challenges and persist even when things get tough (Sriram, 2020). It's important students understand that failure is just the first attempt in learning. Consider creating or sharing mistake-friendly posters, like the one in figure 6.3. See page 176 for a reproducible version of this poster.

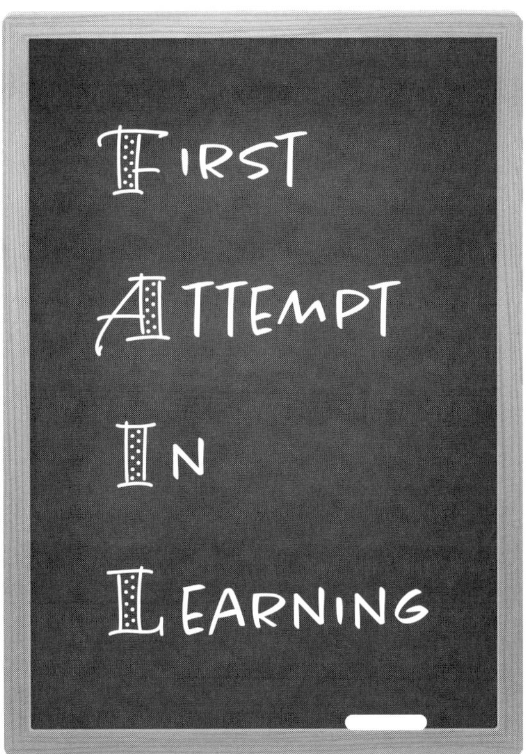

Figure 6.3: Classroom poster on failure.

In 2015, I visited Fuji Kindergarten outside Tokyo. This innovative early-years school was getting lots of attention for its unique design features. The school's architect had specifically created the circular roof as an area for running around—and that's exactly what the four-to seven-year-old students did lots of there. When I was at the school, one visitor asked the host about the skylight boxes that were raised up in various places on the rooftop to allow natural light into the classrooms below.

"So many kids are running around wildly! Don't some of them fall and hit the edges of these skylights?"

The host solemnly replied, "Yes, they do."

"So, what happens?" asked the visitor.

"They learn to be more skillful" was the host's response.

This approach reflects a Jewish proverb that psychologist Wendy Mogel (2001) references in her book *The Blessing of a Skinned Knee*, which reminds us that "treating children's daily distresses as an expected and unalarming part of life is an effective way to discourage them from turning small difficulties into big dramas" (pp. 112–113). Allowing students to experience failures during learning builds up some resiliency—both for learning and during high-stakes tests.

When a student works on a task or assignment, there should be a formative assessment built into the learning sequence. Through the formative assessment, the teacher can determine whether the student made an error or has not yet completed the task correctly. Then the teacher can give the student feedback, allowing the student time to reflect on the suggestions. After doing formative assessments and receiving frequent, useful feedback, students may then be ready for *do-overs*, or second chances at demonstrating their understanding. Do-overs are important because if the brain doesn't have the opportunity to rewire a correct connection, the wrong pattern may remain in the brain unchallenged (Schroder et al., 2017). We don't want incorrect answers to become established patterns. Second or third chances to work on a problem or rewrite a draft story will show students that mistakes are expected and that if they fail in their first attempt, they can always work to improve. Incorporating opportunities for do-overs during the learning process can help students persevere through difficult assignments and tasks. When students learn how to persevere during the learning process, they will be more likely to persevere in a testing environment.

Do-overs are also important because they allow teachers to help students determine (*see* or *recognize*) patterns in their results. "How is this answer different than your first try?" "Do you see any similarities?" "What does this remind you of?" As we take in new information, we connect it to other things we know or have experienced. These connections begin to form a schema in the brain.

Just as Hart (2002) describes, when learners have an opportunity to do a task or activity more than once, they can start to discover patterns. With multiple attempts, they can determine and analyze similarities and differences. Students can look for discrepant events, test hypotheses, and make modifications. Multiple rehearsals and do-overs help the brain form a template for future reference. Our brains become optimized to remember important information by forming knowledge structures, or *schemas*. These schemas are what students can draw on when taking a test.

According to authors James Hiebert and Douglas A. Grouws (2007), when students put in time and effort to grapple with perplexing problems or to make sense of challenging concepts, they engage in a process of *productive struggle*, or effortful practice, that goes beyond passive learning. This productive struggle, which involves challenges that are neither too easy nor too hard, helps build useful, long-term understanding and skill. Redoing challenging tasks actually spurs the production of *myelin*, a fatty substance that increases the strength of neural connections in the brain (Sriram, 2020). Do-overs can help the brain hardwire new schema.

Students who have already developed a growth mindset will have more motivation and eagerness toward new challenges and productive struggle, rather than having a fear of failure. Developing grit and tenacity requires multiple rehearsals with content and skills. Persisting with the challenges compels learners to repeatedly retrieve the information and process new learning over time. This stimulation strengthens neural connections and helps wire the information into long-term memory, which will allow for quicker retrieval and flexible transfer of the information to new contexts—or a high-stakes test—in the future.

Cramming for an upcoming test and learning fast do not always result in the deepest and best learning (Francisco, 2019). This is important information for students to understand. Students who have opportunities for multiple rehearsals and do-overs over a period of time often understand things at a deeper level and are more successful during testing. Spacing or distributing practice sessions over time and locations has been shown to produce lasting learning. *Distributed practice* refers to reviews and do-overs that take place after the original learning event. If we want students to learn something that they can recall during a test, studying the information or practicing the task just once isn't enough.

Formative Assessment Strategies

Using a single data point, such as a well-designed miniquiz, doesn't usually provide enough information to help teachers plan the next steps in their instruction. To check for student understanding along the way, teachers can use any number of formative assessment strategies. Since frequent, multiple check-ins are crucial, they need to be low prep, low stakes, and easy to apply and provide nearly instant feedback. The check-ins during learning ensure students are prepared to demonstrate their learning before a high-stakes exam.

Consider prompts or questions to check for understanding.

- "What are three things you learned today, two things you're still wondering about, and one thing you still don't understand?"
- "Was there anything that was a challenge for you today?"
- "What part of the lesson do you still need some time with?"
- "Regarding today's lesson, what would be three questions the teacher should put on a quiz (include your own answers)?"
- "What parts of today's lesson came easily to you?"
- "What part of today's lesson did you find most interesting and why?"

Teachers can consider checking in with students as they enter or exit the classroom.

- **Entry tickets:** As students arrive, post a quick question about the previous day's work, and ask students to respond in their learning logs or journals, on a slip of paper, or on an online form such as a Google Doc.
- **Exit slips:** Allow a few minutes at the end of a class for students to respond to a question or prompt about the lesson to check for understanding. This can be used as a ticket out.
- ***Twexit* cards:** Twexit cards are exit slips completed as a Twitter post. Challenge students to write a summary statement about the lesson using fewer than 280 characters, reflective of the allotment for Twitter posts. These can be done using an index card or on an online board such as Padlet (https://padlet.com).

Illustrations and graphic organizers also provide meaningful ways to check-in.

- **Illustrations:** Students demonstrate understanding by creating a visual representation of a lesson, whether it involves a scientific process or a historical event.

- **Mind maps:** Students can create mind maps that represent key concepts using a digital diagram-making tool like Inspiration (www.inspiration-at.com) or MindMeister (www.mindmeister.com).

Students can demonstrate their understanding through video and photo responses.

- **Screencastify:** Screencastify (www.screencastify.com) is a free, easy-to-use Chrome extension. Students can record a thirty-second to one-minute response to a prompt and post it to the class's online folder.
- **Screenshots and quick pics:** Students can share their work, notes, or drawings by taking a screenshot or photo on their device.

Digital quizzes or polls are also quick ways to check for understanding.

- **Clicker response system:** Students can use classroom clickers or smartphones to respond to a lesson through a polling app, such as Poll Everywhere (www.polleverywhere.com).
- **Digital Socratic seminar:** Students respond to questions online via a program such as Socrative (www.socrative.com).
- **Google Forms and Flubaroo:** The teacher uses Google Forms (www.google.com/forms) to create a nongraded miniquiz and uses an add-on from Flubaroo (www.flubaroo.com) to provide feedback on student responses.
- **Padlet:** Through Padlet (https://padlet.com), students post their responses to the prompt digitally on an online class wall of comments.

There are also alternative formative assessments teachers can use to determine where students are at in their learning, called *dipsticks* or *pulse checks*.

- **Key vocabulary definitions:** Students provide definitions in their own words for key vocabulary from a lesson.
- **Examples and nonexamples:** Students list, draw, or show three items that exemplify a set of criteria and three items that are similar but not examples.
- **Miniconference:** The teacher conducts a three- to four-question miniconference to find out how a student is doing.
- **Teacher-observation checklist:** The teacher observes students in action and records progress.

Students can also self-assess their own learning.

- **Emoji check-in:** Using emojis, students can reveal how the day's lesson went for them. They'll circle the image that applies. (See figure 6.4.)

GOT IT! Feel Great!	ALMOST THERE Working on it!	TIRED But I did it!	FRUSTRATED Confused
		zZZ	

Figure 6.4: Emoji check-in.

Visit ***go.SolutionTree.com/assessment*** *for a free reproducible version of this figure.*

- **Rubric:** Students use a multicriteria rubric to self-assess their achievement. (See the sample rubric for group participation in figure 6.5).

Criteria	Exceptional	Proficient	Basic	Unacceptable
Workload	Did a full share of the work and often more	Did an equal share of the work as needed	Did almost as much work as others	Did less work than others
Organization	Took the lead in getting the group organized	Always attended to meeting times and came prepared	Often had to be reminded about meeting times; often unprepared	Did not meet at agreed times; unprepared
Participation	Shared ideas and feelings; encouraged others	Participated in discussions and activities as needed	Showed up but mostly listened; some participation	Rarely participated

Figure 6.5: Group participation rubric.

Visit ***go.SolutionTree.com/assessment*** *for a free reproducible version of this figure.*

- **Student-made quiz:** Students write higher-order questions about a text or task and choose two questions to answer.
- **One-minute write:** In one minute, students describe (on paper or post on a Google Doc) the most important thing they learned during the lesson and describe an area of confusion.

Conclusion

Throughout their school years, students should have multiple opportunities to check for understanding during learning. Formative assessments can provide critical data to the teacher about the effectiveness of instruction, as well as show targeted information regarding students' success toward the learning targets. Experiencing failures, setbacks, and challenges can help students further develop resilience and perseverance. Giving students immediate, meaningful, and constructive feedback along with time to reflect can provide them with the guidance they need to retry a task and make the necessary adjustments. This cycle of assessment with feedback and do-overs creates a pattern of success and helps students develop a growth mindset that carries into taking high-stakes exams.

ACADEMIC VOCABULARY INSTRUCTION

The research is clear, and we know vocabulary is a huge predictor of success . . . in life, in school, and even on those dreaded standardized tests.

—DAVIES

The task of preparing students for standardized tests can be daunting, in part because the breadth of content in individual disciplines allows for a vast range of questions. Even students who routinely perform well academically may feel a high level of anxiety as they approach the testing event. Our goal as teachers is to help students de-stress their test experience and approach these tests with a degree of confidence. We must equip students with vocabulary knowledge that will help them navigate a variety of test questions and reading passages with confidence. The research is clear, students' success in school and on tests is directly tied to their vocabulary knowledge (Davies, n.d.; Levine et al., 2020; Marzano, 2020).

When children arrive in kindergarten, they may already have a significant gap in their background knowledge and their *receptive* and *expressive* vocabularies. *Receptive vocabulary*, which begins development earliest, includes words that a person can understand, including spoken and written words. *Expressive vocabulary* refers to words that a person can express or produce by speaking or writing. Language development in the first three years of children's lives most depends on what parents and caregivers say and do with the children on a daily basis (Levine et al., 2020). The frequency and the quality of talk going on in a family's household has a direct impact on a child's future success in school. Here are some benchmarks of typical vocabulary development in the early years (Loraine, 2008).

- **Two years old:** A child will have a 200- to 300-word vocabulary.
- **Four years old:** A child will have a 1,500- to 1,600-word vocabulary.
- **Five years old:** A kindergartener will have a 2,100- to 2,200-word vocabulary.
- **Six years old:** A child has about a 2,600-word expressive vocabulary and a receptive vocabulary of 20,000 to 24,000 words.
- **Twelve years old:** A child will have developed a receptive vocabulary of over 50,000 words.

According to researcher Dani Levine and her team (2020), a family's socioeconomic status (SES) directly influences the child's vocabulary size and language development skills. Children entering kindergarten from low-SES families are already one to two years behind the skills of mid-SES peers (Levine et al., 2020). This huge word gap as children begin school highlights the powerful role that socioeconomic status has in a student's vocabulary development.

According to the *Princeton Review* (n.d.), U.S. students need a strong vocabulary (and a vocabulary strategy) to do well on the SAT. Prior to March 2016, the SAT had questions that explicitly tested difficult vocabulary words. The SAT and other high-stakes tests ask students to identify the meaning of an unknown word based on its use within a text passage. When students have learned how to study words and know how to use context clues to determine word meaning, they will be more confident when they encounter unfamiliar words in a passage. This confidence is a key component to success on high-stakes testing and, more important, in life.

Vocabulary development is a critical area of reading instruction. In *The New Art and Science of Teaching Reading*, Simms and Marzano (2019) present a research-based model of instruction for reading development. The authors' reading model is structured around five key areas: (1) foundational skills, (2) word recognition, (3) fluency, (4) vocabulary, and (5) comprehension. Students who arrive at school with large oral vocabularies will be able to more easily decode words and better understand words in passages that they read. Students who read well tend to read more often and this process continues to help build their range of vocabulary. Students with large vocabularies become more successful independent readers and, therefore, will be better able to read directions and comprehend questions on tests. Students who have a limited vocabulary tend to read less and miss opportunities to build a bank of vocabulary.

Explicitly teaching vocabulary is a high-impact instructional strategy. According to Douglas Fisher, Nancy Frey, and John Hattie (2017), in their book *Teaching Literacy in the Visible Learning Classroom, Grades K–5*, vocabulary programs have an effect size of 0.67, placing them seventeenth on a list of 150 different educational influences.

However, given the importance of vocabulary knowledge on academic success, explicit vocabulary instruction has been found to be lacking in most schools (Simms & Marzano, 2019).

Building a strong vocabulary is crucial for student success during instruction and during tests. It is a fundamental component of literacy. If a test involves reading directions or text passages, vocabulary knowledge could be a game changer. Rigorous vocabulary instruction can have a particularly significant impact on students who do not come from academically advantaged backgrounds or for students whose vocabularies are limited or not yet developed, such as English learners.

Let's take a closer look at the three tiers of vocabulary before exploring strategies for explicitly teaching academic vocabulary.

Three Tiers of Vocabulary

According to Isabel L. Beck, Margaret G. McKeown, and Linda Kucan (2013), there are three broad categories, or *tiers*, of vocabulary that can increase students' ability to comprehend new information and to perform well on tests (see figure 7.1).

1. **Tier one words:** Everyday words used in conversation
2. **Tier two words:** General academic words found across the curriculum
3. **Tier three words:** Domain-specific academic words particular to a content area

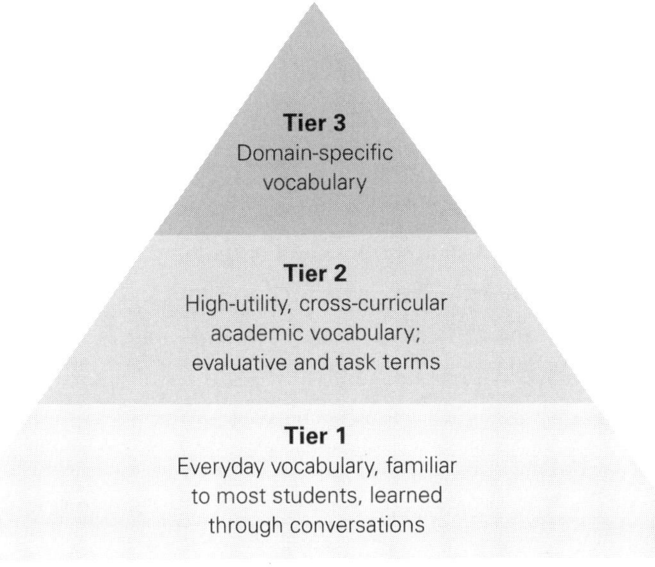

Figure 7.1: Vocabulary tiers.

Tier one includes basic words of everyday life that most students learn through conversations with family, friends, and caregivers (for example, *clock*, *baby*, *house*, and *family*). Most students know these basic, concrete terms that rarely have multiple meanings and often don't require explicit instruction. Tier one words are generally simple and do not express complex concepts or abstract ideas.

Unless students are English learners, these words require less formal attention in school. Tier one vocabulary includes basic *sight words* that students should recognize instantly and use to help them build reading fluency. There are two common lists of sight words. The Dolch Sight Word List includes the 315 most common words encountered in children's books—95 nouns and 220 words that aren't nouns (Sight Words, n.d.a). The Fry Sight Word List contains the 1,000 most-used words in writing and reading (Sight Words, n.d.b). Knowing these sight words is critical in early reading development because they represent high-frequency words, including those that are difficult to sound out or illustrate. Visit www.k12reader.com/dolch/dolch_frequency_by_grade.pdf and https://sightwords.com/sight-words/fry/#lists to access these lists.

Tier two includes more abstract and general academic words that students encounter across content areas in the school curriculum, in written language, and in textbooks (for example, *vary*, *predict*, *explain*, *summarize*, and *layer*). These words convey relatively simple ideas in more precise ways. They are key to success on tests because they often appear in test directions and questions as evaluative or task words. This instructional language is used in many contexts and across multiple domains. Novels, essays, short stories, and poetry are likely to contain these vocabulary, and students in the upper grades should use the words in their writing. Students learn academic vocabulary with deliberate effort—unlike tier one words, which they learn from conversation. This tier of words is often neglected in terms of explicit instruction. Targeting instruction of these words will better prepare students for the language of tests.

Tier three includes subject- or domain-specific vocabulary, made up of highly specialized words. Subject areas such as mathematics, science, social studies, and art each have a specific vocabulary that describes the events, methods, categories, labels, and so forth unique to that domain. Students need to acquire these specific vocabularies in order to understand the content of these various disciplines. Tier three vocabulary words can often be challenging because they occur infrequently in most texts and conversations, students may lack the necessary conceptual background, and the words may have Latin or Greek roots (for example, *hypotenuse* and *cubism*). See *Teaching Basic, Advanced, and Academic Vocabulary* (Marzano, 2020) for more than 8,000 tier one, tier two, and tier three words in 444 semantic clusters.

Preparing students for standardized testing is a challenging task with many aspects to consider, but explicitly teaching tier two academic vocabulary—the language of testing—is a powerful strategy that can help students better understand the test directions and questions. When students encounter unfamiliar words during a test, not only will it cause them to struggle with the correct response but it may trigger a reflex response. Struggling with even a single unknown word might throw off students and ultimately affect their responses on the remainder of the test. Familiarizing students with critical vocabulary across all grade levels can be a game changer and potentially de-stress reactions during a test.

Everyday language, or tier one vocabulary, often suffices up to third grade, but once academic vocabulary (including many process verbs, such as *summarize*, *classify*, and *investigate*) is included in text passages and instructions, many students fall behind across the curriculum. Lack of tier two vocabulary may be a roadblock to their successfully understanding school texts, completing assignments, and performing well on tests in many disciplines. The gap will be even wider for students who already have a language disadvantage (Beck et al., 2013). Consider the following direct links between academic-vocabulary knowledge and student success (Davies, n.d.; Levine et al., 2020; Marzano, 2020).

- Learning academic vocabulary improves overall reading comprehension and fluency, important skills when reading test passages with complex text.
- The more students study academic vocabulary and how to pick up on context clues, the more comfortable they will feel identifying the meanings of unfamiliar words in a test passage.
- After reading a test passage, students may be asked to write an essay. When they use more complex vocabulary, they will score higher.
- After reading a test passage, students may be asked to support their responses with evidence from the text. Knowing how to use context clues to determine a word's meaning can help them select the correct words and phrases to support their answers.

So, what tier two words should teachers target? The following list of fifteen evaluative or task-based verbs and their definitions, adapted from Marilee Sprenger (2013), Robert J. Marzano and Julia A. Simms (2013), Vocabulary.com (2020), and Sadlier School (n.d.), is based on an analysis of the words likely to appear in question stems, answer options, and test directions in grades 3–12.

1. ***Analyze***: Break down into parts; critically examine each of the facts.
2. ***Compare***: Identify how the facts or ideas are alike or similar.
3. ***Contrast***: Identify how the facts or ideas are different.
4. ***Define***: Set forth the meaning or make something clear.
5. ***Discuss***: Present a detailed argument or consideration.
6. ***Evaluate***: Determine the value, significance, or worth of something.
7. ***Identify***: Establish and point out the essential characteristics of something.
8. ***Illustrate***: Make clear by citing examples, or use images to explain something.
9. ***Infer***: Draw a conclusion based on given facts, generalize, or read between the lines.
10. ***Interpret***: Present the subject at hand in understandable terms.
11. ***Justify***: Show or prove to be right or reasonable.
12. ***Sequence***: Arrange in a meaningful order, from beginning to end.
13. ***Summarize***: Explain or make a short statement about the main points, considering the *who*, *what*, *when*, *where*, *why*, and *how*.
14. ***Synthesize***: Combine various parts to create a more complex product.
15. ***Trace***: Follow the development of something, or find through investigation.

See page 177 for a reproducible list of additional critical verbs and nouns that students should know prior to taking high-stakes tests.

Sprenger (2013) identifies the grade levels at which the Common Core State Standards, Partnership for Assessment of Readiness for College and Careers, and Smarter Balanced assessments introduce many of these and other critical verbs.

- Kindergarten—Compare, contrast, describe, distinguish, identify, retell
- First—Demonstrate, determine, draw, explain, locate, suggest, support
- Second—Comprehend, develop
- Third—Organize, refer
- Fourth—Infer, integrate, interpret, paraphrase, summarize
- Fifth—Analyze
- Sixth—Articulate, cite, delineate, evaluate, trace
- Eleventh—Synthesize (p. 31)

Many of these key vocabulary words are interrelated. Research indicates that teaching related words together can benefit students learning the new vocabulary (Reading Rockets, n.d.). For example, *comparing* and *contrasting* go hand in hand, but teachers do not always connect them or teach them together. The brain is better able to store information if it can connect the new information to prior knowledge. It also stores words more effectively if the words are related and are taught in categories. When the brain learns one term, it is the perfect time to link the term to other related vocabulary.

Common vocabulary groupings are as follows.

- **Prefixes and suffixes:** *Pre-, un-, dis-, semi-, -ness, -able, -ly, -ing*
- **Root words (Latin and Greek):** *Geo, struct, graph, morph, bio*
- **Literary techniques:** *Foreshadowing, tone, proverb, imagery*
- **Figurative language:** *Metaphor, simile, personification, symbolism*
- **Analysis terms:** *Compare, contrast, organize, delineate*

To prepare students for high-stakes tests, teachers can explicitly teach key tier two words. Familiarity with the testing language will keep students from experiencing a reflex response when they encounter the vocabulary during exams, and it will positively impact their performance.

The Need for Tier Two Vocabulary Instruction

During the first year that the Smarter Balanced tests were administered to assess the Common Core State Standards in California, I was teaching part time at a charter school and in charge of administering the tests to fourth graders. At the assigned times, the students would come to my room and set up their Chromebooks to complete the tests. During one of the English language arts tests, I noticed a student sitting with his elbow on the table and his head cradled in his hand. I asked him, "Are you OK? Is there anything you would like some help with?" He looked up at me quite forlornly and said, "I can't remember what a detail is!" Because I could offer only limited assistance during the test, I encouraged him to reread the passage and the instructions. I reflected on this afterward—I didn't know whether I'd ever considered that my students wouldn't understand the word *detail* and could have benefitted from receiving explicit instruction!

Strategies for Explicitly Teaching Academic Vocabulary

As Marzano (2020) puts it, "There is little if any argument anymore regarding the importance of directly teaching vocabulary. Unfortunately, there is still a major problem associated with vocabulary instruction—it is virtually impossible to directly teach all the new terms students will encounter" (p. 4). Therefore, finding the most powerful strategies to build student vocabulary should be an explicit goal for all teachers, regardless of grade or discipline. Ensuring students deeply learn academic vocabulary terms and can quickly recall the definitions when they encounter the terms in text will take multiple rehearsals with differentiated strategies. This vocabulary instruction should go beyond the traditional, tedious student work of recording a word's definition and then using the word in a sentence. Actively processing the new words in a variety of ways over time will promote long-term retention.

Start with proven beginning strategies such as Robert J. Marzano's (2020) six-step process for teaching academic vocabulary, and then add in several more creative strategies. Marzano's (2020) six-step process for teaching academic vocabulary is as follows.

1. Provide a description, explanation, or example of the new term. Share a personal story or how the term might be used. Include a nonlinguistic representation of the term, which is especially helpful for English learners.

   Examples—Tell or read a story that includes the new term. Show a video or a picture that might help students understand the term. Create a firsthand experience, such as an experiment or field trip, to introduce the new term.

2. Ask students to restate the description, explanation, or example in their own words. This important step helps students link the new word to prior knowledge. Allow English learners whose primary existing knowledge base is still in their native language to respond in their native language.

   Examples—Students can record their explanation in their vocabulary learning logs. Have students describe the term to a partner. Students can record a thirty-second video clip of their own description and post it on Flipgrid (https://flipgrid.com).

3. Ask students to construct a picture, symbol, or graphic representing the term. This helps learners represent the word visually—a good indicator that they understand it.

Examples—Students do a quick illustration in their vocabulary learning logs. Model some simple drawings or graphics that students can copy. Have students select emojis or gifs to represent the new term.

4. Have students keep a vocabulary notebook. Routinely engage students in activities that help them add to their knowledge of the terms.

   Examples—Use a highlighter to note root words, prefixes, and suffixes. Have students list synonyms or antonyms for the new term. Create a list of related words.

5. Periodically ask students to use the new vocabulary in conversations with one another. Look for ways to integrate the new terms into daily instruction. When appropriate, allow these conversations to be in students' native languages.

   Examples—Use a think-pair-share, and have students share their descriptions and pictures with a partner. Encourage students to offer help and suggestions to clarify understanding.

6. Periodically involve students in games that allow them to play with new terms.

   Examples—Set aside some time to incorporate a vocabulary game. *Pictionary* is a great format to help students review terms and recreate images that represent them. Have students create the clues and set up a *Jeopardy!*-style game using PowerPoint slides.

Once you've gone through this six-step process, consider using the following specific strategies for helping students process new words.

- **Word window (also known as *word four square* or the *Frayer model* [Buehl, 2017]):** In the first quadrant, students write the definition of a new term in their own words. In the second quadrant, they draw a nonlinguistic representation of the vocabulary word. In the third quadrant, they list nonexamples or antonyms. In the fourth quadrant, they use the word in a sentence (see figure 7.2, page 145).
- **Crossword-puzzle generator:** Instruct students to use graph paper or a free web application or website (such as https://crosswordhobbyist.com) to create a crossword puzzle featuring at least six vocabulary words.

- **Flipbook or foldable:** Ask students to put together an illustrated minidictionary of at least six vocabulary words. Try https://the-room-mom.com/foldable-booklets for simple step-by-step foldable instructions.
- **TV game-show format:** For *Password*, have students pair up, with one student giving one-word clues to try to get his or her partner to guess a vocabulary word. For *Jeopardy!*, given a vocabulary word, students must provide the definition in the form of a question.
- **Mind map or concept map:** Have students create a web for the new term. Include categories such as part of speech, derivatives, synonyms, antonyms, and more for a given vocabulary word (see figure 7.3).
- **Charades:** Invite students to act out the meaning of a vocabulary word or to write a skit to help everyone remember the word's meaning and usage.
- **Websites or apps:** There are tons of clever apps and websites to help students study and review vocabulary words. Vocabulary.com is a great place to start, and the Vocabulary Builder app from Magoosh (https://magoosh.com/vocabulary-builder) guides teachers through dozens of vocabulary lists for students to learn exam-level words. You might also try the Exam Vocabulary Builder app. A favorite game of students' is a variation of Ellen DeGeneres's *Heads Up!* app. Teachers can use this free application in the classroom with any vocabulary list you have by purchasing the inexpensive *custom-deck extension*. (Or go old school and create a deck of the vocabulary words using index cards.) See page 177 for a reproducible of critical verbs and nouns to use.

Conclusion

Understanding academic vocabulary is a key for a student's success on a high-stakes test. More important, building students' vocabulary background knowledge builds their overall confidence. The more students understand tier two words that they'll encounter on high-stakes tests, the easier it will be for them to understand the directions and comprehend text passages they must read. Students from academically disadvantaged environments or English learners may arrive to school with gaps in their vocabulary background knowledge. If not addressed, this may have long-term consequences for literacy development and success in school. Explicitly teaching academic vocabulary "is probably the strongest action a teacher can take to ensure that students have the academic background knowledge they need to understand the content they will encounter in school" (Marzano & Pickering, 2005, p. 1).

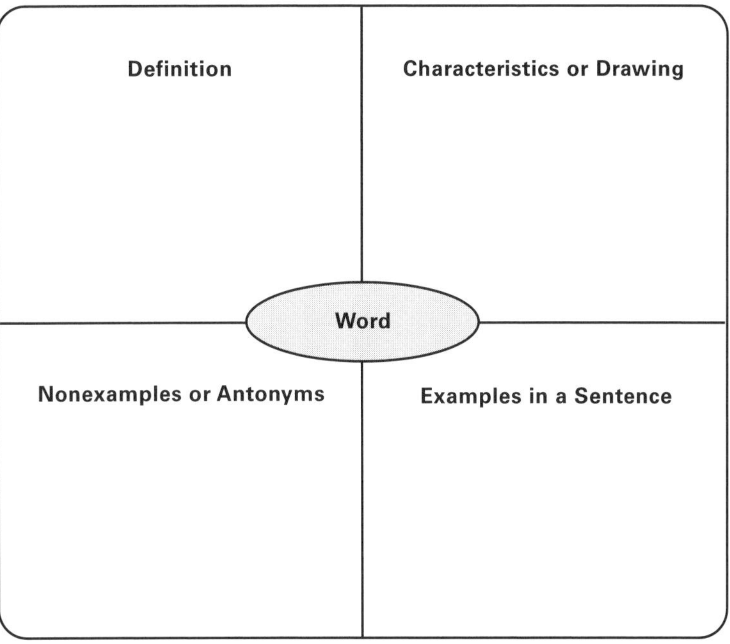

Figure 7.2: Word window.

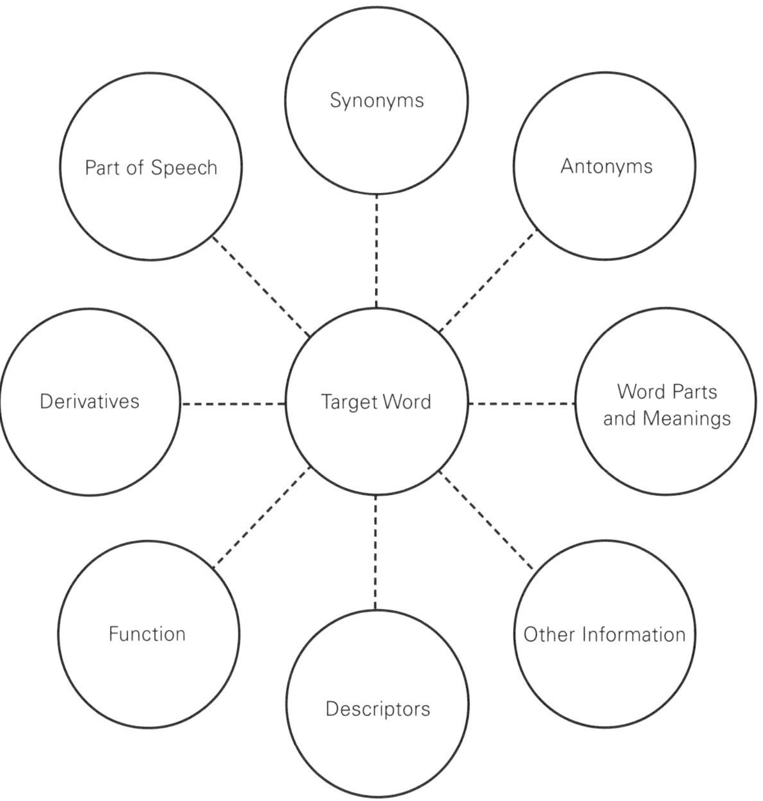

Figure 7.3: Mind map or concept map.

TEST PREP FOR STUDENTS AND TEACHERS

Don't be afraid. Be focused.
Be determined. Be hopeful.
Be empowered.

—MICHELLE OBAMA

It's quite possible that some readers have turned immediately to this chapter without having read the previous chapters' suggestions about preparing for high-stakes tests throughout the year. But truly de-stressing the test for our students requires a long-term effort in how we prepare our students' knowledge base, mindsets, confidence, and self-regulation skills. This chapter does include many helpful test-prep strategies that students can use during the actual exam event, but if you haven't put the previous chapters' knowledge, strategies, and preparations in place, these hints may be a moot point.

Unfortunately, many schools do attempt to get students' parents to make last-minute arrangements the week before testing. Inevitably, the administration sends parents a letter that outlines important things they must do to ensure the students will perform well on the upcoming exams. These parent actions include the following.

- Make sure students have a good breakfast on the day of the test.
- Make sure students get a good night's sleep before the test.
- Make sure students have their own water bottle for during the test.
- Make sure students come to school on time—no tardies.
- Make sure students don't miss school and they avoid being absent.

These letters to parents always confuse me. Shouldn't schools encourage parents to do all these things *every day*, not just on the day of the test? If parents attend to these things throughout the school year, then students will be much more prepared. The strategies in this book should be developed *during* the learning process.

This chapter includes some general test-prep techniques that can help students feel prepared to take high-stakes tests, rather than anxious about the unknown. Developing some good study habits and meeting basic needs on the days leading up to the test are important first steps. Prepare for the *stress mess* that often accompanies high-stakes tests, and practice ways to de-escalate the anxiety before, during, and after the exam, making sure that you, as the teacher, are just as prepared. Then, after the test, helping students recover from test stress will be crucial. Please consider the variety of test-taking tips included in this chapter.

Developing Good Study Habits

When teachers design brain-friendly learning environments and incorporate these strategies throughout the year, students will be much more prepared when tasked with taking a high-stakes test. Students who have opportunities to develop self-efficacy, a growth mindset, and perseverance during the learning process approach exams with a positive mindset. De-stressing the test involves integrating all these strategies, which will serve the students beyond the day of the test.

Lots of instruction, preparation, and studying will have happened by the time the test day finally arrives. Students who have had good attendance, completed assignments, asked questions when they didn't understand, responded to feedback, taken part in discussions, and worked to develop a growth mindset will have a great advantage when taking the test. In the days leading up to the test, teachers can help students dedicate some time to develop some good study habits. Encourage students to adopt the following good study habits (U.S. Department of Education, 2003; Whitbourne, 2011).

- **Determine a dedicated study space:** Students should create a comfortable area in their home in which to read, study, and do homework. It should be well lit and have some necessary supplies (such as pens and paper) easily accessible. Tell students to try to eliminate distractions—including turning off their phones for periods of time—and ask family members to respect and not interrupt their studying time.
- **Pace themselves:** Students should review test material several days ahead of time and in various ways (for example, by writing flash cards one day and taking practice tests the next). In other words, they should not cram.

When studying, students should take frequent breaks. Recommend that students study in chunks, using fifteen-or twenty-minute time frames to try to tackle a section of problems or a reading passage. After twenty minutes of intensive study time, many young brains will begin to lose focus and get bored or distracted (Ward, 2020). Suggest students set a timer, work for the chunk of time, and then get up and move or grab a snack once the time is up.

- **Study with friends:** Students studying with a group of people who are learning the same things as they are can be a great way for them to prepare for a big test. They can quiz one another, reteach material, and make sure that everyone is on the same page. Teaching someone else is the best way to learn. After teaching others, students will know the subject more thoroughly and ultimately do better in class and on tests (Najam, 2017). Online study buddies can be a great help, so students might use Zoom, Google Meet, or FaceTime to study virtually with friends.
- **Study, sleep, and repeat:** After students study, they should sleep on it—sleep strengthens one's memory and embeds the new learning in the brain (Ro, 2018). According to sleep researcher Jakke Tamminen, "Even though you're not studying when you sleep, your brain is still studying. It's almost like it's working on your behalf. You can't really get the full impact of the time you put into your studies unless you sleep" (as cited in Ro, 2018). Caution students against pulling an all-nighter before a test. Neurology professor Clifford B. Saper (as cited in Barzilay, 2012) explains, "Trying to stay up late and cram for a test is probably the very worst thing you could do."
- **Use mnemonics:** A *mnemonic* is a memory aid that helps people remember an idea or phrase with a pattern of letters, numbers, or relatable associations. Mnemonic devices include special rhymes, acronyms, images, songs, and other tools that tie the concepts people want to memorize to prior knowledge for efficient storage and retrieval. Mnemonics help connect new information and associate it with something meaningful. The devices will allow students to quickly and successfully learn and remember spellings, the order of items, and key concepts. For example, *PEMDAS* (or *please excuse my dear aunt Sally*) is a common mnemonic for remembering the order of operations in prealgebra: parentheses, exponents, multiplication, division, addition, and subtraction.

Meeting Basic Needs

Teachers and parents can encourage students to maintain healthy habits all year long. When the test day is finally in sight, remind students that meeting their bodies' basic needs before the test will help them perform well even if they experience some anxiety. With the following needs satisfied, students' brains and bodies will be ready to optimally support them. (See chapter 3, page 53, for more on the hierarchy of basic needs [Maslow, 1968].)

- **Sleep:** Students should get enough sleep for several nights before the test day. Explain that they should go to bed at the same reasonable time and wake up at the same time for at least three to five days before the test. To be the most alert on the test day, they should try to get seven to eight hours of sleep each of these nights, including the night before. Rather than staying up late to cram the night before the test, students should, if need be, wake up a little early and do some more studying in the early morning (Paruthi et al., 2016). Consider the following sleep recommendations from the American Academy of Sleep Medicine (Paruthi et al., 2016).
    - Children three to five years of age should sleep ten to thirteen hours per twenty-four hours (including naps) on a regular basis.
    - Children six to twelve years of age should sleep nine to twelve hours per twenty-four hours on a regular basis.
    - Teenagers thirteen to eighteen years of age should sleep eight to ten hours per twenty-four hours on a regular basis.
- **Food:** Increasing the amount of healthy foods they eat on the days leading up to the exam may help students with their test performance. Eating a healthy dinner the night before, or a healthy breakfast the morning of, a test will help tremendously (University of the People, n.d.). According to Score at the Top Learning Centers and Schools (2013), the best brain foods are as follows.
    - *Fish for omega-3s*—Omega-3s will help students maintain concentration, brain capacity, and general alertness. The best source for omega-3s is oily cold-water fish like wild Alaskan salmon, sardines, and herring. Vegetarians can get omega-3s from other sources such as eggs, spinach, walnuts, flax seeds, or soybeans.

- *Antioxidant-rich foods*—Eating foods with naturally occurring antioxidants can provide a natural defense against many diseases and improve brain health. The most beneficial antioxidants are obtained through eating whole foods, rather than just taking supplements. Foods especially high in antioxidants include blueberries, red and black beans, prunes, apples, and pecans.
- *Complex carbohydrates*—Our brains need twice the amount of energy as the rest of the cells in our bodies, and the brain uses sugar for fuel. The best sources of this fuel are complex, minimally processed carbohydrates. Sugar found in sodas or candy doesn't provide steady energy. Some great sources of complex carbohydrates include whole grains (oatmeal is a great pretest breakfast), fresh fruits and vegetables, and beans.
- *Quality protein*—Protein is important for sustained energy, and protein-rich foods increase mental clarity and concentration and can lessen anxiety—quite useful on the test day. Healthy protein sources should be low in fat. Some great breakfast proteins include lean meats like Canadian bacon or turkey bacon, eggs, milk, soy-based foods (soy milk or soy meat substitutes), and whole-grain cereals.

- **Hydration:** Adequate hydration is necessary to support optimal brain function. Drinking water in the morning and then throughout the day can enhance mental focus. Signs of dehydration include fatigue, hunger, and headaches—symptoms students don't want to have during a test.
- **Movement:** Stretching, doing yoga, and going for a quick jog could all help energize students' brains before test taking. Just a ten-minute session of aerobic exercise can give the brain a jolt, boosting students' decision-making processes and improving their focus, according to researchers Ashna Samani and Matthew Heath (2018). Just a few minutes of moderate-intensity exercise can improve the brain's task-switching efficiency and executive function.
- **Comfort:** Taking a test is not a comfortable activity, but students can make sure they aren't in *discomfort*. Students should choose comfortable clothes that won't distract them in any way. They should also take care of personal needs (for example, having a bathroom break) just before the test begins.

Preparing for the Stress Mess

Students commonly feel anticipatory anxiety when getting ready to take a big test. Looping negative thoughts and negative self-talk can often start to throw students off and distract them. Knowing a variety of mindfulness and stress-reduction strategies can help students relax and focus on the task at hand. Even with lots of preparation for high-stakes tests, test anxiety can cause students to react in ways that ultimately sabotage their ability to show what they know. Remind students that mindfulness is not about denying stress but about controlling how they react to stress.

In the days leading up to the testing event, teachers can start reminding students of the things they can do to make sure their brains and bodies are as ready and calm as they can be on the day of the test. Billy Calder (2018), a test-prep expert, reminds us that while it's important to focus on academic preparation, it is just as important to plan a routine for the night before and the hours leading up to a big test. There are a few simple strategies students can do to reduce stress and create a calm and confident mindset on the big day.

- **Prepare the night before:** Suggest that students gather any materials they will need for the test the next day. In some instances, a student may need to have pencils, calculators, photo identification, and an entry ticket (for tests such as the SAT). It may also be helpful to select clothes, fill a water bottle, pack a mask or hand sanitizer, and make a lunch or snack. Being organized the night before may help relieve some unnecessary stress in the morning.
- **Plan a calming early-morning routine:** Explain that students should do things that can calm their nerves and also get their heads in the zone: go for a ten-minute walk, take a long shower or bath, get up early so they aren't rushed, or listen to some music.
- **Practice mindful breathing:** Recommend students try a three- to five-minute mindfulness meditation before they leave home the morning of the test. (See chapter 5, page 95, for more mindfulness practices.) They should focus on breathing and being in the present moment, and they might try a sitting meditation before the test to increase mindfulness and awareness. This can be done before they leave for school as well as just before the test. For the sitting meditation, students should:
    - Sit in a chair with their feet firmly on the ground or sit on the floor with their legs crossed in a quiet, relaxing environment

    - Close their eyes and draw their attention to everything their bodies do
    - Begin taking deep belly breaths
    - Gradually let everything fade away except how their bodies feel
    - Focus only on the present moment

- **Make use of positive self-talk:** Encourage students to try to ignore any voices in their minds that tell them they are not smart enough or they won't do very well. They should give themselves pep talks—"I'll just do my best," "I'm going to show what I know," "I've got what it takes to be successful today," and so forth. See page 178 for a reproducible activity to practice positive self-talk.
- **Visualize success:** The power of positive thinking can really help on test day. The brain can do amazing things. Jack Canfield (n.d.), former teacher, transformational speaker, and cofounder of the *Chicken Soup for the Soul* empire, says that using visualization can give you superpowers! Research indicates that visualization can affect one's performance. Some studies have shown that mentally picturing something can be almost as effective as actually doing it (Shobe, 2005). Tell students to take a little time to visualize themselves taking the test with ease. They should also visualize what it will feel like when they are finished. If the brain thinks something is possible, it is (Ranganathan, Siemionow, Liu, Sahgal, & Yue, 2004).

Taking Midtest Brain and Body Breaks

During a test, sometimes an especially tricky question will pop up. When students encounter a surprise or difficult challenge, their brains may start to go into a reflex response—which is not helpful while taking a test (Kaufeldt, 2019). By monitoring their bodies' stress levels, students can determine when they should insert a little brain and body break, several strategies for which follow. Ideally, teachers should introduce these strategies for students to practice weeks before the test, during quiet independent work times. Teachers need to establish clear procedures for when and how students can use them during a test. (Have students help determine these protocols ahead of time.) Students can do some strategies quietly at one's seat; no need to get up or disturb other test-takers. For some students, a brief chance to stand and stretch can provide an opportunity to refocus. Teachers or test monitors should remind students to simply stand behind their seat so as not to distract other students. Students will begin to notice how a brief brain and body break can help them during challenging test times (Education Corner, n.d.; Kaufeldt, 2019; Whitbourne, 2011).

- **Look away:** Many tests occur online. The eyes aren't designed to focus on a screen. Looking away from their computer from time to time during a test can help students. That is, looking away from the test and switching their focus to something twenty feet away several times an hour can help reduce eye strain. When the eyes focus on something farther away, they relax, and the muscles don't work as hard. Invite students to adopt the twenty-twenty-twenty routine, looking twenty feet away for twenty seconds every twenty minutes. If the test is a written (pencil-and-paper) test, looking away from the test packet and following the same strategy can still help relax one's eyes. Teachers can put up a poster of a pleasant scene or mandala near the clock and encourage students to use that as a focal point. This can help alleviate "wandering eyes" in an exam environment.
- **Relax your muscles:** Sitting at a desk or looking at a computer screen for an extended period of time can increase tension in one's back, neck, and shoulders. At intervals during the exam, students should take time to do a quick relaxation exercise. What follows are a few simple movements to relieve stress.
    - *Stop, drop, and roll*—Students pause for a mindful moment; drop their pencil (or let go of the computer mouse); and slowly roll their head around in a big circle, going in one direction and then the other to release tension.
    - *Head, shoulders, knees, and toes*—Students slowly and gently roll their head three times, bringing their chin to their chest, their right ear to their right shoulder, their chin up and their head back, and their left ear to their left shoulder. Then they reverse the direction and repeat the movement three more times. They should then shrug their shoulders up to their ears and then relax their shoulders, rolling them forward and backward several times before clasping their hands behind their back to stretch. Finally, students should activate their knees and calf muscles to stimulate blood flow from their legs up to their brains; they can do knee bends, toe-ups, or lunges or walk or jog in place. For some students, this type of stretching movement may be helpful

several times during a test. Make sure everyone knows the procedures that will work for all students.

- **Breathe:** Explain to students that if they suddenly feel anxious or upset, they should try doing a simple breathing exercise. Tell students to close their eyes, touch their middle fingers to their thumbs, and breathe deeply through their nose. They should aim to divide their focus among the feeling of their fingers touching, the feeling of their chest and belly rising, and the feeling of air going in and out of their nostrils. As thoughts enter their mind, they should acknowledge them and try to let them go.
- **Try the starfish hand meditation:** This simple meditation combines breathing with the use of touch to refocus and center the mind, thus allowing students to take control of their emotions and calm down. Consider the following directions. (See chapter 5, page 95, for more mindfulness practices.)

    a. Spread the fingers of one of your hands out like a starfish, and place your hand palm down on your table or desk.

    b. Using your other hand's index finger, slowly trace up and down around each finger of your starfish hand.

        - Inhale deeply when you trace up a finger.
        - Exhale slowly when you trace down a finger.

    c. Concentrate only on how it feels, and let other thoughts go.

    d. Continue until you feel relaxed and calm.

- **Hydrate:** Remind students to have a water bottle with them to keep hydrated and energized throughout the day. Sitting through the test with a dry throat and rumbling tummy will frustrate and distract them.
- **Stand and stretch:** Depending on the rules and protocols surrounding test taking, you might give students permission to take a moment to stand up behind their chair. They can twist or rotate their body and, if possible, do squats to energize their legs and get the blood flowing.

Utilizing General Test-Taking Tips and Tricks

There are a variety of preparations one can do *before* the testing event. There are some tried-and-true techniques that teachers should review with students beforehand. The following list includes some general test-taking tips and tricks to provide students as the test nears.

- **Read the instructions:** Directions are the first thing students must get right on a test. Tell students to carefully read all the initial instructions once (or even twice) and then scan through as many items as they can on the test to get an idea of how much time it will take. They should ask questions if they need any clarification. See page 179 for a clever reproducible emphasizing how important it is to read *all* of the directions *before* beginning a test.
- **Monitor your time:** Explain to students that it's important to budget time appropriately. Suggest that students consider how many questions they need to answer and how much time is available and then develop a plan. Calculate about how much time they can spend on each section. They should check the time at the beginning of the test and then frequently check the time throughout to stay on track. Caution them against spending a lot of time on any one question. If they notice that they are spending too much time on a question, suggest that they attempt an answer, but flag the question (or note the item number on a piece of paper) and come back to it later if there's time. For elementary students, teachers can be helpful by monitoring the time and letting students know how much time is still left by noting the time on the whiteboard or chalkboard.
- **Understand computer-adaptive, or tailored, testing:** A *computer-adaptive test* or a *tailored test* is a computer-based test that continually adapts to the student's ability level. Be sure to let students know that many online tests are now computer adaptive. Students should respond to every question because each answer they give then determines which questions, or set of questions, the test will ask next. If a student gives a correct answer, it prompts a possibly harder question next. If a student gives an incorrect answer, a slightly easier question will come up soon. Explaining this to students often helps reduce stress. When they realize that they will have a second chance to get a test item right, they are more likely to give it a go. Likewise, if progressively harder questions come up, they will know they are actually doing OK.
- **Review the test questions:** If all the test questions have equal value, explain to students that, if allowed, they should consider going through

that section of the test and completing the easiest questions first. If some questions carry more weight or points than others, they should consider attempting those first and then going back and completing the less important ones. If students get stuck on a question for too long, they should consider moving on and returning to it if they have time. (They may not have the option of skipping questions if the test is computer adaptive.)

- **Give it a go:** Explain to students that when giving a wrong answer doesn't have a penalty, it is better to take a guess than to leave a space blank. If they aren't 100 percent sure of an answer, students should reread all the possible choices, eliminate any that they know are obviously wrong, and continue to narrow down the choices before giving their best guess.
- **Check and double-check:** Some questions may have tricky wording. Students should take extra care to read and reread those questions and the answer choices before selecting a response. Especially tricky are questions that begin with "All of the following are true *except* for . . ." or "Which of the following *best* describes . . . ?" If students are using computers, they should be sure to take time to review all their answers before submitting their test. If students are using paper answer sheets or Scantron forms, they should double-check that they have completely filled in their answer bubbles on the correct lines.
- **Make sure *confidence* doesn't become *carelessness*:** Stress to students that even if they have studied and prepared for the test, they should not rush through it. They should instead read all questions and answers carefully. It might be tempting to quickly pick a response and move on, but there might be some tricky wording or a better answer choice. Carelessness is often a characteristic of successful and engaged students, not just struggling students. San Pedro et al. (2014) determine that 20 percent of student errors were deemed "careless." Overconfidence was often associated with making careless mistakes.

Before administering a high-stakes test, teachers should take a little time to review the following top-ten basic test-taking tips. See page 180 for a reproducible version of this list. Teachers could display it as a poster or provide it as a handout to students the day before the test.

1. Pay careful attention to written and verbal directions.
2. Scan through the full test first—if allowed—to determine your strategy.

3. Know the rules about skipping questions or guessing.
4. Monitor your time and pacing.
5. Closely read all questions and answers. Reread any items that are confusing or complex.
6. Double-check your answers.
7. On reading comprehension items, it may help to read the questions before reading the passage.
8. Don't forget to show your work if questions ask you to do so. (Mathematics questions may often ask you to show your work.)
9. If allowed, skip over difficult questions, and come back to them later.
10. If you're not sure about a question, narrow down the possible answers, and take an educated guess.

For even more test-taking tips, check out these websites.

- **Education Corner's (n.d.) "Test Taking Strategies":** www.educationcorner.com/test-taking-strategies.html
- **The Test Taking Tips website:** www.testtakingtips.com
- **Jennifer Findlay's Online Testing Strategies:** https://jenniferfindley.com/online-testing-strategies
- ***Psychology Today*'s "10 Failsafe Test-Taking Tips" (Whitbourne, 2011):** www.psychologytoday.com/us/blog/fulfillment-any-age/201110/10-failsafe-test-taking-tips

Doing Teacher Test-Day Preparations

Preparing students for high-stakes tests is a big job and takes time. Not only must teachers provide successful instruction, but they must also develop their students' abilities to self-regulate, calm themselves, and keep going despite challenges. As the test day approaches, teachers can attend to several things that will contribute to a successful event with few upsets. In many cases, test preparations can begin days and weeks before the actual testing event. Establishing patterns for what to expect will reduce test anxiety (Eitland et al., 2017; Manca et al., 2020).

- **Prepare students for what will be different:** The brain's attention goes to things that are new, different, unusual, interesting, or possibly threatening. During testing, changes often need to be made to the classroom environment. Any things that are different from on a normal day could end up distracting students. If the changes are quite different, students could even perceive them as possible threats, and the changes could end up triggering a reflex response in some students. Here are some things that might distract students on the test day. (See chapter 3, page 37, for more about body- and brain-friendly classrooms and testing environments.)

- *Different location*—Testing commonly involves room changes. Students may need to go to a different classroom to take the test. In some schools, students rotate into a computer room to take the test. Large groups of students may also spread out in a library or multipurpose room. Any changes in their regular physical environment could be a stress trigger for some students and result in a reflex response. Even a rearrangement of desks and seating assignments in their classroom can distract some students. Review these possibilities with students *prior* to the test day, and even visit the other locations together as practice.
- *Different people*—Just as some students may get upset, frustrated, or confused when they have a substitute teacher, students may feel stressed if they discover someone other than their teacher administering the test. Prepare students for this situation. If a different teacher will be administering the test, have that person visit your students before the test day if possible.
- *Different schedule*—Test days commonly involve alterations to the daily schedule. For some students, these changes can be upsetting. Review with students ahead of time any schedule changes and what those might look like. Students always need to know if their break or lunch times are going to be different.
- *Different procedures and protocols*—On test days, there are usually some more rigid rules in place. Students who are used to getting out of their seats, working with others, getting drinks of water when needed, and so on may feel a little oppressed. Review the testing procedures ahead of time, and practice doing a few lessons using the stricter rules. Introducing the changes on the test day may throw off some students.

- **Create mindful moments:** Before the test begins, guide students through a relaxing mindfulness activity. Use a strategy that they are already familiar with, such as belly breathing or mandala breathing introduced in chapter 5 (pages 103–105). During the test, it may be possible to prompt students to take a quick break to move, stretch, or calm themselves. If students have *not* had prior experiences with mindful practices, this could be more of a distraction than a benefit. Help students learn and practice mindful moments throughout the school year. This is a worthwhile skill to rehearse and use often.

In my classrooms, my students and I created a midtest mindfulness prompt that aligned with testing rules and protocols. I arranged to give students a cue for an attention break depending on the length of the test and the age of the students (every twenty minutes for elementary students, and every thirty or more minutes for secondary students). I would sound a quiet chime that cued the students to look away from their screen and roll their shoulders and head to relax their hackles. I said nothing. I rang the chime again at the end of the attention break time—usually less than thirty seconds—and students would resume the test. This was an *optional* prompt. We had already practiced this strategy many times in class—even during silent reading and working periods. The students knew that it was helpful and used it to reset their brains and bodies to continue with the test. This method has worked successfully for my students in a variety of grade levels.

- **Use growth-mindset language:** Throughout the year, you can help students develop a growth mindset by encouraging them to work hard and persevere even when experiencing setbacks, and on the test day, it is more important than ever to maintain growth-mindset language when communicating with students. (See chapter 4, page 71, for more on developing a growth mindset.) During the testing event, consider using the following types of phrases to encourage students.
    - "You are really sticking with this!"
    - "I know you are getting tired, but you can keep going a little while more."
    - "Even if you don't think you know all the answers, you are giving it your best."
    - "I am impressed with your perseverance."
    - "You look like you are pacing yourself and getting it done."
    - "Even when you come to something that is difficult, you are trying hard."

  - "This test will show only some things that you know—I know how smart you are."
  - "I am so proud of how you are trying your very best."

- **Check in on your own teacher stress:** Students look to their teachers to get a pulse check on stress levels, and test days can be stressful for teachers as well as students. Test-day schedule changes, technology setups, absences, and behavioral issues can all impact a teacher's own stress level. Take time to do a brief mindfulness check-in with yourself. Breathe deeply and focus on the present moment. Check that your voice's tone and volume are communicating a sense of calmness rather than tension and sharpness. Smile! Exude a sense of calm expectation that students can easily interpret.

Preparing Students for Testing Technology

With 21st century learning comes more and more student assessments that rely on digital competencies. Among classrooms, there is a huge disparity regarding the routine use of technology. Some classrooms have computers or laptops for every student, yet others have limited access to technology. It is critical that teachers address the digital literacies students must have in order to perform well on technology-based assessments. If students are not already used to it, teachers need to frequently integrate technology use. Providing multiple opportunities for students to develop and practice their technology skills on school computers prepares them for the online tests. There may be students who do not have any technology available to them at home and do not have opportunities for daily use. As educators quickly learned during the COVID-19 pandemic, when in-person classroom instruction came to a halt, technology access is crucial. Researchers for *Education Week* report that more than one-fifth of U.S. households lack reliable access to a computer or other digital device and one-quarter don't have dependable internet (Harwin & Furuya, 2021). Make sure all students have access to the necessary technology to ensure equity. This is one way to level the playing field.

If we expect students to do well on high-stakes tests, we must give them prior experiences with the testing formats. Many of the high-stakes tests provide practice tests that use the same online format. Reviewing sample test questions will allow students to see what they will encounter during testing. This helps students learn how the test works, what's expected of them, and what kind of questions will be included on the actual test.

Learners need opportunities to build a level of comfort with the actual keyboard, screen, and external mouse or touch pad that they'll use during the assessments. Have students practice:

- Highlighting text
- Drawing lines
- Creating graphs
- Operating an online calculator and dictionary
- Using a scroll bar
- Manipulating drop-down menus

Stacey Pusey, an adjunct instructor at Wilmington University, recommends, "Whatever is used for testing should flow naturally from what the students have already encountered in their lessons. An assessment should not be the first time students use a piece of technology" (as cited in Planbook, n.d.).

Edcite (https://edcite.com) is a free program to help familiarize students with online standardized tests. This helpful service allows educators to join over 200,000 teachers who are committed to engaging their students with state-aligned digital practice. There are literally thousands of online practice tests in their assignment library and question banks, or teachers can make up their own.

In a 2017 *Edutopia* article, Heather Wolpert-Gawron reminds us that some students may be given opportunities to use a feature on the test that reads the text aloud to them. Make sure students know how to look for this tool before the test. Prior to the testing event, develop lessons that ask students to access applications that may read aloud the text. The Read&Write extension for Google Chrome is an easy, free application for students to become familiar with documents being read to them (Wolpert-Gawron, 2017).

Recovering From Test Stress

In *The New Art and Science of Teaching*, Robert J. Marzano (2017) states that the most basic issues a teacher can consider are establishing and communicating learning goals, tracking student progress, and *celebrating* successes. The teacher and students can celebrate those successes by acknowledging all the hard work, effort, and knowledge gains the students have made (Marzano, 2017). Immediately following a stressful testing event, there are a few things educators can do to celebrate and help students' brains and bodies return to homeostasis.

- **Have minicelebrations:** Teachers often give students a reward or treat at the conclusion of high-stakes tests. While providing a reward for taking a test may not be pedagogically sound, the idea of having a minicelebration for completing a challenging task seems perfectly appropriate. Celebrations, including some food, games, movement, and opportunities to visit and chat, can help the brain and body acknowledge that the immediate stress is over and that students should have a feeling of relief.
- **Allow for rest and recuperation:** Often after a stressful event, people need some recovery time. The military has known this for centuries. After stressful battles or extremely long periods of deployment, soldiers and sailors get leave time to rest and recuperate away from imminent danger areas. This designated time allows the brain and body a little respite. Some free class time, quiet reading time, or extra break time could help students' brains and bodies recuperate from the stressful event.
- **Switch gears:** The old *Monty Python* comedy series used to have a segment that would always begin with "And now for something *completely* different!" (And Now for Something Completely Different, n.d.). The brain loves novelty. An unexpected activity can redirect and engage the brain if it is something totally different. A surprise activity such as a favorite game, a guest speaker, or a movie can help the brain and body switch gears and get some relief from the stress.
- **Talk about it:** After a day or two of recovery, a class discussion about the testing event may be appropriate. Sometimes a debriefing or sense-making discussion allows students to reflect on the test experience and share their feelings with classmates. The conversation may help them understand some of their own feelings they experienced and realize they are not alone (Favero & Hendricks, 2016). A brief self-reflection survey could help students organize their thoughts and feelings about the test. See figure 8.1 (page 164).

What changes do you think you could make that might help you prepare for the next test? Please check all that apply.

- ☐ Manage my time better with other classes and after-school activities.
- ☐ Start studying sooner—don't wait till the last minute.
- ☐ Come to class more prepared, and keep up with assignments.
- ☐ Pay more attention to figures, graphics, and illustrations.
- ☐ Make concept or mind maps to organize information.
- ☐ Try actively in class to solve the problems instead of just waiting for the answer.
- ☐ Find and take some online practice quizzes before the test.
- ☐ Make vocabulary lists or flash cards to study terms and definitions.
- ☐ Get more sleep, and eat breakfast before the test.
- ☐ Don't panic! Use mindfulness strategies to calm my brain and body.
- ☐ Add any other change you want to make that's not listed here:

____

____

____

____

____

Figure 8.1: Test self-reflection.

Visit ***go.SolutionTree.com/assessment*** *for a free reproducible version of this figure.*

Encouraging Parents to Help With Test Prep

Educators can enlist and encourage parents to help prepare students to do their best on high-stakes tests. Testing is just one part of a student's education, but some parents have skewed expectations about what the tests can prove or how the scores might be used. Their own stress, anxiety, and concerns can contribute to their children's views and even their fears about the tests. Communicating this impact to parents is important.

Introductory back-to-school parent-night presentations or parent-education meetings can provide information about how parents can promote a growth mindset and include stress-reduction strategies that will be useful all year long. Keeping parents updated on exams and grades is important. Memos should reflect suggestions for how parents can support and help their children and keep their expectations within reason. Encourage parents to keep in touch with the school and their child's teachers throughout the year; for example, ask parents to take the following actions.

- Attend school meetings, open houses, and teacher conferences.
- Use phone calls, email, web postings, Google Classroom, and the like to keep in touch with teachers regarding assignments and student progress or concerns.
- Keep tabs on their children's progress by checking in each day and asking to see their work.

Remind parents to remain positive. Staying calm will help their child stay calm. Share with parents the suggestions from the U.S. Department of Education (2003), www2.ed.gov/parents/academic/help/succeed/part9.html, which includes some of the following dos and don'ts for parents about tests and testing.

- Talk to children about high-stakes tests. It's helpful for them to understand why schools give tests and to know the different kinds of tests they will take.
- Explain that tests are a way to measure what teachers, schools, states, and provinces are teaching and how well students are learning. The results of some tests tell schools that they need to strengthen courses or change teaching methods.
- Explain that a standardized test uses the same standards to measure student achievement performance across the state or province or even across the country. Every student takes the same test according to the same rules.
- Parents should praise children for the things they work hard at and do well. This will help them do their best on a test, and they will be less likely to fear failing, become anxious, or make mistakes.
- Parents should meet with their child's teacher several times a year to discuss the child's progress. Teachers can suggest activities to do at home to help students prepare for tests and improve their understanding of schoolwork.
- Remember that one test is simply one test. Parents shouldn't let a single test score upset them. Many things could influence how students do on tests.

- Don't lose sight of children's well-being. Too much pressure can affect test performance. In addition, children may come to think that a parent's love depends on whether they do well on tests.

Conclusion

Preparing students for high-stakes tests is a high priority for teachers. Beyond the instruction of rigorous content and 21st century skills, teachers can also provide students with strategies and mindsets that will allow them to do their very best under even the most stressful testing conditions. Of course, no strategies work all of the time for all students, but we can tip the scales in the students' favor by adequately preparing them for tests. On the actual test day, we will see students who have an appropriate level of good stress without falling apart or drawing a blank because they know how to handle the stress mess.

EPILOGUE

Don't stress. Do your best. Forget the rest.

—UNKNOWN

The message throughout this book has been to consider how our students' brains learn best and how they might react when put under excess pressure and stress. When teachers have a better grasp on the conditions that can maximize student learning, they can design and orchestrate brain-friendly classroom environments. This includes so many best practices of educational pedagogy: social-emotional learning, trauma-sensitive classrooms, restorative justice, mindfulness practices, cultural responsiveness, student health and nutrition, movement and exercise, growth mindsets, and student agency; the list can go on and on. When teachers follow the suggestions presented in this book to *de-stress the test*, they will also incorporate evidence-based teaching and learning strategies that can help students become powerful, engaged learners. De-stress the test, *and* you will also maximize learning.

Many parents, educators, school leaders, and even policymakers disagree about the kinds of tests to administer to students, how often to test students, and how to use the scores. Standardized tests and current grading systems are not perfect, and every format has limitations, but it is important for teachers to help students prepare as best they can for any tests that may be administered.

Teachers should consider the following when creating a brain-friendly, relaxed, and engaging classroom.

- Teach students about their brains and how they react to stress and perceived threats. This knowledge can be empowering.
- Teach students mindfulness practices to reduce stress and enhance focus and awareness. Model and practice these on a regular basis.

- Orchestrate a brain-friendly classroom climate and environment. Maintain a sense of belonging and collaboration for all students. Make sure the classroom is a clean, healthy, and safe place to learn.
- Promote a growth mindset every day with encouragement, positive language, and chances for do-overs. Help students develop a healthy attitude about failures, perseverance, and a willingness to persist despite challenges.
- Find a way to frequently integrate technology use. This helps level the playing field. As educators quickly learned during the COVID-19 pandemic, all students should have access to the necessary technology to ensure equity.
- Integrate targeted talks with selected tier two vocabulary into everyday classroom activities. Help students learn these important academic vocabulary words.
- Give students regular opportunities to participate in independent activities to develop perseverance. Promote student self-regulation and choice to encourage self-direction.
- Encourage students to bring healthy snacks, take breaks, move around, get a good night's sleep, and so on. Don't wait till just before the test to provide this encouragement; these should be everyday actions!
- Remember that distractions can derail anyone.

See page 181 for a reproducible checklist of some chapter-by-chapter strategies to plan to de-stress the test.

A Possible Shift in Testing Culture

In the 2020–2021 school year, education abruptly changed. Around the globe, the COVID-19 pandemic brought in-person classroom instruction to a halt. In the United States, the yearly federally mandated high-stakes tests were suspended in most places, as were the SAT and ACT tests. Many states requested a waiver for the 2021 tests. In September 2020, U.S. Education Secretary Betsy DeVos said the waivers would be denied and insisted that all schools were required to test students. Due to the inequitable instruction and resources provided during the year, many felt this was unfair to the students, the teachers, and ultimately the schools (as cited in Planbook, n.d.).

Josh Godinez, president of the California Association of School Counselors, said, "We have created such a testing culture among the kids, to tell them all of a sudden that the tests don't matter, it's a hard one for them to swallow even though it's a reality" (as cited in Planbook, n.d.). So perhaps there is a chance that testing culture *is* changing? Due to the COVID-19 pandemic, there has been a shift back to standardized tests collecting data rather than acting as accountability measures.

On February 22, 2021, the U.S. Department of Education confirmed that states must resume the annual testing of students in grades 3–8 and report the results because it is "vitally important that parents, educators, and the public have access to data on student learning and success" (as cited in Kamenetz, 2021). However, there are a few exceptions that lower the stakes on high-stakes tests (Kamenetz, 2021).

- States may request waivers of the requirement that they use the test data to identify failing schools.
- States can be flexible in how their schools give the tests, such as by shortening the tests, administering them remotely, or even offering alternate dates that could go into the summer and even the fall.
- The results of the standardized tests will not be used to penalize schools in terms of funding or ranking.

States like Georgia, Michigan, South Carolina, and New York requested to skip standardized testing altogether in 2021 (Field, 2021), even though the federal government required tests for grades 3–8. On March 29, 2021, Westchester County in New York announced that it would only give standardized tests to students whose parents requested it. All tests must be taken in person, so fully remote students wouldn't be eligible. The New York State Education Committee determined that these tests couldn't be used for any teacher evaluations or school rankings this year (News 12 Staff, 2021). Again, the move to collect data but reduce accountability measures effectively lowers the stakes on these high-stakes tests. The *high-stakes* aspect of the exams has been nearly eliminated. Ryan Brown, chief communications officer for the South Carolina Department of Education, states, "It's a lot of anxiety and stress in a year that has already had an unprecedented amount of stress" (as cited in Field, 2021).

Becky Pringle, president of the National Education Association, urged states to seek maximum flexibility on waivers: "High-stakes standardized tests administered during the global health crisis should not determine a student's future, evaluate educators, or punish schools; nor should they come at the expense of precious learning time that students could be spending with their educators" (as cited in Kamenetz, 2021).

At the time of this book's publication, the details of how federally mandated standardized tests will be administered, and to what degree the results will have an impact, are in question. If individual student test scores are simply compared to their last tests, then we can begin to see student growth or lack of. However, not every student will be taking the test, and every district will have a different percentage of students taking the exam. The tests that are given to the sampling of students can only provide a snapshot of the learning that occurred. As Scott Marion, executive director of the nonprofit National Center for the Improvement of Educational Assessment, puts it, "Bad data is worse than no data, because people will still make decisions based on bad data" (as cited in Field, 2021).

Mike Huber, the assistant superintendent of instruction and assessment in Portage, Michigan, says, "I think what we're trying to do is what best meets the needs of our students in light of the waiver on accountability being granted but not the waiver to administer assessments" (as cited in Miller, 2021).

Perhaps then, it's possible that this devastating pandemic has begun to change the high-stakes testing culture. We have a chance, worldwide, to re-examine the role that high-stakes tests play in accountability systems, or at least to reduce the burden they place on schools.

A Look Beyond the Test

As stated at the beginning of this book, testing, in one form or another, will always be a part of learning and life. When educators orchestrate learning within a brain-friendly environment, teach mindfulness practices, and help students develop healthy attitudes about failures and perseverance, we will empower our students to be successful in whatever they attempt. It may be possible that by helping them de-stress for the test, we can help them de-stress about life.

APPENDIX: Reproducibles

Personal-Praise Statements and Process-Praise Statements

Personal-Praise Statements	Process-Praise Statements
To discourage a fixed mindset, avoid personal-praise statements such as these. • "You're so smart." • "You are a talented athlete." • "You are a born artist." • "You are such a good boy."	To encourage a growth mindset, offer process-praise statements such as these. • "Your paper shows that you put a lot of effort into the research." • "I noticed that you redid several problems—way to go!" • "This story shows me that you are really expanding your use of descriptive words." • "I noticed you showed initiative and got started right away."
Notes	Notes

Activity to Evaluate Inner Thoughts

Our inner voices are constantly telling us what we think we can do. This internal dialogue may be sending us messages that confirm a fixed mindset. With practice, students can begin to identify their negative thoughts and learn ways to turn them into positive messages. This activity can help students distinguish between three types of common inner voices so they will be able to evaluate whether their own inner thoughts reflect a fixed mindset or a growth mindset.

1. **Stuck-up:** An inner stuck-up voice also sends fixed-mindset messages, but these messages emphasize one's current capabilities. This confident, know-it-all attitude often keeps a person from even considering putting in more effort or trying to improve: "I've done this before; I don't have to prove myself," "This is so easy that I'm not even going to try," "It's not *my* fault it didn't work out; it's someone else's fault," and "My parents say I'm the best player on the team."
2. **Stuck-down:** An inner stuck-down voice sends fixed-mindset messages that seem to confirm someone isn't smart or talented and shouldn't even try to improve: "I'm not smart," "I'm a loser," "Why should I even try? I always mess up," "Nobody in my family is good at this," and "If my team loses, my teammates will probably blame me because I'm not a very good player."
3. **Coach:** Coach's motto is "With effort, you can do it!" An inner coach voice always says encouraging statements that promote a growth mindset, such as, "Keep trying," "Give it another shot," "Think about what you can do better next time," "You can learn from this," and "Stick with it."

This activity has two parts. For part 1, select four students to role-play the following scenarios. One student sits in a chair and reads out loud the scenario description. The other three students stand behind the chair and act as the seated student's potential inner voices, offering their thoughts about the scenario task. Encourage them to really add gestures and tone to emphasize their points of view.

After the four students have role-played, part 2 of this activity involves opening up a class discussion about each character's statements. Ask students to give examples of times they've experienced similar inner voices. Then, ask all students in the class to write their own scenarios, whether they're made-up scenarios or situations that the students have encountered. Invite students to share and act out new dialogues.

page 1 of 3

Scenario 1

This scene is about trying new things. The assignment is that I must give a PowerPoint presentation to the class.

1. **Stuck-up:** "This is a stupid assignment. I've been making and posting viral videos online for years. I did PowerPoint presentations back in second grade! Forget it!"
2. **Stuck-down:** "Oh, great! I know that my presentation will suck. There will probably be technical problems, and I'll look like an idiot. I'll never have enough time to get it finished. I don't have anybody to help me anyway."
3. **Coach:** "Yikes! This could be a little scary, but I've always wanted to learn how to do a PowerPoint presentation. I wonder who I could ask to help me. I guess I'd better not wait till the last minute for this. I might actually learn something!"

Scenario 2

This scene is about sticking with something. I have just joined a soccer team, and I'm thinking of quitting.

1. **Stuck-up:** "I don't know why I should keep going to practice. I'm one of the best players on the team, and I really don't feel challenged. Most of the other players are real losers. I'm way above this level of play."
2. **Stuck-down:** "Ugh! This is so hard! I've never even played this level of soccer before. These players have all played *way* more than me. My ankle's been bothering me, so that would be a good excuse. I think I'd rather be at home playing video games."
3. **Coach:** "Even though I don't really look forward to practice, I still always end up having a great time. I've been watching a few of the other players to see what they do. I think my running is getting better, and I'm definitely playing better with my teammates. I'm actually having some fun out there."

page 2 of 3

Scenario 3

This scene is about setbacks and failures. I just got my grade on the mathematics test—I got a D!

1. **Stuck-up:** "This was a ridiculous test! There were hardly any problems on it. I'm used to way harder tests than this. The problems weren't even like the ones I've had before. I could have easily passed this if there had been more time."
2. **Stuck-down:** "Here we go again—another chance to show everyone how bad I am at mathematics! Everyone saw my grade. I give up! Mathematics is hard for my brother too, so I think it runs in the family. I'm going to act like I don't even care."
3. **Coach:** "Darn! I was hoping that my grade was a little better than this. I guess I will have to study more next time. Maybe I can ask my classmate who sits in front of me if she could help me learn."

page 3 of 3

Classroom Poster on Failure

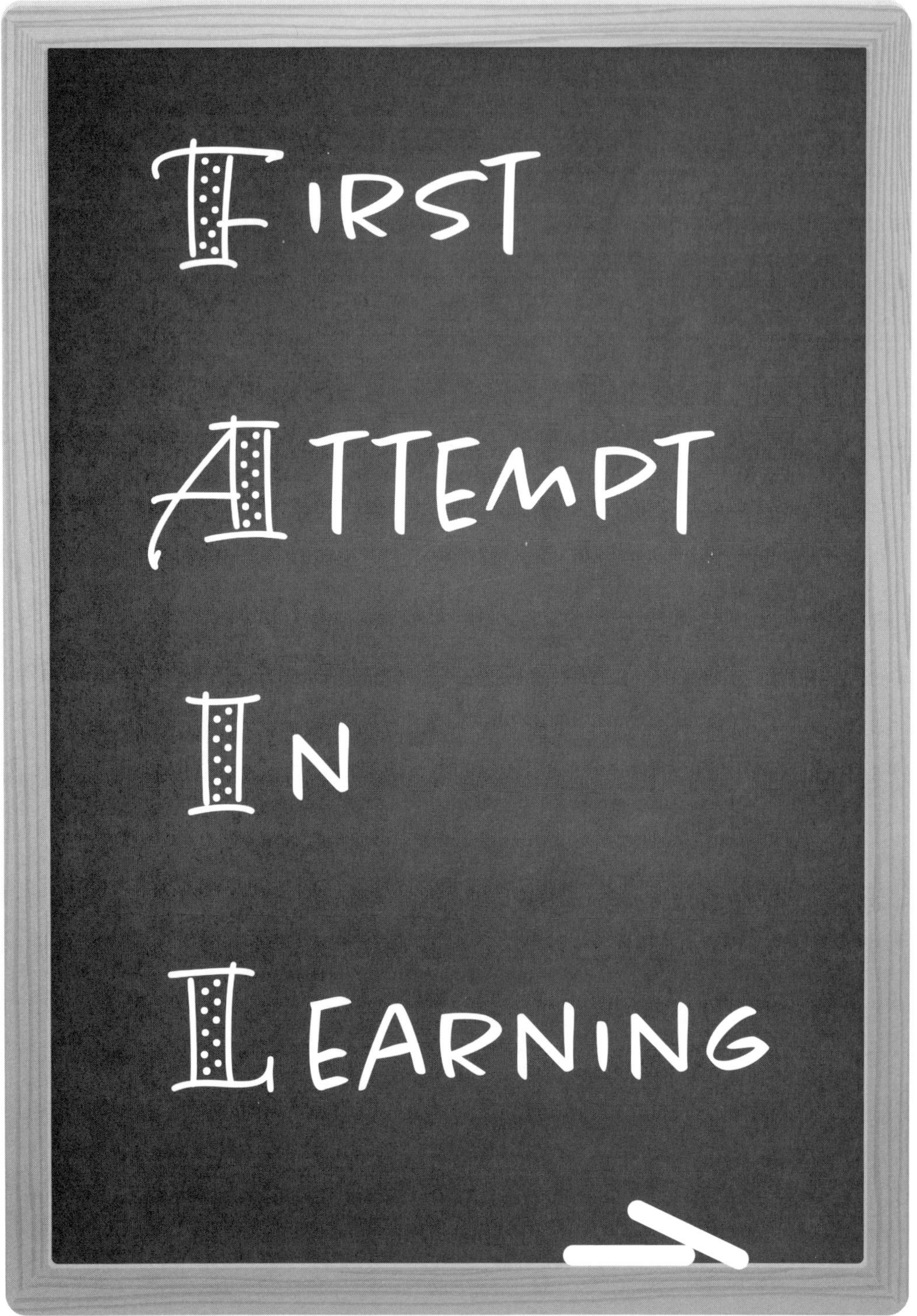

Critical Academic Vocabulary

Critical Verbs	Critical Nouns
Allude	*Argument* or *counterargument*
Appeal	*Author's purpose*
Articulate	*Conclusion*
Capture	*Data*
Categorize	*Details*
Characterize	*Evidence*
Cite	*Figurative language*
Claim	*Graph*
Classify	*Hypothesis*
Comprehend	*Illustrations*
Conclude	*Interaction*
Delineate	*Item*
Demonstrate	*List*
Describe	*Metaphor*
Determine	*Mood*
Develop	*Narrator*
Distinguish	*Perspective*
Draw	*Point of view*
Foreshadow	*Rhetoric*
Formulate	*Simile*
Imply	*Stanza*
Locate	*Summary*
Organize	*Table*
Paraphrase	*Theme*
Persuade	*Tone*
Predict	
Recognize	
Recount	
Refer or *reference*	
Retell	
Suggest	
Support	

Practicing Positive Self-Talk

Directions: Revise each of the following statements as a realistic, yet optimistic, replacement thought.

- "I'm just not good at drawing."

- "My hair is looking so weird!"

- "I can't trust anyone else. I need to rely only on myself."

- "That's the way we always do it in my family."

- "It's just too difficult—why try?"

Come up with one of your own! What's a negative or limiting thought you've had about yourself or your learning that you could simply reframe?

Can You Follow Instructions?

Directions: Read all the items before you begin to carry out each instruction. Work as quickly as you can. You have three minutes to finish this activity. Good luck!

1. Write your name at the top of the paper.

2. Write today's date in the upper-right-hand corner of the paper.

3. Fold your paper in half horizontally so there is a crease.

4. Draw an *X* in the lower-left-hand corner of this paper.

5. In the lower-right-hand corner of this paper, write your age.

6. Add 35 and 25. Write your answer underneath your name at the top of the paper.

7. Underline the phrase *Good luck* at the top of the paper.

8. Circle all the numbers on this paper.

9. Draw a rectangle around the word *crease* in item 3.

10. Now that you have finished reading everything carefully, don't do items 1 through 9.

Top-Ten Test-Taking Tips

1. Pay careful attention to written and verbal directions.

2. Scan through the full test first—if allowed—to determine your strategy.

3. Know the rules about skipping questions or guessing.

4. Monitor your time and pacing.

5. Closely read all questions and answers. Reread any items that are confusing or complex.

6. Double-check your answers.

7. On reading comprehension items, it may help to read the questions before reading the passage.

8. Don't forget to show your work if questions ask you to do so. (Mathematics questions may often ask you to show your work.)

9. If allowed, skip over difficult questions, and come back to them later.

10. If you're not sure about a question, narrow down the possible answers, and take an educated guess.

Planning to De-Stress the Test

Strategies	Before Testing			
	One to Three Weeks	Four to Seven Weeks	Two to Three Months	Four to Six Months
Teach students simple mindfulness strategies to lower stress and calm anxiety. See chapter 5, "Mindfulness Practices for the Classroom" (page 95).	X	X	X	X
Prepare students with basic test-taking strategies as well as with experience navigating the technology that they will use when the test is administered. See chapter 8, "Test Prep for Students and Teachers" (page 147).	X	X	X	X
Explicitly teach students the academic vocabulary (tier two words for the appropriate grade level) that makes up the language of most testing discourse. See chapter 7, "Academic Vocabulary Instruction" (page 135).		X	X	X
Teach students about how their brains' capabilities are minimized when they perceive threats or are anxious. See chapter 2, "The Stress of High-Stakes Testing" (page 19).		X	X	X
Foster a growth mindset in students to build their self-efficacy, encouraging students to work hard and persevere even when experiencing setbacks. See chapter 4, "The Development of Student Agency Through Self-Efficacy, Growth Mindset, and Perseverance" (page 71).			X	X
Orchestrate and maintain a brain-friendly classroom environment that reduces perceived threat and minimizes stress throughout the year. See chapter 3, "Body- and Brain-Friendly Classrooms and Testing Environments" (page 37).				X
Integrate a variety of formative assessments during learning, and provide students with constructive feedback along with additional time to make the necessary adjustments. See chapter 6, "Feedback and Formative Assessments" (page 119).				X

REFERENCES AND RESOURCES

Abdelbary, M. (2017, August 9). Learning in motion: Bring movement back to the classroom. *Education Week*. Accessed at www.edweek.org/tm/articles/2017/08/08/learning-in-motion-bring-movement-back-to.html on October 29, 2020.

Abeles, V. (Director). (2014). *Beyond measure* [Film]. United States: Reel Link Films.

Abeles, V. (2015). *Beyond measure: Rescuing an overscheduled, overtested, underestimated generation*. New York: Simon & Schuster.

Abeles, V., & Congdon, J. (Directors). (2009). *Race to nowhere* [Film]. United States: Reel Link Films.

Adams, S. (2020). *Forbes investigation: How the SAT failed America*. Accessed at www.forbes.com/sites/susanadams/2020/09/30/the-forbes-investigation-how-the-sat-failed-america/?sh=6edc014d53b5 on March 10, 2021.

Albrecht, K. (2010). *Stress and the manager: Making it work for you*. New York: Simon & Schuster.

Alexander, D., & Lewis, L. (2014). *Condition of America's public school facilities: 2012–13—First look* (NCES 2014–022). Washington, DC: National Center for Education Statistics. Accessed at https://nces.ed.gov/pubs2014/2014022.pdf on January 12, 2021.

American Institute of Stress. (2012, August 10). *Take a deep breath*. Accessed at www.stress.org/take-a-deep-breath on December 22, 2020.

American Psychological Association. (n.d.). *Stress relief is within reach*. Accessed at www.apa.org/topics/stress on January 12, 2021.

American Psychological Association. (2019). *Identifying signs of stress in your children and teens*. Accessed at www.apa.org/topics/stress/children on March 15, 2021.

American Test Anxieties Association. (n.d.). *Test anxiety: Prevalence*. Accessed at www.amtaa.org on February 26, 2021.

Amrein, A. L., & Berliner, D. C. (2003). The effects of high-stakes testing on student motivation and learning. *Educational Leadership*, *60*(5), 32–38.

And Now for Something Completely Different. (n.d.). In *Wikipedia*. Accessed at https://en.wikipedia.org/wiki/And_Now_for_Something_Completely_Different on April 10, 2021.

Anderson, J. (2021). *The agile learner: Where growth mindset, habits of mind, and practice unite*. Bloomington, IN: Solution Tree Press.

Ankrom, S. (2021). 8 deep breathing exercises to reduce anxiety. *VeryWellMind*. Accessed at www.verywellmind.com/abdominal-breathing-2584115 on March 26, 2021.

Anxiety and Depression Association of America. (n.d.). *Stress*. Accessed at https://adaa.org/understanding-anxiety/related-illnesses/stress on October 29, 2020.

Anxiety and Stress Management Institute. (n.d.). *Stress*. Accessed at www.stressmgt.net/cherry-services/stress on October 29, 2020.

ASCD. (2015, January 25). *Reduce the reliance on standardized testing* [Conference agenda]. Leadership Institute for Legislative Policy, Washington, DC. Accessed at www.ascd.org/ASCD/pdf/siteASCD/conferences/LILA15/LILA15_Leg_Agenda_Key_Points_Testing.pdf on April 30, 2021.

Babbage, S. (2019, August 30). *Overcoming the fear of feedback* [Blog post]. Accessed at www.emilywray.com/blog/2019/8/30/overcoming-the-fear-of-feedback on October 29, 2020.

Bandura, A. (1977). *Social learning theory*. Englewood Cliffs, NJ: Prentice Hall.

Bandura, A. (1989). Human agency in social cognitive theory. *American Psychologist, 44*(9), 1175–1184.

Bandura, A. (Ed.). (1997a). *Self-efficacy in changing societies*. New York: Cambridge University Press.

Bandura, A. (1997b). *Self-efficacy: The exercise of control*. New York: Freeman.

Barber, R. (2019, December 9). "Llamapalooza" offers students opportunity to de-stress before finals. *The Daily Californian*. Accessed at www.dailycal.org/2019/12/09/llamapalooza-offers-students-opportunity-to-de-stress-before-finals on October 29, 2020.

Barzilay, J. A. (2012, October 21). *Sleeping tips for optimal exam performance*. Accessed at www.thecrimson.com/flyby/article/2012/10/21/sleep-tips-dr-saper on December 18, 2020.

Beck, I. L., McKeown, M. G., & Kucan, L. (2013). *Bringing words to life: Robust vocabulary instruction* (2nd ed.). New York: Guilford Press.

Beilock, S. (2010). *Choke: What the secrets of the brain reveal about getting it right when you have to*. New York: Free Press.

Bekker, H. L., Legare, F., Stacey, D., O'Connor, A., & Lemyre, L. (2003). Is anxiety a suitable measure of decision aid effectiveness? A systematic review. *Patient Education and Counseling, 50*(3), 255–262.

Bergland, C. (2013, January 22). *Cortisol: Why the "stress hormone" is public enemy no. 1* [Blog post]. Accessed at www.psychologytoday.com/us/blog/the-athletes-way/201301/cortisol-why-the-stress-hormone-is-public-enemy-no-1 on October 29, 2020.

Berner, M. M. (1993). Building conditions, parental involvement, and student achievement in the District of Columbia public school system. *Urban Education, 28*(1), 6–29.

Bertin, M. (2015). *Mindful parenting for ADHD: A guide to cultivating calm, reducing stress and helping children thrive*. Oakland, CA: New Harbinger.

Bertin, M. (2016, October 12). *Body scan for kids*. Accessed at www.mindful.org/body-scan-kids on October 29, 2020.

Bjork, R. A. (1994). Memory and metamemory considerations in the training of human beings. In J. Metcalfe & A. P. Shimamura (Eds.), *Metacognition: Knowing about knowing* (pp. 185–205). Cambridge, MA: MIT Press.

Black, B. (2020). *Are active shooter drills doing more harm than good?* Accessed at www.psycom.net/active-shooter-drills on March 18, 2021.

Blanchard, K., & Johnson, S. (2015). *The new one minute manager*. New York: HarperCollins.

Boys & Girls Club of America. (2020, June 16). *Is my child OK? Warning signs kids and teens are stressed about COVID-19*. Accessed at www.bgca.org/news-stories/2020/June/Warning-Signs-Kids-and-Teens-are-Stressed-and-How-to-Help on March 12, 2021.

BrainyQuote. (n.d.). *Lucius Annaeus Seneca quotes*. Accessed at www.brainyquote.com/quotes/lucius_annaeus_seneca_107581 on May 4, 2021.

Bransford, J. D., Brown, A. L., & Cocking, R. R. (Eds.). (2000). *How people learn: Brain, mind, experience, and school* (Expanded ed.). Washington, DC: National Academies Press.

Briggs, S. (2013, June 25). *The perils of standardized testing: Six ways it harms learning*. Accessed at www.opencolleges.edu.au/informed/features/the-perils-of-standardized-testing on March 25, 2021.

Briggs, S. (2015, November 21). *Eight alternatives to high-stakes standardised tests.* Accessed at www.opencolleges.edu.au/informed/features/8-alternatives-to-standardized-testing on March 9, 2021.

Bronson, P. (2007, February 9). How not to talk to your kids. *New York Magazine.* Accessed at https://nymag.com/news/features/27840 on October 29, 2020.

Brown, P. C., Roediger, H. L., III, & McDaniel, M. A. (2014). *Make it stick: The science of successful learning.* Cambridge, MA: Belknap Press of Harvard University Press.

Brown, S. (2009). *Play: How it shapes the brain, opens the imagination, and invigorates the soul.* New York: Penguin.

Buehl, D. (2017). *Developing readers in the academic disciplines* (2nd ed.). Portland, ME: Stenhouse.

Bullmaster-Day, M. L. (n.d.). *Productive struggle for deeper learning* [White paper]. Accessed at www.academia.edu/22763598/Productive_Struggle_for_Deeper_Learning on October 29, 2020.

Burdick-Will, J. (2018). Neighborhood violence, peer effects, and academic achievement in Chicago. *Sociology of Education, 91*(3), 205–223.

Burrows, B. (2020). *What is a standardized test?* Accessed at www.studyusa.com/en/a/1284/what-is-a-standardized-test on March 5, 2021.

Calder, B. (2018, March 8). Staying sharp on test day: 14 practical mindfulness tips for reducing stress on standardized tests. *Forbes.* Accessed at www.forbes.com/sites/noodleeducation/2018/03/08/staying-sharp-on-test-day-mindfulness-tips/#4e6fe6d913f4 on October 29, 2020.

Campbell, L., & Campbell, B. (2009). *Mindful learning: 101 proven strategies for student and teacher success* (2nd ed.). Thousand Oaks, CA: Corwin Press.

Canfield, J. (n.d.). *Visualization techniques to affirm your desired outcomes: A step-by-step guide* [Blog post]. Accessed at www.jackcanfield.com/blog/visualize-and-affirm-your-desired-outcomes-a-step-by-step-guide on April 9, 2021.

Cardozo, L. T., Ramos de Azevedo, M. A., Carvalho, M. S. M., Costa, R., Oliveira de Lima, P., & Marcondes, F. K. (2020). Effect of an active learning methodology combined with formative assessments on performance, test anxiety, and stress of university students. *Advances in Physiology Education, 44*(4), 744–751.

Carlson, L. E., & Garland, S. N. (2005). Impact of mindfulness-based stress reduction (MBSR) on sleep, mood, stress and fatigue symptoms in cancer outpatients. *International Journal of Behavioral Medicine, 12*(4), 278–285.

Carter, S. B. (2012, March 14). *Why mess causes stress: 8 reasons, 8 remedies* [Blog post]. Accessed at www.psychologytoday.com/us/blog/high-octane-women/201203/why-mess-causes-stress-8-reasons-8-remedies on October 29, 2020.

Catalyst. (2020). *People of colour in Canada: Quick* take. Accessed at www.catalyst.org/research/people-of-colour-in-canada on May 3, 2021.

Center for Teaching and Learning at Washington University in St. Louis. (n.d.). *Reducing stereotype threat: Strategies for instructors.* Accessed at https://ctl.wustl.edu/resources/reducing-stereotype-threat on June 11, 2021.

Center on the Developing Child. (n.d.). *What are ACEs? And how do they relate to toxic stress?* Accessed at https://developingchild.harvard.edu/resources/aces-and-toxic-stress-frequently-asked-questions on October 29, 2020.

Centers for Disease Control and Prevention. (n.d.). *About the CDC-Kaiser ACE study.* Accessed at www.cdc.gov/violenceprevention/childabuseandneglect/acestudy/about.html on October 29, 2020.

Cherry, K. (2020). *Signs and symptoms of test anxiety.* Accessed at www.verywellmind.com/the-symptoms-of-test-anxiety-2795367 on March 11, 2021.

Cherry, K. (2021a). *How experience changes brain plasticity.* Accessed at www.verywellmind.com/what-is-brain-plasticity-2794886 on March 24, 2021.

Cherry, K. (2021b). *What is self-esteem?* Accessed at www.verywellmind.com/what-is-self-esteem-2795868 on March 21, 2021.

Cheryan, S., Ziegler, S. A., Plaut, V. C., & Meltzoff, A. N. (2014). Designing classrooms to maximize student achievement. *Policy Insights From the Behavioral and Brain Sciences, 1*(1), 4–12. Accessed at https://journals.sagepub.com/doi/full/10.1177/2372732214548677 on October 29, 2020.

Churchill, A. (2015). *Bless the tests: Three reasons for standardized testing.* Accessed at https://fordhaminstitute.org/national/commentary/bless-tests-three-reasons-standardized-testing on March 25, 2021.

Cohn, D., & Caumont, A. (2016, March 31). *10 demographic trends shaping the U.S. and the world in 2016.* Accessed at www.pewresearch.org/fact-tank/2016/03/31/10-demographic-trends-that-are-shaping-the-u-s-and-the-world on October 29, 2020.

Collaborative for Academic, Social, and Emotional Learning. (n.d.). *SEL is . . . .* Accessed at https://casel.org/what-is-sel on January 10, 2021.

Collaborative for Academic, Social, and Emotional Learning. (2015). *CASEL guide: Effective social and emotional learning programs* (Middle and high school ed.). Chicago: Author. Accessed at https://casel.org/middle-and-high-school-edition-casel-guide on June 11, 2021.

Cooper, H., Robinson, J. C., & Patall, E. A. (2006). Does homework improve academic achievement? A synthesis of research, 1987–2003. *Review of Educational Research, 76*(1), 1–62.

Council of the Great City Schools. (2015). *Student assessments in public schools not strategic, often redundant* [Press release]. Accessed at www.cgcs.org/cms/lib/DC00001581/Centricity/Domain/4/Testing%20Report.pdf on March 24, 2021.

Curry, O., Rowland, L., Van Lissa, C., Zlotowitz, S., McAlaney, J., & Whitehouse, H. (2018). Happy to help? A systematic review and meta-analysis of the effects of performing acts of kindness on the well-being of the actor. *Journal of Experimental Social Psychology, 76*, 320–329.

Daring Authenticity. [daringauthenticity]. (2011, April 12). *5 minute breathing exercise* [Video file]. Accessed at www.youtube.com/watch?v=5f5N6YFjvVc on January 22, 2021.

Darling-Hammond, L., Flook, L., Cook-Harvey, C., Barron, B., & Osher, D. (2020). Implications for educational practice of the science of learning and development. *Applied Developmental Science, 24*(2), 97–140.

Davies, R. (n.d.). *Vocabulary is destroying your test scores. Here's how to fix it!* Accessed at www.differentiatedteaching.com/how-vocabulary-is-destroying-your-test on April 4, 2021.

Davis, K. L., & Panksepp, J. (2018). *The emotional foundations of personality: A neurobiological and evolutionary approach.* New York: Norton.

Deci, E., & Cascio, W. (1972, April 19). *Changes in intrinsic motivation as a function of negative feedback and threats.* Paper presented at the Eastern Psychological Association Meeting, Boston.

Dell'Antonia, K. J. (2014, March 12). *Homework's emotional toll on students and families* [Blog post]. Accessed at https://parenting.blogs.nytimes.com/2014/03/12/homeworks-emotional-toll-on-students-and-families on October 29, 2020.

Department of Veterans' Affairs. (2012). *Allostatic load: A review of the literature.* Canberra, Australia: Author. Accessed at www.dva.gov.au/sites/default/files/files/consultation%20and%20grants/healthstudies/allostatic/allostatic.pdf on January 12, 2021.

Desautels, L. (2017, October 23). *Quick classroom exercises to combat stress.* Accessed at www.edutopia .org/article/quick-classroom-exercises-combat-stress on October 29, 2020.

Devaney, E., O'Brien, M. U., Resnik, H., Keister, S., & Weissberg, R. P. (2006). *Sustainable schoolwide social and emotional learning (SEL): Implementation guide and toolkit.* Chicago: Collaborative for Academic, Social, and Emotional Learning.

Doidge, N. (2007). *The brain that changes itself: Stories of personal triumph from the frontiers of brain science.* New York: Penguin.

Driscoll, R. (2004). Who's afraid of the big bad test. *Our Children: The National PTA Magazine, 29*(6), 7.

Duckworth, A. (2016). *Grit: The power of passion and perseverance.* New York: Scribner.

Durlak, J. A., Weissberg, R. P., Dymnicki, A. B., Taylor, R. D., & Schellinger, K. B. (2011). The impact of enhancing students' social and emotional learning: A meta-analysis of school-based universal interventions. *Child Development, 82*(1), 405–432.

Dweck, C. S. (1999). Caution—Praise can be dangerous. *American Educator, 23*(1), 4–9.

Dweck, C. S. (2016). *Mindset: The new psychology of success* (Updated ed.). New York: Random House.

Dweck, C. S. (2017). *Mindset* (Updated ed.)*: Changing the way you think to fulfil your potential.* London: Little, Brown.

Dweck, C. S., Walton, G. M., & Cohen, G. L. (2014). *Academic tenacity: Mindsets and skills that promote long-term learning.* Seattle, WA: Bill & Melinda Gates Foundation.

Education Corner. (n.d.). *Test taking strategies.* Accessed at www.educationcorner.com/test-taking -strategies.html on January 18, 2021.

Educator's School Safety Network. (2019). *2018–2019 violence in schools report.* Accessed at http:// eschoolsafety.org/violence on October 29, 2020.

Eitland, E., Klingensmith, L., MacNaughton, P., Laurent, J. C., Spengler, J., Bernstein, A., et al. (2017). *Schools for health: Foundations for student success: How school buildings influence student health, thinking and performance.* Boston: Harvard Center for Health and the Global Environment.

Elementary and Secondary Education Act of 1965, Pub. L. No. 89–10, 20 U.S.C. § 6301 (1965).

Fallows, J. (2013, May 23). Linda Stone on maintaining focus in a maddeningly distractive world. *The Atlantic.* Accessed at www.theatlantic.com/national/archive/2013/05/linda-stone-on -maintaining-focus-in-a-maddeningly-distractive-world/276201 on December 22, 2020.

FairTest. (2019). *Graduation test update: States that recently eliminated or scaled back high school exit exams.* Accessed at www.fairtest.org/graduation-test-update-states-recently-eliminated on March 11, 2021.

FairTest Examiner. (2013). *Common Core brings a new chapter of high-stakes test horrors.* Accessed at www.fairtest.org/Common-Core-Testing-Horror-Stories on February 26, 2021.

Faraone, S. V., Sergeant, J., Gillberg, C., & Biederman, J. (2003). The worldwide prevalence of ADHD: Is it an American condition? *World Psychiatry, 2*(2), 104–113.

Farrington, C. A., Roderick, M., Allensworth, E., Nagaoka, J., Keyes, T. S., Johnson, D. W., et al. (2012). *Teaching adolescents to become learners: The role of noncognitive factors in shaping school performance—A critical literature review.* Chicago: University of Chicago Consortium on Chicago School Research. Accessed at https://consortium.uchicago.edu/sites/default/files/2018 -10/Noncognitive%20Report_0.pdf on January 12, 2021.

Favero, T. G., & Hendricks, N. (2016). Student exam analysis (debriefing) promotes positive changes in exam preparation and learning. *Advances in Physiology Education*, *40*(3), 323–328.

Felitti, V. J., Anda, R. F., Nordenberg, D., Williamson, D. F., Spitz, A. M., Edwards, V., et al. (1998). Relationship of childhood abuse and household dysfunction to many of the leading causes of death in adults. *American Journal of Preventive Medicine*, *14*(4), 245–258.

Ferguson, R. F., Phillips, S. F., Rowley, J. F. S., & Friedlander, J. W. (2015). *The influence of teaching beyond standardized test scores: Engagement, mindsets, and agency.* Cambridge, MA: Achievement Gap Initiative at Harvard University. Accessed at www.agi.harvard.edu/projects /TeachingandAgency.pdf on January 12, 2021.

Fertman, C. I., & Primack, B. A. (2009). Elementary student self efficacy scale development and validation focused on student learning, peer relations, and resisting drug use. *Journal of Drug Education*, *39*(1), 23–38. Accessed at www.ncbi.nlm.nih.gov/pmc/articles/PMC3008354 on December 20, 2020.

Field, K. (2021). *To test or not to test? Educators weigh the value of standardized testing during a pandemic.* Accessed at https://hechingerreport.org/to-test-or-not-to-test-educators-weigh-the -value-of-standardized-testing-during-a-pandemic on May 5, 2021.

Fink, G. (2016, April 26). *Stress: The health epidemic of the 21st century.* Accessed at http:// scitechconnect.elsevier.com/stress-health-epidemic-21st-century on October 29, 2020.

Fisher, D., Frey, N., & Hattie, J. (2017). *Teaching literacy in the visible learning classroom, grades K–5.* Thousand Oaks, CA: Corwin Press.

Flintoff, J.-P. (2013, July 27). Brené Brown: People are sick of being afraid all the time. *The Guardian.* Accessed at www.theguardian.com/lifeandstyle/2013/jul/27/brene-brown-people-sick-being -afraid on March 25, 2021.

Floyd, K. (2017, April 18). *Five breathing techniques for kids* [Video file]. Accessed at www.youtube .com/watch?v=b_nOeQNP7vA on January 22, 2021.

FluentU. (n.d.). *Extra! Extra! We've got the cure for foreign language anxiety* [Blog post]. Accessed at www.fluentu.com/blog/educator/foreign-language-anxiety on October 29, 2020.

Francisco, A. (2019). *Ask the cognitive scientist: Distributed practice.* Accessed at https://digitalpromise .org/2019/05/08/ask-the-cognitive-scientist-distributed-practice on April 4, 2021.

Freshwater, S. (2018). *Three types of stress and health hazards.* Accessed at https://spacioustherapy .com/3-types-stress-health-hazards on March 12, 2021.

Frey, N., Hattie, J., & Fisher, D. (2018). *Developing assessment-capable visible learners, grades K–12: Maximizing skill, will, and thrill.* Thousand Oaks, CA: Corwin Press.

Fulton, B. A. (2016). *The relationship between test anxiety and standardized test scores* [Doctoral dissertation, Walden University]. Walden Dissertations and Doctoral Studies Collection. Accessed at https://scholarworks.waldenu.edu/cgi/viewcontent.cgi?article=3361&context =dissertations on April 30, 2021.

Galanakis, M. J., Palaiologou, A., Patsi, G., Velegraki, I.-M., & Darviri, C. (2016). A literature review on the connection between stress and self-esteem. *Psychology*, *7*(5), 687–694. Accessed at http://dx.doi.org/10.4236/psych.2016.75071 on October 29, 2020.

Galloway, M., Conner, J., & Pope, D. (2013). Nonacademic effects of homework in privileged, high-performing high schools. *Journal of Experimental Education*, *81*(4), 490–510.

Gandy, L. (2016, January 11). Don't believe the hype: Standardized tests are good for children, families and schools. *Education Post.* Accessed at https://educationpost.org/dont-believe-the -hype-standardized-tests-are-good-for-children-families-and-schools on March 25, 2021.

Gaumer Erickson, A. S., & Noonan, P. M. (2012). *College and career competency framework* (3rd ed.). Lawrence, KS: University of Kansas Center for Research on Learning.

Gaumer Erickson, A. S., & Noonan, P. M. (2018). *The skills that matter: Teaching interpersonal and intrapersonal competencies in any classroom*. Thousand Oaks, CA: Corwin Press.

Gaumer Erickson, A. S. & Noonan, P. M. (2021). *Self-efficacy assessment suite: Technical report*. Accessed at http://researchcollaboration.org/uploads/Self-EfficacyAssessSuiteTech.pdf on April 28, 2021.

Gibbs, J. (2006). *Reaching all by creating tribes learning communities*. Windsor, CA: CenterSource Systems.

Gladden, R. M., Vivolo-Kantor, A. M., Hamburger, M. E., & Lumpkin, C. D. (2014). *Bullying surveillance among youths: Uniform definitions for public health and recommended data elements* (Version 1.0). Atlanta, GA: Centers for Disease Control and Prevention. Accessed at www.cdc.gov/violenceprevention/pdf/bullying-definitions-final-a.pdf on January 12, 2021.

Glossary of Education Reform. (2014). *High-stakes test*. Accessed at www.edglossary.org/high-stakes-testing on January 12, 2021.

Goldsmith, M. (2007). *Feedforward: leadership excellence*. Accessed at www.marshallgoldsmith.com/articles/1438 on March 30, 2021.

Goleman, D. (2019). *The emotionally intelligent leader*. Boston: Harvard Business Review Press.

GoNoodle. (2016, October 4). *Trolls: Can't stop the feeling* [Video file]. Accessed at www.youtube.com/watch?v=KhfkYzUwYFk on October 29, 2020.

Gopnik, A., Meltzoff, A. N., & Kuhl, P. K. (1999). *The scientist in the crib: Minds, brains, and how children learn*. New York: Morrow.

Gregory, G., & Kaufeldt, M. (2015). *The motivated brain: Improving student attention, engagement, and perseverance*. Alexandria, VA: Association for Supervision and Curriculum Development.

Hallowell, E. M. (2006). *CrazyBusy: Overstretched, overbooked, and about to snap!—Strategies for handling your fast-paced life*. New York: Ballantine Books.

Hallowell, E. M. (2015). *Driven to distraction at work: How to focus and be more productive*. Boston: Harvard Business Review Press.

Hamed, A. M., Kauer, A. J., & Stevens, H. E. (2015). Why the diagnosis of attention deficit hyperactivity disorder matters. *Frontiers in Psychiatry*, *6*(12), 168. Accessed at www.doi.org/10.3389/fpsyt.2015.00168 on October 29, 2020.

Hamilton, J. (2008, October 2). *Think you're multitasking? Think again*. Accessed at www.npr.org/templates/story/story.php?storyId=95256794 on October 29, 2020.

Hammond, Z. (2015). *Culturally responsive teaching and the brain: Promoting authentic engagement and rigor among culturally and linguistically diverse students*. Thousand Oaks, CA: Corwin Press.

Hansen, M. M., Jones, R., & Tocchini, K. (2017). Shinrin-yoku (forest bathing) and nature therapy: A state-of-the-art review. *International Journal of Environmental Research and Public Health*, *14*(8), 851. Accessed at https://doi.org/10.3390/ijerph14080851 on October 29, 2020.

Harris, N. B. (2018). *The deepest well: Healing the long-term effects of childhood adversity*. New York: Houghton Mifflin Harcourt.

Hart, B., & Risley, T. R. (2003). The early catastrophe: The 30 million word gap by age 3. *American Educator*, *27*(1), 4–9. Accessed at www.aft.org/pdfs/americaneducator/spring2003/TheEarlyCatastrophe.pdf on October 29, 2020.

Hart, L. A. (2002). *Human brain and human learning* (3rd ed.). Covington, WA: Books for Educators.

Harvard Health Publishing. (2019). *Benefits of mindfulness: Practices for improving emotional and physical well-being*. Accessed at www.helpguide.org/harvard/benefits-of-mindfulness.htm on March 15, 2021.

Harwin, A., & Furuya, Y. (2021, January 19). Where families are feeling pandemic impacts the worst. *Education Week*. Accessed at www.edweek.org/leadership/where-families-are-feeling-pandemic-impacts-the-worst/2021/01 on May 5, 2021.

Hattie, J. (2009). *Visible learning: A synthesis of over 800 meta-analyses relating to achievement*. New York: Routledge.

Hattie, J. (2015, October 27). We aren't using assessments correctly. *Education Week*. Accessed at www.edweek.org/policy-politics/opinion-we-arent-using-assessments-correctly/2015/10 on October 29, 2020.

Hattie, J., & Clarke, S. (2019). *Visible learning: Feedback*. New York: Routledge.

Hattie, J., & Timperley, H. (2007). The power of feedback. *Review of Educational Research, 77*(1), 81–112.

HeartMath Institute. (2002). *The inside story: Understanding the power of feelings*. Boulder Creek, CA: Author.

Heath, M., & Shukla, D. (2020). A single bout of aerobic exercise provides an immediate "boost" to cognitive flexibility. *Frontiers in Psychology, 11*, 1106. Accessed at www.doi.org/10.3389/fpsyg.2020.01106 on October 29, 2020.

Heissel, J. A., Adam, E. K., Doleac, J. L., Figlio, D. N., & Meer, J. (2018). *Testing, stress, and performance: How students respond physiologically to high-stakes testing*. Cambridge, MA: National Bureau of Economic Research. Accessed at www.nber.org/papers/w25305 on January 12, 2021.

Hiebert, J. S., & Grouws, D. A. (2007). The effects of classroom mathematics teaching on students' learning. In F. K. Lester Jr. (Ed.), *Second handbook of research on mathematics teaching and learning* (pp. 371–404). Charlotte, NC: Information Age.

Hines, E. W. (1996). *Building condition and student achievement and behavior* [Unpublished doctoral dissertation]. Virginia Polytechnic Institute and State University, Blacksburg, Virginia.

Hutton, T. L. (2008). *Three tiers of vocabulary and education*. Accessed at www.superduperinc.com/handouts/pdf/182_VocabularyTiers.pdf on October 29, 2020.

Ito, C. (1999). *I think I did it, but I can't find it: Assisting students who lack organizational skills*. Williamsburg, VA: William and Mary School of Education. Accessed at https://education.wm.edu/centers/ttac/resources/articles/learndisable/ithinkididit/index.php on October 29, 2020.

Jacobsen, E. (2020). A *(mostly) brief history of the SAT and ACT tests*. Accessed at www.erikthered.com/tutor/sat-act-history-printable.html on March 1, 2021.

Jennings, P. A. (2015). *Mindfulness for teachers: Simple skills for peace and productivity in the classroom*. New York: Norton.

Jensen, E. (2005). *Teaching with the brain in mind* (2nd ed.) Alexandria, VA: Association for Supervision and Curriculum Development.

Johnson, S. (2019, January 9). *The 12 high-school cliques that exist today, and how they differ from past decades*. Accessed at https://bigthink.com/culture-religion/modern-high-school-cliques-study on October 29, 2020.

Jones, J. M. (2018, August 24). *More parents, children fearful for safety at school*. Accessed at https://news.gallup.com/poll/241625/parents-children-fearful-safety-school.aspx on October 29, 2020.

K12 Reader. (n.d.). *Dolch word list: Sorted by frequency by grade level*. Accessed at www.k12reader.com/dolch/dolch_frequency_by_grade.pdf on January 14, 2021.

Kabat-Zinn, J. (2003). Mindfulness-based interventions in context: Past, present, and future. *Clinical Psychology: Science and Practice, 10*(2), 144–156.

Kagan, S. (2014). *Brain-friendly teaching: Tools, tips, and structures*. San Clemente, CA: Kagan.

Kamenetz, A. (2021, February 23). *States must test student learning this year, Biden administration says.* Accessed at www.npr.org/sections/coronavirus-live-updates/2021/02/23/970520559/states-must-test-student-learning-this-spring-biden-administration-says on April 11, 2021.

Kaufeldt, M. (Ed.). (2010). *Begin with the brain: Orchestrating the learner-centered classroom* (2nd ed.). Thousand Oaks, CA: Corwin Press.

Kaufeldt, M. (2019, October 14). *The stress mess: Improving learning from the inside out activity* [Conference session]. Achievement for Students in Poverty: Poor Students, Rich Teaching Institute, Orlando, FL.

Kirschenbaum, D. S., Ordman, A. M., Tomarken, A. J., & Holtzbauer, R. (1982). Effects of differential self-monitoring and level of mastery on sports performance: Brain power bowling. *Cognitive Therapy and Research, 6*(3), 335–42.

Klassen, E. (2015, December 15). *Triangle breathing, 1 minute* [Video file]. Accessed at www.youtube.com/watch?v=u9Q8D6n-3qw on October 29, 2020.

Kohn, A. (1999). *Punished by rewards: The trouble with gold stars, incentive plans, A's, praise, and other bribes.* New York: Houghton Mifflin.

Lakshmi, R. (2015). These Indian parents climbed a school wall to help their kids cheat on an exam. *The Washington Post.* Accessed at www.washingtonpost.com/news/worldviews/wp/2015/03/19/these-indian-parents-climbed-a-school-wall-to-help-their-kids-cheat-on-an-exam on March 24, 2021.

Lally, P., van Jaarsveld, C. H. M., Potts, H. W. W., & Wardle, J. (2010). How are habits formed? Modelling habit formation in the real world. *European Journal of Social Psychology, 40*(6), 998–1009. Accessed at https://doi.org/10.1002/ejsp.674 on October 29, 2020.

Langer, E. J. (2016). *The power of mindful learning* (2nd ed.). Boston: Da Capo Lifelong Books.

Layous, K., Chancellor, J., & Lyubomirsky, S. (2014). Positive activities as protective factors against mental health conditions. *Journal of Abnormal Psychology, 123*(1), 3–12.

Lazarín, M. (2014, October 16). *Testing overload in America's schools.* Accessed at www.americanprogress.org/issues/education-k-12/reports/2014/10/16/99073/testing-overload-in-americas-schools on October 29, 2020.

Learning A-Z. (n.d.). *Common Core: Academic vocabulary.* Accessed at www.learninga-z.com/site/what-we-do/standards/common-core/academic-vocabulary on March 30, 2021.

Levine, D., Pace, A., Luo, R., Hirsh-Pasek, K., Golinkoff, R M., deVilliers, J., et al. (2020). Evaluating socioeconomic gaps in preschoolers' vocabulary, syntax and language process skills with the Quick Interactive Language Screener (QUILS). *Early Childhood Research Quarterly, 50*(1), 114–128.

Lopez-Garrido, G. (2020). *Self-efficacy theory.* Accessed at www.simplypsychology.org/self-efficacy.html on March 22, 2021.

Lopez, S. J., & Snyder, C. R. (Eds.). (2009). *The Oxford handbook of positive psychology* (2nd ed.). New York: Oxford University Press.

Loraine, S. (2008). *Vocabulary development.* Accessed at www.superduperinc.com/handouts/pdf/149_VocabularyDevelopment.pdf on May 5, 2021.

Louisiana State University Shreveport. (2017, October 13). *What is a culturally responsive learning environment?* Accessed at https://online.lsus.edu/articles/education/culturally-responsive-learning-environment.aspx on October 29, 2020.

Luscombe, R. (2019, April 19). Generation Columbine: How mass shootings changed America's schools. *The Guardian.* Accessed at www.theguardian.com/us-news/2019/apr/19/columbine-parkland-how-mass-shootings-changed-us-schools on October 29, 2020.

MacWhinney, B. (n.d.). *Language acquisition—The basic components of human language, methods for studying language acquisition, phases in language development.* Accessed at https://education.stateuniversity.com/pages/2153/Language-Acquisition.html#ixzz6pm6ghTqr on March 19, 2021.

Maddux, J. E. (2009). Self-efficacy: The power of believing you can. In S. J. Lopez & C. R. Snyder (Eds.), *The Oxford handbook of positive psychology* (2nd ed., pp. 335–343). New York: Oxford University Press.

Makhlouf, J. (2015). *Multitasking vs. continuous partial attention.* Accessed at https://elmlearning.com/multitasking-vs-continuous-partial-attention on March 24, 2021.

Marmolejo, A. (1991, April). *The effects of vocabulary instruction with poor readers: A meta-analysis.* Paper presented at the annual meeting of the American Educational Research Association, Chicago.

Manca, S., Cerina, V., Tobia, V., Sacchi, S., & Fornana, F. (2020). The effect of school design on users' responses: A systemic review (2008–2017). *Sustainability, 12*(8), 1–37.

Maree, R. (2020). *Meditation in motion: The new way to meditate.* Accessed at https://medium.com/mind-body-soul/meditation-in-motion-273359912e7c on March 26, 2021.

Marteau, T. M., & Bekker, H. (1992). The development of a six-item short-form of the state scale of the Spielberger State-Trait Anxiety Inventory (STAI). *British Journal of Clinical Psychology, 31*(3), 301–306.

Marthe Creations. [marthe-Creations]. (2015, October 6). *Breathing exercise for relaxation: Reduce stress and anxiety* [Video file]. Accessed at www.youtube.com/watch?v=KePf3G7dUyY on January 22, 2021.

Marzano, R. J. (2017). *The new art and science of teaching.* Bloomington, IN: Solution Tree Press.

Marzano, R. J. (2020). *Teaching basic, advanced, and academic vocabulary: A comprehensive framework for elementary instruction.* Bloomington, IN: Marzano Resources.

Marzano, R. J., Norford, J. S., & Ruyle, M. (2019). *The new art and science of classroom assessment.* Bloomington, IN: Solution Tree Press.

Marzano, R. J., & Pickering, D. J. (2005). *Building academic vocabulary: Teacher's manual.* Alexandria, VA: Association for Supervision and Curriculum Development.

Marzano, R. J., & Simms, J. A. (2013). *Vocabulary for the Common Core.* Bloomington, IN: Marzano Resources.

Maslow, A. (1968). *Toward a psychology of being* (2nd ed.). Princeton, NJ: Van Nostrand.

Mason, C., Rivers Murphy, M. M., & Jackson, Y. (2018). *Mindfulness practices: Cultivating heart centered communities where students focus and flourish.* Bloomington, IN: Solution Tree Press.

Mason, C., Rivers Murphy, M. M., & Jackson, Y. (2020). *Mindful school communities: The five Cs of nurturing heart centered learning.* Bloomington, IN: Solution Tree Press.

McDonald, A. (2001). The prevalence and effects of test anxiety in school children. *Educational Psychology, 21*(1), 89–101.

McEwen, B. S. (2002). *The end of stress as we know it.* Washington, DC: Joseph Henry Press.

McEwen, B. S., & Gianaros, P. J. (2010). Central role of the brain in stress and adaptation: Links to socioeconomic status, health, and disease. *Annals of the New York Academy of Sciences, 1186*(1), 190–222.

Meador, D. (2019). *Examining the pros and cons of standardized testing.* Accessed at www.thoughtco.com/examining-the-pros-and-cons-of-standardized-testing-3194596 on March 25, 2021.

Mental Health Foundation. (n.d.). *Stress.* Accessed at www.mentalhealth.org.uk/a-to-z/s/stress on December 10, 2020.

Merriam-Webster. (n.d.a). *Perseverance*. Accessed at www.merriam-webster.com/dictionary/perseverance on March 24, 2021.

Merriam-Webster. (n.d.b). *Words we're watching: Infomania in the Information Age*. Accessed at www.merriam-webster.com/words-at-play/infomania-in-the-information-age on December 22, 2020.

Metcalf, J. (2017). Learning from errors. *Annual Review of Psychology*, *68*, 465–489.

Miller, K. (2021). *Michigan students still have to take standardized tests this year and reactions are mixed, varied, assorted, diverse*. Accessed at www.mlive.com/news/2021/04/michigan-students-still-have-to-take-standardized-tests-this-year-and-reactions-are-mixed-varied-assorted-diverse.html on April 12, 2021.

Mills, H., Reiss, N., & Dombeck, M. (n.d.). *Stress reduction and management: Distraction and humor in stress reduction*. Accessed at www.gulfbend.org/poc/view_doc.php?type=doc&id=15671 on March 27, 2021.

Mind Tools. (n.d.). *Albrecht's four types of stress: Managing common pressures*. Accessed at www.mindtools.com/pages/article/Albrecht-stress.htm on October 29, 2020.

Ming, G.-L., & Song, H. (2011). Adult neurogenesis in the mammalian brain: Significant answers and significant questions. *Neuron*, *70*(4), 687–702.

Mogel, W. (2001). *The blessing of a skinned knee: Using Jewish teachings to raise self-reliant children*. New York: Scribner.

Moldoveanu, M., & Langer, E. J. (2002). When "stupid" is smarter than we are: Mindlessness and the attribution of stupidity. In R. J. Sternberg (Ed.), *Why smart people can be so stupid* (pp. 212–231). New Haven, CT: Yale University Press.

Montgomery, J. K. (2008). *MAVA: Montgomery assessment of vocabulary acquisition* [Video file]. Greenville, SC: Super Duper.

Moreno, R. (2004). Decreasing cognitive load for novice students: Effects of explanatory versus corrective feedback in discovery-based multimedia. *Instructional Science*, *32*(1), 99–113.

Morin, A. (2019). *Activities to increase emotional vocabulary*. Accessed at www.thoughtco.com/activities-to-increase-emotional-vocabulary-2086623 on March 26, 2021.

Mott, M. S., Robinson, D. H., Walden, A., Burnette, J., & Rutherford, A. S. (2012). Illuminating the effects of dynamic lighting on student learning. *SAGE Open*, *2*(2), 1–9. Accessed at https://doi.org/10.1177/2158244012445585 on October 29, 2020.

Muhammad, A. (2015). *Overcoming the achievement gap trap: Liberating mindsets to effect change*. Bloomington, IN: Solution Tree Press.

Munsey, C. (2010). The kids aren't all right: New data from APA's Stress in America survey indicate parents don't know what's bothering their children. *Monitor Staff*, *41*(1). Accessed at www.apa.org/monitor/2010/01/stress-kids on October 29, 2020.

Najam, F. (2017). *Best way to learn is to teach someone else*. Accessed at www.linkedin.com/pulse/best-way-learn-teach-someone-else-farah-najam on April 8, 2021.

National Association of School Psychologists & National Association of School Resource Officers. (2017). *Best practice considerations for schools in active shooter and other armed assailant drills*. Bethesda, MD: Authors. Accessed at www.nasponline.org/resources-and-publications/resources-and-podcasts/school-climate-safety-and-crisis/systems-level-prevention/best-practice-considerations-for-schools-in-active-shooter-and-other-armed-assailant-drills on October 29, 2020.

National Center on Safe Supportive Learning Environments. (2018). *Creating a safe and respectful environment in our nation's classrooms*. Washington, DC: Author. Accessed at https://safesupportivelearning.ed.gov/creating-safe-and-respectful-environment-our-nations-classrooms on October 29, 2020.

National Child Traumatic Stress Network. (n.d.). *Essential elements.* Accessed at www.nctsn.org/trauma-informed-care/trauma-informed-systems/schools/essential-elements on March 16, 2021.

National Commission on Excellence in Education. (1983). *A nation at risk: The imperative for educational reform.* Washington, DC: Author. Accessed at https://files.eric.ed.gov/fulltext/ED226006.pdf on January 14, 2021.

National Institute of Mental Health. (n.d.). *5 things you should know about stress.* Accessed at www.nimh.nih.gov/health/publications/stress/index.shtml on October 29, 2020.

National Reading Panel. (2000). *Teaching children to read: An evidence-based assessment of the scientific research literature on reading and its implications for reading instruction—Reports of the subgroups.* Bethesda, MD: National Institutes of Health. Accessed at www.nichd.nih.gov/sites/default/files/publications/pubs/nrp/Documents/report.pdf on January 12, 2021.

National Research Council. (2007). *Green schools: Attributes for health and learning.* Washington, DC: National Academies Press. Accessed at https://doi.org/10.17226/11756 on October 29, 2020.

Neighmond, P. (2013, December 2). *School stress takes a toll on health, teens and parents say.* Accessed at www.npr.org/sections/health-shots/2013/12/02/246599742/school-stress-takes-a-toll-on-health-teens-and-parents-say on October 29, 2020.

Neill, M., & Guisbond, L. (2017). *Test reform victories surge in 2017: What's behind the winning strategies?* Boston: National Center for Fair and Open Testing. Accessed at www.fairtest.org/sites/default/files/FairTest-TestReformVictoriesReport2017.pdf on January 12, 2021.

News 12 Staff. (2021, March 29). *Some school districts to only give standardized tests to students whose parents request it.* Accessed at https://westchester.news12.com/some-school-districts-to-only-give-standardized-tests-to-students-whose-parents-request-it on April 10, 2021.

Nichols, S. L., & Berliner, D. C. (2007). *Collateral damage: How high-stakes testing corrupts America's schools.* Cambridge, MA: Harvard Education Press.

No Child Left Behind (NCLB) Act of 2001, Pub. L. No. 107–110, § 115, Stat. 1425 (2002).

Noonan, P. M., & Gaumer Erickson, A. S. (2018). *The skills that matter: Teaching interpersonal and intrapersonal competencies in any classroom.* Thousand Oaks, CA: Corwin Press.

OER4Schools. (2013, November 11). *Shirley Clarke video on feedback* [Video file]. Accessed at www.youtube.com/watch?v=DGNp0AJte_c on October 29, 2020.

Ogle, D. M. (1986). K-W-L: A teaching model that develops active reading of expository text. *Reading Teacher, 39*(6), 564–570.

Ohanian, S. (2002, March 14). *Collateral vomitage.* Accessed at www.sacbee.com/content/news/education/story/1852977p-1949391c.html on February 14, 2014.

Ohio State University. (2018). *This is your brain detecting patterns: It is different from other kinds of learning, study shows.* Accessed at www.sciencedaily.com/releases/2018/05/180531114642.htm on March 15, 2021.

Our Family Wizard. (n.d.). *Signs and symptoms of stress in children.* Accessed at www.ourfamilywizard.com/blog/signs-and-symptoms-stress-children#:~:text=Common%20physical%20symptoms%20of%20stress,asleep%2C%20or%20having%20frequent%20nightmares on March 13, 2021.

Oxford University Press. (2021). Stress. In *Lexico.com dictionary.* Accessed at www.lexico.com/en/definition/stress on March 12, 2021.

Oxford Learning. (2018, May 28). *Common causes of school stress for students.* Accessed at www.oxfordlearning.com/causes-of-school-stress on October 29, 2020.

Panksepp, J. (1998). *Affective neuroscience: The foundations of human and animal emotions.* New York: Oxford University Press.

Panksepp, J., & Biven, L. (2012). The archaeology of mind: Neuroevolutionary origins of human emotions. New York: Norton.

Parmentier, F. B. R., García-Toro, M., García-Campayo, J., Yañez, A. M., Andrés, P., & Gili, M. (2019) Mindfulness and symptoms of depression and anxiety in the general population: The Mediating roles of worry, rumination, reappraisal and suppression. *Frontiers in Psychology, 10*(506). Accessed at www.frontiersin.org/articles/10.3389/fpsyg.2019.00506/full on April 28, 2021.

Paruthi, S., Brooks, L. J., D'Ambrosio, C., Hall, W. A., Kotagal, S., Lloyd, R. M., et al. (2016) Recommended amount of sleep for pediatric populations: A consensus statement of the American Academy of Sleep Medicine. *Journal of Clinical Sleep Medicine, 12*(6), 785–786.

Penn State. (2018) *Mindful movement may help lower stress, anxiety.* Accessed at www.sciencedaily.com/releases/2018/06/180621112007.htm on April 28, 2021.

Piper, W. (1930). *The little engine that could.* New York: Platt & Munk.

Planbook. (n.d.). *How can teachers help prepare students for exams in the 2020–2021 school year?* [Blog post]. Accessed at https://blog.planbook.com/2021-exams on April 10, 2021.

Poon, J. D. (2018, September 11). *Part 1: What do you mean when you say "student agency"?* Accessed at https://education-reimagined.org/what-do-you-mean-when-you-say-student-agency on October 29, 2020.

Pope, D., Brown, M., & Miles, S. (2015). *Overloaded and underprepared: Strategies for stronger schools and healthy, successful kids.* San Francisco: Jossey-Bass.

Popham, W. J. (2005, March 23). Standardized testing fails the exam. *Edutopia.* Accessed at www.edutopia.org/standardized-testing-evaluation-reform on October 29, 2020.

Popham, W. J. (2011). *Transformative assessment in action: An inside look at applying the process.* Alexandria, VA: Association for Supervision and Curriculum Development.

Power You Are. [ThePowerYouAre]. (2015, March 11). *HRV resonant breathing exercise: 5.5–6BPM* [Video file]. Accessed at www.youtube.com/watch?v=DUbAHGPtNM4 on January 22, 2021.

Princeton Review. (n.d.). *SAT vocabulary.* Accessed at www.princetonreview.com/college-advice/sat-vocabulary# on April 5, 2021.

ProCon.org. (2020, December 7). *Do standardized tests improve education in America?* Accessed at https://standardizedtests.procon.org on January 12, 2021.

Promises Behavioral Health. (2013, July 2). *Teens are feeling more anxious than ever* [Blog post]. Accessed at www.promisesbehavioralhealth.com/addiction-recovery-blog/teenagers-are-feeling-more-anxious-than-ever on January 12, 2021.

Rana, R., & Mahmood, N. (2010). The relationship between test anxiety and academic achievement. *Bulletin of Education and Research, 32*(2), 63–74.

Ranganathan, V. K., Siemionow, V., Liu, J. Z., Sahgal, V., & Yue, G. H. (2004). From mental power to muscle power—Gaining strength by using the mind. *Neuropsychologia, 42*(7), 944–956. Accessed at https://doi.org/10.1016/j.neuropsychologia.2003.11.018 on October 29, 2020.

Rathey, A. (2019). *The healthy and safe facility handbook* (School and college ed.). San Francisco: Healthy Facilities Institute-University.

Reading Rockets. (n.d.). *Vocabulary: In practice.* Accessed at www.readingrockets.org/teaching/reading101-course/modules/vocabulary/vocabulary-practice on April 5, 2021.

Ro, C. (2018). *Why sleep should be every student's priority.* Accessed at www.bbc.com/future/article/20180815-why-sleep-should-be-every-students-priority on April 8, 2021.

Rock, D. (2011). Introducing the healthy mind platter. *HuffPost*. Accessed at www.huffpost.com/entry/healthy-mind-platter_b_870664 on June 5, 2021.

Roser, M. (2017). *Teachers and professors*. Accessed at https://ourworldindata.org/teachers-and-professors on April 30, 2021.

RULER. (n.d.). *What is RULER?* Accessed at www.rulerapproach.org/about/what-is-ruler on October 29, 2020.

Sacks, P. (1999). *Standardized minds: The high price of America's testing culture and what we can do to change it*. Cambridge, MA: Perseus Books.

Sadlier School. (n.d.). *Vocab Gal's favorite test prep resources kit*. Accessed at https://go.sadlier.com/school/vocab-gals-favorite-test-prep-resources on January 8, 2021.

Salaky, K. (2018). *What standardized tests look like in ten places around the world*. Accessed at www.insider.com/standardized-tests-around-the-world-2018-9 on March 24, 2021.

Samani, A., & Heath, M. (2018). Executive-related oculomotor control is improved following a 10-min single-bout of aerobic exercise: Evidence from the antisaccade task. *Neuropsychologia, 108*, 73–81. Accessed at www.sciencedirect.com/science/article/abs/pii/S0028393217304591?via%3Dihub on October 29, 2020.

San Pedro, M. O. Z., Baker, R. S. J. d., & Rodrigo, M. M. T. (2014). Carelessness and affect in an intelligent tutoring system for mathematics. *International Artificial Intelligence in Education Society, 24*, 189–210.

Sapolsky, R. M. (1998). *Why zebras don't get ulcers: An updated guide to stress, stress-related diseases, and coping*. New York: Freeman.

Sapolsky, R. M. (2004). *Why zebras don't get ulcers* (3rd ed.). New York: Holt.

Sarason, S. B., Davidson, K. S., Lighthall, F. F., Waite, R. R., & Ruebush, B. K. (1960). *Anxiety in elementary school children: a report of research*. New York: Wiley.

Saudino, K. J. (2005). Behavioral genetics and child temperament. *Journal of Developmental and Behavioral Pediatrics, 26*(3), 214–223. Accessed at https://doi.org/10.1097/00004703-200506000-00010 on October 29, 2020.

Schimelpfening, N. (2020, December 3). *How genetics can play a role in depression*. Accessed at https://verywellmind.com/is-depression-genetic-1067317 on June 16, 2021.

Schroder, H. S., Fisher, M. E., Lin, Y., Lo, S. L., Danovitch, J. H., & Moser, J. S. (2017). Neural evidence for enhanced attention to mistakes among school-aged children with a growth mindset. *Developmental Cognitive Neuroscience, 24*, 42–50. Accessed at https://doi.org/10.1016/j.dcn.2017.01.004 on October 29, 2020.

ScienceDaily. (2008, September 28). *Most elementary schools in California will fail to meet proficiency requirements by 2014, study shows*. Accessed at www.sciencedaily.com/releases/2008/09/080925144619.htm#:~:text=A%20new%20study%20shows%20that,Left%20Behind%20Act%20of%202001 on October 29, 2020.

Score at the Top Learning Centers and Schools. (2013, June 20). *Brain food: 5 best foods to eat before a test* [Blog post]. Accessed at www.scoreatthetop.com/blog/brain-food-5-best-foods-to-eat-before-a-test on January 9, 2021.

Scott, E. (2021, March 19). *All about acute stress: What you should know about acute stress*. Accessed at https://verywellmind.com/all-about-acute-stress-3145064 on June 16, 2021.

Scott, E. (2020, April 8). *What you should know about acute stress*. Accessed at www.verywellmind.com/all-about-acute-stress-3145064#:~:text=Acute%20stress%20is%20one%20of,either%20physical%2C%20emotional%20or%20psychological on March 12, 2021.

Segal, J., Smith, M., Segal, R., & Robinson, L. (2020). *Stress, symptoms, signs, and causes.* Accessed at www.helpguide.org/articles/stress/stress-symptoms-signs-and-causes.htm on March 15, 2021.

Segool, N. K., von der Embse, N. P., Mata, A. D., & Gallant, J. (2013). *Cognitive behavioral model of test anxiety in a high-stakes context: An exploratory study.* New York: Springer Science + Business Media.

Selye, H. (1974). *Stress without distress.* Philadelphia: Lippincott.

Shapiro, A. (2019, June 22). *Dr. Marijuana Pepsi won't change her name "to make other people happy."* Accessed at www.npr.org/2019/06/21/734839666/dr-marijuana-pepsi-wont-change-her-name-to-make-other-people-happy on October 29, 2020.

Shapiro, E., & Shapiro, D. (2017) *Mindfulness and meditation: What's the difference?* Accessed at https://medium.com/thrive-global/mindfulness-meditation-whats-the-difference-852f5ef7ec1a on March 26, 2021.

Sharma, V. K., Trakroo, M., Subramaniam, V., Rajajeyakumar, M., Bhavanani, A. B., & Sahai, A. (2013). Effect of fast and slow pranayama on perceived stress and cardiovascular parameters in young health-care students. *International Journal of Yoga*, *6*(2), 104–110.

Sharp Health News. (2019, January 23). *Yes, mess causes stress.* Accessed at www.sharp.com/health-news/yes-mess-causes-stress.cfm on October 29, 2020.

Shepard, L. A. (n.d.). *Testing: Standardized tests and high-stakes assessment.* Accessed at https://education.stateuniversity.com/pages/2500/Testing-STANDARDIZED-TESTS-HIGH-STAKES-ASSESSMENT.html on February 26, 2021.

Shobe, E. R. (2005). A simple visualization exercise for reducing test anxiety and improving performance on difficult math tests. *Journal of Worry and Affective Experience, 1*(1), 34–52.

Shute, V. J. (2007). *Focus on formative feedback.* Princeton, NJ: Educational Testing Service. Accessed at https://files.eric.ed.gov/fulltext/EJ1111586.pdf on October 29, 2020.

Siegel, D. (n.d.). *The healthy mind platter.* Accessed at https://drdansiegel.com/healthy-mind-platter on October 29, 2020.

Sight Words. (n.d.a). *Dolch sight words list.* Accessed at https://sightwords.com/sight-words/dolch on January 7, 2021.

Sight Words. (n.d.b). *Fry sight words list.* Accessed at https://sightwords.com/sight-words/fry on January 7, 2021.

Simms, J. A., & Marzano, R. J. (2019). *The new art and science of teaching reading.* Bloomington, IN: Solution Tree Press.

Sincero, S. M. (n.d.). *Three different kinds of stress.* Accessed at https://explorable.com/three-different-kinds-of-stress on October 29, 2020.

Smith, A., & Scherrer, P. (2013, August 5). *Who benefits from the "Common Core" curriculum in US schools?* Accessed at www.wsws.org/en/articles/2013/08/05/core-a05.html on October 29, 2020.

Smith, M. (2017). Hyperactive around the world? The history of ADHD in global perspective. *Social History of Medicine*, *30*(4), 767–787.

Smith, W. C. (2016). An introduction to the global testing culture. In W. C. Smith (Ed.), *The global testing culture: Shaping education policy, perceptions, and practice* (pp. 7–23). Oxford, England: Symposium Books.

Solochek, J. S. (2021, April 9). Florida removes high-stakes consequences from spring testing. *Tampa Bay Times.* Accessed at www.tampabay.com/news/education/2021/04/09/florida-removes-high-stakes-consequences-from-spring-testing on June 5, 2021.

Sparks, S. D. (2019, March 12). Why teacher-student relationships matter. *Education Week*. Accessed at www.edweek.org/ew/articles/2019/03/13/why-teacher-student-relationships-matter.html on October 29, 2020.

Sprenger, M. (2013). *Teaching the critical vocabulary of the Common Core: 55 words that make or break student understanding*. Alexandria, VA: Association for Supervision and Curriculum Development.

Sriram, R. (2020). The neuroscience behind productive struggle. *Edutopia*. Accessed at www.edutopia.org/article/neuroscience-behind-productive-struggle on April 4, 2021.

Stein, B. D., Jaycox, L. H., Kataoka, S. H., Wong, M., Langley, A. K., Avila, J. L., et al. (2011) *Helping children cope with violence and trauma: A school-based program that works*. Santa Monica, CA: RAND.

Stenger, M. (2014, August 6). *Five research-based tips for providing students with meaningful feedback* [Blog post.]. Accessed at https://edutopia.org/blog/tips-providing-students-meaningful-feedback-marianne-stenger on June 17, 2021.

Stevens, J. (2015, November 9). *How does sitting too long in school affect the students?* [Blog post]. Accessed at https://scienceleadership.org/blog/how_does_sitting_too_long_in_school_affect_the_students on October 29, 2020.

Stinson, A. (2018, April 25). *Experts say stress can change your personality, so here's how to stay true to yourself*. Accessed at www.elitedaily.com/p/can-stress-change-your-personality-heres-how-to-stay-true-to-yourself-no-matter-what-8856456 on March 10, 2021.

Stone, L. (n.d.). *FAQ*. Accessed at https://lindastone.net/faq on October 29, 2020.

Strauss, V. (2011, April 26). *Unanswered questions about standardized tests* [Blog post]. Accessed at www.washingtonpost.com/blogs/answer-sheet/post/unanswered-questions-about-standardized-tests/2011/04/26/AFNRPlmE_blog.html on October 29, 2020.

Strauss, V. (2013, November 21). N.Y. school principals write letter of concern about Common Core tests. *The Washington Post*. Accessed at www.washingtonpost.com/news/answer-sheet/wp/2013/11/21/n-y-school-principals-write-letter-of-concern-about-common-core-tests on October 29, 2020.

Strauss, V. (2021, February 1). What you need to know about standardized testing. *The Washington Post*. Accessed at www.washingtonpost.com/education/2021/02/01/need-to-know-about-standardized-testing on March 25, 2021.

Street, E. (2018, April 4). *How some schools are improving school safety*. Accessed at www.learningliftoff.com/how-some-schools-are-improving-school-safety on October 29, 2020.

Summer Institute for the Gifted. (2020, March 31). *4 ways to support gifted children with anxiety* [Blog post]. Accessed at https://blog.giftedstudy.org/4-ways-to-support-gifted-children-with-anxiety on October 29, 2020.

Svinicki, M. (1993–1994). *UIC TA handbook: What they don't know can hurt them—The role of prior knowledge in learning*. Chicago: University of Illinois Chicago. Accessed at https://grad.uic.edu/academic-support/ta-enrichment/uic-ta-handbook/uic-ta-handbook-what-they-dont-know-can-hurt-them-the-role-of-prior-knowledge-in-learning on October 29, 2020.

Tahmassian, K., & Jalali Moghadam, N. (2011). Relationship between self-efficacy and symptoms of anxiety, depression, worry and social avoidance in a normal sample of students. *Iranian Journal of Psychiatry and Behavioral Sciences*, *5*(2), 91–98.

Thorton, C. (2018, September 4). *When it comes to learning, social emotional health is a prerequisite* [Blog post]. Accessed at https://inservice.ascd.org/when-it-comes-to-learning-social-emotional-health-is-a-prerequisite on March 22, 2021.

Tornio, S. (2019, March 14). *More kids than ever are dealing with test anxiety, and we need to help.* Accessed at www.weareteachers.com/test-anxiety on March 12, 2021.

Tough, P. (2012). *How children succeed: Grit, curiosity, and the hidden power of character.* New York: Houghton Mifflin Harcourt.

Tran, H. (2016, October 17). *Foreign language anxiety* [Blog post]. Accessed at https://amvietnam.com/foreign-language-anxiety on December 14, 2020.

Turner, C. (2014, April 30). *U.S. tests teens a lot, but worldwide, exam stakes are higher* [Radio broadcast transcript]. All Things Considered. Accessed at www.npr.org/2014/04/30/308057862/u-s-tests-teens-a-lot-but-worldwide-exam-stakes-are-higher on March 24, 2021.

United Nations Educational, Scientific and Cultural Organization, Education Sector. (2019). *Behind the numbers: Ending school violence and bullying.* Accessed at https://unesdoc.unesco.org/ark:/48223/pf0000366483 on March 18, 2021.

United Nations Educational, Scientific and Cultural Organization, Education Sector. (2020). *COVID-19 education response webinar: Managing high-stakes exams and assessments during the Covid-19 pandemic.* Accessed at https://unesdoc.unesco.org/ark:/48223/pf0000373247 on March 24, 2021.

United Nations Office of the Special Representative of the Secretary-General on Violence Against Children. (2016). *Tackling violence in schools: A global perspective.* Accessed at https://violenceagainstchildren.un.org/sites/violenceagainstchildren.un.org/files/documents/publications/10._tackling_violence_in_schools_a_global_perspective.pdf on March 17, 2021.

University of California, San Francisco Institute for Global Health Sciences. (n.d.). *Globally Reduce Adverse Childhood Experience (GRACE) Initiative.* Accessed at https://globalhealthsciences.ucsf.edu/our-work/mental-health/globally-reduce-adverse-childhood-experience-initiative on May 3, 2021.

University of the People. (n.d.). *Stress-free eating tips for exams.* Accessed at www.uopeople.edu/blog/what-to-eat-the-night-before-a-test on April 8, 2021.

U.S. Congress, Office of Technology Assessment. (1992). *Testing in American schools: Asking the right questions.* Washington, DC: Government Printing Office.

U.S. Department of Education. (2000). *Impact of inadequate school facilities on student learning.* Washington, DC: Author.

U.S. Department of Education. (2003). *Helping your child with test-taking: Helping your child succeed in school.* Accessed at www2.ed.gov/parents/academic/help/succeed/part9.html on October 29, 2020.

U.S. Department of Health and Human Services. (2018). *Physical activity guidelines for Americans* (2nd ed.). Washington, DC: Author.

USQ Social Hub. (2019). *The five stages of stress every student needs to know.* Accessed https://social.usq.edu.au/wellbeing/articles/5-stages-of-stress-article on April 28, 2021.

Vatterott, C. (2018). *Rethinking homework: Best practices that support diverse needs* (2nd ed.). Alexandria, VA: Association for Supervision and Curriculum Development.

Vocabulary.com. (2020, December 22). *The new SAT: Language of the test—List 1.* Accessed at www.vocabulary.com/lists/877974 on January 8, 2021.

von der Embse, N., Jester, D., Roy, D., & Post, J. (2018). Test anxiety effects, predictors, and correlates: A thirty-year meta-analytic review. *Journal of Affective Disorders, 227,* 483–493.

Vygotsky, L. S. (1978). *Mind in society: The development of higher psychological processes.* Boston: Harvard University Press.

Walker, T. (2016, July 25). Is stress in the classroom contagious? *NEA Today*. Accessed at www.neatoday.org/2016/07/25/is-stress-in-the-classroom-contagious on October 29, 2020.

Walker, T. (2020, February 25). Unannounced active shooter drills scaring students without making them safer. *NEA Today*. Accessed at www.nea.org/advocating-for-change/new-from-nea/unannounced-active-shooter-drills-scaring-students-without on March 19, 2021.

Ward, C. M. (2020, July 28). *What are normal attention spans for children?* [Blog post]. Accessed at www.kids-houston.com/2020/08/21/what-are-normal-attention-spans-for-children on April 6, 2021.

Warren, E. (n.d.). *Teaching visualization can improve academic achievement for students at any age*. Accessed at https://minds-in-bloom.com/teaching-visualization-can-improve on March 23, 2021.

We Are Teachers. (2019). *What teachers need to know about restorative justice*. Accessed at www.weareteachers.com/restorative-justice on March 20, 2021.

Wells, C. (1899). The jingle book. New York: Macmillan.

Whitbourne, S. K. (2011, October 8). *10 failsafe test-taking tips* [Blog post]. Accessed at www.psychologytoday.com/us/blog/fulfillment-any-age/201110/10-failsafe-test-taking-tips on October 29, 2020.

Willis, J. (2009). Inspiring middle school minds: Gifted, creative, and challenging. Scottsdale, AZ: Great Potential Press.

Willis, J. (2017, April 7). *Brain-based strategies to reduce test stress*. Accessed at www.edutopia.org/article/brain-based-strategies-reduce-test-stress-judy-willis on October 29, 2020.

Wolpert-Gawron, H. (2017, March 15). *Test prep doesn't have to be overwhelming* [Blog post]. Accessed at www.edutopia.org/blog/preparing-students-state-standardized-tests on April 10, 2021.

World Health Organization. (n.d.). *Adverse childhood experiences international questionnaire (ACE-IQ)*. Accessed at https://who.int/violence_injury_prevention/violence/activities/adverse_childhood_experiences/questionnaire.pdf on June 18, 2021.

World Health Organization. (2007). Promoting physical activity in schools: An important element of a health-promoting school. In *WHO information series on school health (Vol. 12)*. Accessed at https://apps.who.int/iris/handle/10665/43733 on May 3, 2021.

Wylie, E. C. (2008). *Formative assessment: Examples of practice*. Washington, DC: Council of Chief State School Officers. Accessed at www.ccsso.org/sites/default/files/2017-12/Formative_Assessment_Examples_2008.pdf on January 12, 2021.

Yang, D. (2019). The myth of multitasking. *BrainWorld*. Accessed at https://brainworldmagazine.com/the-myth-of-multitasking on March 25, 2021.

Zakrzewski, V. (2013). How to help kids overcome fear of failure. *Greater Good Magazine*. Accessed at https://greatergood.berkeley.edu/article/item/how_to_help_kids_overcome_fear_of_failure on May 4, 2021.

Zhao, Y. (2009). *Catching up or leading the way: American education in the age of globalization*. Alexandria, VA: Association for Supervision and Curriculum Development.

INDEX

C

F

G

H

I

J

K

L

M

N

T

U

V

W

X

Y

Z

Think Big, Start Small
Gayle Gregory and Martha Kaufeldt
You don't have to be a neuroscientist to understand how your students absorb knowledge. This easy-to-understand guide pares down the vast field of neuroscience and provides simple brain-compatible strategies that will make a measurable difference in your differentiated classrooms.
BKF471

Best Practices at Tier 1, Elementary
Gayle Gregory, Martha Kaufeldt, and Mike Mattos
Created specifically to target core instruction in grades K–5, this book provides proven response to intervention strategies to differentiate instruction, engage students, increase success, and avoid additional interventions. Discover how to create a brain-friendly learning environment, shift processes to support collaboration, and more.
BKF650

Best Practices at Tier 1, Secondary
Gayle Gregory, Martha Kaufeldt, and Mike Mattos
Created specifically to target core instruction in grades 6–12, this book provides proven response to intervention strategies to differentiate instruction, engage students, increase success, and avoid additional interventions. Discover how to create a brain-friendly learning environment, shift processes to support collaboration, and more.
BKF651

Softening the Edges
Katie White
Discover how to design, deliver, and differentiate instruction and assessment to address learners' diverse intellectual and emotional needs. By creating an effective assessment architecture, you can ensure your students are invested in their own learning and have the confidence to face any learning challenge.
BKF781

Visit SolutionTree.com or call 800.733.6786 to order.

Solution Tree